Confessions

of the Letter Closet

Confessions
of the Letter Closet

Epistolary Fiction and Queer Desire
in Modern Spain

PATRICK PAUL GARLINGER

UNIVERSITY OF MINNESOTA PRESS

MINNEAPOLIS • LONDON

The University of Minnesota Press gratefully acknowledges assistance from the Northwestern University Research Grants Committee, which has provided partial support for the publication of this book.

Portions of chapter 2 were previously published as "Lost Lesbian Love Letters? Epistolary Erasure and Queer Readers in Martín Gaite's *El cuarto de atrás,*" *Bulletin of Hispanic Studies* (Glasgow) 76, no. 4 (1999): 513–33, http://www.tandf.co.uk/journals/titles/14753820.html, reprinted by permission of Carfax Publishing, Taylor & Francis Ltd.; and as "Corresponding with Carmen Martín Gaite: The Death of the Letter Writer," *Revista de Estudios Hispánicos* 36, no. 1 (2002): 191–208; reprinted by permission of the editors of *Revista de Estudios Hispánicos.* An early version of chapter 5 previously appeared in *Bulletin of Hispanic Studies* 80, no. 1 (2003): 83–104; reprinted by permission of Liverpool University Press.

Published by the University of Minnesota Press
111 Third Avenue South, Suite 290
Minneapolis, MN 55401-2520
http://www.upress.umn.edu

Library of Congress Cataloging-in-Publication Data

Garlinger, Patrick Paul.
  Confessions of the letter closet : epistolary fiction and queer desire in modern Spain / Patrick Paul Garlinger.
    p. cm.
  Includes bibliographical references and index.
  ISBN 0-8166-4493-4 (hc : alk. paper) — ISBN 0-8166-4494-2 (pb : alk. paper) 1. Epistolary fiction, Spanish—History and criticism. 2. Spanish fiction—20th century—History and criticism. 3. Homosexuality in literature. I. Title.
  PQ6147.E65G37 2005
  863'.609353—dc22

                                                    2005005396

Printed in the United States of America on acid-free paper

The University of Minnesota is an equal-opportunity educator and employer.

12 11 10 09 08 07 06 05   10 9 8 7 6 5 4 3 2 1

CONTENTS

Acknowledgments vii

Introduction: Confession, Sexuality, Epistolarity ix

PART I. QUEER TRACES

1. Archival Resurrections of Queer Desire in
Miguel de Unamuno 3
2. Specters of Lesbian Desire: Love Letters and
Queer Readers in Carmen Martín Gaite 31

PART II. CLOSET CONFESSIONS

3. The Ethics of Outing in Luis Antonio de Villena 59
4. A Witness to Mourning: Memory and Testimony
in Carme Riera 87

PART III. EPISTOLARY POLITICS

5. Pleasurable Insurrections: Sexual Liberation and
Epistolary Anarchy 115
6. E-mail, AIDS, and Virtual Sexuality in Lluís Fernàndez 149

Postscript 177
Notes 189
Bibliography 215
Index 235

ACKNOWLEDGMENTS

Writing a book depends fundamentally on the assistance, support, and guidance of others. I would like to thank first and foremost Carlos Alonso and Hazel Gold, whose commitment to critical rigor and clarity of expression has shaped me as a scholar more than they know. I owe a great debt to Annabel Martín, who displayed remarkable patience and a keen critical eye, gently pushing me in new directions. Over the years, Mark Jordan has shown great support and a generosity for reading my work. In addition to reviewing the manuscript for the University of Minnesota Press, Brad Epps has consistently offered invaluable feedback and immense support during various stages of the book's composition, and Josiah Blackmore provided excellent suggestions for improving the manuscript. Several friends and colleagues kindly read and commented on portions of the manuscript, offered advice on the publishing process, and served at various moments as intellectual interlocutors. My thanks to Andrew Bush, Kathy Glenn, Christopher Lane, Tom Lewis, Elisa Martí-López, Alberto Mira, José Quiroga, H. Rosi Song, and Akiko Tsuchiya. I am profoundly grateful to Dara Goldman for her support and friendship over the years. A special thanks to my parents, Gil and Kate Fellers, who have never ceased to believe in me, and to Alisha, Alan, and Erin for the support that only siblings can provide. The person who has most influenced this project, personally and intellectually, is James Meyer. Without his love and support, I could not have finished this book.

I would also like to thank several other mentors, colleagues, and friends for their encouragement and support, both professional and personal, at various moments during the writing process: Rob Baird, Daniel Balderston, Mark Bauerlein, Robin Blaetz, María Mercedes Carrión, Walter Dobrian, Denise Filios, Emma Martinell Gifre, Suzanne Guerlac, Laura Gutiérrez, Christopher Herbert, Ellen Lewin, Tom Lewis, Judith Liskin-Gasparro, Jay Grossman, Jeffrey Masten, Dwight McBride, Adriana Méndez, Emilia Navarro, Miriam Peskowitz, Helena Reckitt, Michael Solomon, Karen Stolley, and Chris Victor. My thanks to the graduate students in my Spring 2002 seminar on confession at Emory University for their critical acumen. I am especially indebted to my colleagues at Northwestern University—Jorge Coronado, Gonzalo Díaz-Migoyo, Darío Fernández Morera, Lucille Kerr, Elisa Martí-López, Yarí Pérez Marín, and Julio Prieto—for their support during the book's completion. My thanks to Jaime Domingo and Imanol Martínez for hosting me during research trips to Madrid, and to Fernando Martín Vallejo for his advice on Spanish law. To my friends in Chicago—in particular, Stephen Kirk, Michael Kowalsky, Lee Nostrant, Jason Pearson, and George Thomson—my gratitude for their understanding and patience when I needed to write. Finally, I cannot thank enough Richard Morrison for his support, professionalism, and enthusiasm for the project, and the staff at the University of Minnesota Press—Laura Westlund, Dan Leary, and Lynn Walterick, in particular—for their keen attention as they shepherded the manuscript through the various stages of production.

The book benefited greatly from institutional support. Northwestern University and the University of Iowa generously provided research funds, and the University Research Grants Committee at Northwestern University offered a subvention. The librarians at the Museo Postal y Telegráfico in Madrid were especially helpful in locating research materials. My thanks also go to the Spanish National Library in Madrid, the Casa-Museo Miguel de Unamuno in Salamanca, and the Interlibrary Loan Department at Northwestern University.

I have used quotations from published translations of primary literary works when available, with occasional modifications. In most instances, original-language quotations are included in the notes. All translations of secondary materials are my own, except where otherwise noted.

Confession, Sexuality, Epistolarity

This book explores the ways in which Spanish authors have used letters and letter correspondence in literature to give voice to homoerotic and homosexual desire. The overarching premise of *Confessions of the Letter Closet* is that epistolary fiction offers a fertile yet unexplored terrain for the investigation of queer subjectivities in modern Spain. The association of letter writing with intimate secrets and sexuality has motivated contemporary critics to investigate authentic letter correspondence for evidence of homoerotic and homosexual relationships. Constance Jones has asserted, for example, that the "confidential aspect of letter writing has made it an especially fertile medium for gay and lesbian relationships, which for so much of history have been banished to the hidden corners of human experience" (7).[1] Literary studies such as Linda Kauffman's *Discourses of Desire,* Ruth Perry's *Women, Letters, and the Novel,* and Elizabeth Goldsmith's edited collection *Writing the Female Voice* have taken their cue from the association of letter writing with women to demonstrate that epistolary fiction is well suited to the exploration of gender, desire, and women's subjectivity. There is, however, no comparable study on queer desire and sexuality, a critical oversight this book aims to rectify.

A closet was traditionally a small room devoted to privacy, reading, devotion, and in some cases letter writing. In *Closet Devotions* Richard Rambuss focuses on the space of the prayer closet in seventeenth-century English literature as a privileged and private location in which to practice religious devotion. His study addresses the ways in which devotion folds into desire, religious affect into homoeroticism, the closet alluding to both the literal space of prayer and the figurative space of homoerotic desire. This study initiates a similar move in that it yokes together the practice of letter writing with the expression of queer desire. The letter replicates the tropological dynamics of the closet as a space that contains intimate thoughts and secret desires, hidden behind the protective veil of an envelope. Many of the thematic, formal, and historical characteristics associated with epistolarity accrue new significance when considered in conjunction with homosexuality: individual privacy and public surveillance; memory, love, and loss; confession and confidentiality; identity politics and the concept of community are topics salient to both letters and homosexual desire. With the phrase "the letter closet," this book conceptualizes the familiar, intimate letter—composed in private, containing personal information, and destined for a specific individual—as a historically specific manifestation of the closet, an argument developed further in the latter half of this introduction. Hence, at its core, this study asks two interrelated questions: How does letter writing emerge and substantially shape the representation of queer desire? What types of queer subjectivities emerge when we train our sights on epistolary fiction?

To answer these questions, *Confessions of the Letter Closet* engages in a series of textual analyses that focus primarily on the role of reading in the representation of queer desire. It is a fundamental tenet in epistolary studies that the role of the reader is central to the narrative plots of letter fiction. Rhetorical treatises have long defined letter writing as a form of *sermo mutuus absentium,* a virtual or deferred dialogue in which both speakers are absent. Formalist studies such as Janet Altman's *Epistolarity* have demonstrated the significance of the formal parameters of epistolary writing—the use of present-tense narration, the explicit naming of an addressee, the necessary distance between interlocutors, and the emphasis on the process of writing itself—for the production of meaning. Epistolary fiction—which in this study encompasses works composed of a single letter, a collection of letters, works with intercalated letters, and even narratives that are thematically engaged with epistolarity—involves the representation of internal readers and writers engaged in a complex practice of reading and interpretation.[2] Inherently metafictional, letter narratives often mirror on an internal level the relationship of external readers to literary texts. This study examines the ways in which fictional correspondents in epistolary fiction communicate and interpret their desires in writing, and by extension, the ways in which our own critical modes of reading refract internal acts of reading and interpretation. By choosing to analyze in depth a genre that has received relatively little attention in queer studies, this work insists that literature and literary form still have a great deal to tell us about the workings of sexuality and desire.

The book's title, *Confessions of the Letter Closet,* clearly evokes Foucault's arguments regarding the secular expansion of confession as part of an "incitement to discourse" that transformed sexual desire into a codified system of *sexuality.* Theoretical approaches to queer reading in literary studies have drawn considerable theoretical strength from Foucault's claims in the first volume of *The History of Sexuality* for the emergence of homosexuality as a discrete category in the late nineteenth century. But a discursive approach is insufficient for understanding the representation of queer desire in epistolary fiction. Reading epistolary fiction is an interpretive exercise that navigates between the conscious intentions of senders and receivers as well as the unconscious demands and wishes that their letters communicate: letters are a site of contestation between the social and the psychic, between the subject's private desires and the social categories used to apprehend them. Queer theory has generally been resistant to psychoanalytic approaches to the subject, in part due to Foucault's own perceived rejection of psychoanalysis as a major contributor to the expansion of sexuality as a discourse.[3] Yet Ann Laura Stoler cogently reminds us that "saying 'yes' to Foucault has not always meant saying 'no' to Freud, not even for Foucault himself" (168). More recently critics have argued that Foucault is not nearly as dismissive of psychoanalysis in volume 1 as many readers assume, in part because he distinguishes the "singular position of psychoanalysis" from the "perversion-heredity-degeneracy system," characterizing the former as a "rupture" within nineteenth-century discourses of sexuality (Davidson xi; Lane, *Burdens* 14). Arnold Davidson has further asserted that Foucault accepted the Freudian discovery of the unconscious, and like Lacan, saw it as a "system of socio-linguistic structures" (209).[4]

This is not to deny that discursive and psychoanalytic theories of the subject take considerably different approaches to the concepts of subjectivity and sexuality, even as they concur in seeing identity as contradictory and incoherent. Foucault's work focuses on the construction of sexuality as a historically unique mode of producing forms of subjectivity that are organized around objects of desire.[5] Queer theory, in turn, has emphasized the instability of sexual identity. The fluidity of the boundaries between homosexuality and heterosexuality, between sameness and difference, suggests that normative patterns of gender and sexuality remain open to rearticulation. In contrast, psychoanalytic approaches (principally Freudian and Lacanian) emphasize the internal psychic tensions that are produced at the level of the unconscious, underscoring the contingent relationship between social norms and psychic repression. Where Foucault theorizes sexuality as the product of medical, religious, and legal discourses, psychoanalysis views sexuality as a gap, a trauma, against which the subject protects itself through repression; language comes to fill the gap left by the original void. For psychoanalysis, the identities produced by discourses are unstable because the psychic structure that governs desire is located in the unconscious and maintains a hostile relationship with the ego.[6] Epistolary fiction plunders the tension between social norms and psychic desires, dramatizing at the level of plot the conflicts that arise between historically contingent concepts of sexuality and the private desires and psychic dilemmas that are often the content of and motivation for writing letters. With an eye to both the convergences and contradictions between Foucault and psychoanalysis, *Confessions of the Letter Closet* maneuvers between a discursive approach that attends to the historical development of sexuality and a psychoanalytic model of desire that underscores the role of the unconscious.

In light of the study's focus on the multiple ways in which epistolary fiction shapes and gives voice to queer desire, the texts included here were chosen for their use of the epistolary form and their historical engagement with the shifting panorama of discourses around sexuality. The authors are by no means necessarily gay or lesbian, nor do they enjoy equal status in literary histories: Miguel de Unamuno (1864–1936) and Carmen Martín Gaite (1925–2000) are canonical figures of Spanish literature; Luis Antonio de Villena and Carme Riera are successful contemporary writers, located in Madrid and Barcelona, respectively; Lluís Fernàndez, a Valencian writer who currently resides in Barcelona, is the least known relative to the others. The selection of texts does not pretend to offer an exhaustive account of epistolary works that engage with topics of sexuality. Instead, the principal thread guiding these authors' inclusion is their use of the epistolary form for the representation of homoerotic and homosexual desire. I have sought in this respect to establish a balance between subgenres of epistolary works (e.g., single or multiple correspondents, wholly epistolary narratives or the use of intercalated letters), narratives that reflect same-sex desire between both male and female correspondents, works that reflect the historical range of the fictional engagement with epistolarity and queer desire (e.g., early-twentieth-century or contemporary works, traditional letter writing or advancements such as facsimile and e-mail), and works in Castilian and Catalan, in order to reflect, albeit partially, the linguistic diversity of literary production in Spain.

The three parts of the book are organized around a series of literary representations of desire and sexuality that reflect the confessional and confidential dimension of familiar, private letters. Concretely, the first section explores the relationship between letter writing, homoeroticism, and sexual identity by examining the fictional use of the letter as a "window to the soul," or a transparent representation of an individual's psyche. Works of letter fiction excel in the representation of secret thoughts and intimate desires, and they often employ letters as points of entry into the sexuality of their protagonists. These first chapters explore the representation of homoeroticism (both male and female) in Unamuno's *La novela de Don Sandalio, jugador de ajedrez* (*The Novel of Don Sandalio, Chessplayer,* 1933) and Martín Gaite's *El cuarto de atrás* (*The Back Room,* 1978), analyzing how these texts engage with discourses of sexuality to articulate enigmatic desires that cannot be fully categorized as "homosexual." The second part of the book expands upon the use of letters for psychological insight and turns to the explicit disclosure of homosexual desire, where the letter functions as a confessional or testimonial document. The analyses in this section focus on how the protagonists of Villena's *Amor pasión* (Love Passion, 1983) and

Riera's short story "Jo pos per testimoni les gavines" ("I Call Upon the Seagulls as Witness," 1977) negotiate the stigma of homosexuality and their own ambivalence toward a gay or lesbian identity. The resistance to and struggle with sexuality as a subjectivity centered on the object of one's desire is expressed both as a psychic, internal struggle and as a concern with confidentiality of correspondence. Both works reflect the potential for private matters to enter the public sphere, a concern that historically has marked the use of letter writing and the expression of queer desire in the Spanish context. The final section of the book addresses the rise of gay and lesbian liberation politics during the transition to democracy and the impact of AIDS during the late 1980s and '90s in Spain in, respectively, Fernàndez's *L'anarquista nu* (*The Naked Anarchist,* 1979) and *Una prudente distancia* (A Prudent Distance, 1998). The analyses focus on the political dimension of private correspondence. The chapters focus on the ways in which the collected letters reflect the increasing visibility of the gay and lesbian community in Spain at the same time as gays and lesbians maintain a profound ambivalence toward official political organization. Where *L'anarquista nu* dramatizes the emergence of gay liberation politics after the death of Franco, *Una prudente distancia* examines the impoverished response of the gay community and the Spanish government to the AIDS epidemic.

The temporal scope of the study thus extends roughly from the early decades of the twentieth century to the late 1990s. Unamuno's and Martín Gaite's works focus on the first half of the twentieth century. The letters in *Don Sandalio,* written in 1930, date from 1910, and *El cuarto de atrás* engages with women's subjectivity during the decades after the Spanish civil war and during the Franco regime. Villena and Riera cover the later decades of the dictatorship and the early years of the transition to democracy. Fernàndez engages with the transition to democracy in *L'anarquista nu* and with the contemporary setting of the so-called second transition from the socialist government to the right-wing Partido Popular in *Una prudente distancia.* Nevertheless, *Confessions of the Letter Closet* does not strive to narrate a seamless, chronological development. Not only do the texts only roughly conform to a chronological order; the analyses, even as they attend closely to the movement of a letter between private and public spaces, are not focused on the increasing explicitness of desire. Readers will find no simple recuperation of queer voices here. Just as Foucault rejected the argument that the Victorian era repressed sex and the modern era liberated it, this study refuses a narrative in which sexuality is first oppressed and then freed, especially after the death of Francisco Franco in 1975 and the subsequent fall of his dictatorship.[7] The epistolary works in this study offer a different narrative of queer desire: they expose the social homophobia and psychic ambivalences around sexuality and identity that were foundational in the emergence of homosexuality as a category and with which gays and lesbians still struggle in spite of legal advances, political shifts, and increased social tolerance.

In studies of sexuality the selection of terminology is neither easy nor innocent. In light of this book's argument for the ambivalence around same-sex desire in the Spanish context, the choice of words becomes all the more pressing. I have opted to use the phrase "queer desire" throughout the study as an umbrella term for sexual desire between two members of the same sex.[8] In my analyses, "homoeroticism," "homosexuality," "gay," and "lesbian" also figure prominently when appropriate. These terms are not meant to be taken as equivalents, although they are closely related; individual chapters develop more fully their respective meanings. For example, homoeroticism is a form of desire or attraction between two members of the same sex, but it does not necessarily disrupt a heterosexual identity. In fact, homoeroticism can also function as an affective bond that strengthens heterosexual ties. In this study, "homoeroticism" and "queer desire" are employed as interchangeable terms when they designate an erotic attraction that disrupts normative patterns of affective relationships, familial arrangements, and modes of conceptualizing gender and sexual identity. "Homosexuality," in constrast, refers to the organization of homoeroticism into an identity based on same-sex object choice. Similarly, "queer subjectivity" designates an identity based on same-sex object choice, coupled with a conscious understanding of sexuality as a discourse.[9] The use of these terms throughout the book reflects the conceptual fluctuations that inform the historical development of same-sex desire in modern Spain.

The development of correspondence as a manifestation of the closet requires that we pay close attention to the historical transformations in epistolary discourses, particularly in relation to gender and sexuality, with an eye to examining their influence on the evolution of letter fiction in Spain. Admittedly, literary studies of narrative genres are rare today, and the genre of epistolary fiction—given its association with the eighteenth century—may seem at first glance an odd choice. Literary histories continually characterize epistolary fiction in terms of a narrative of rise and decline. The genre is said to culminate in the eighteenth century and then wane in the nineteenth, becoming virtually absent in the twentieth century. But not only did epistolarity not go by the wayside, persisting throughout the nineteenth and twentieth centuries, it remains a powerful presence in everyday lives and interpersonal relationships. The renaissance of epistolary communication in the form of e-mail, to offer one example, has resuscitated our awareness of the presence of written communication in mediating human relations. As an autobiographical form of writing, letters are considered a potent tool for examining the evolution of subjectivity and sexuality, texts whose intimate and confidential nature ostensibly provides a unique insight into the lives of their authors.

Letters nonetheless distinguish themselves from autobiography in subtle yet significant ways that are fundamental to the development of the letter closet. In their correspondence, letter writers often review the recent events of their lives, probe the motives behind their actions, analyze the reactions of others, and negotiate relationships with their interlocutors. Letters are snapshots of a life, written at various points, but usually not with the intention of producing a coherent biographical narrative. Autobiographies encompass the span of a subject's lifetime; in contrast, the letter is more focused on the author's relationship with a specific interlocutor. Both letters and autobiographies may share highly personal information, but letters tend to be more closely associated with confidentiality; they are embedded in a history of suspicion, secrecy, and surveillance. Autobiographies, on the other hand, are usually public in address. This is not to suggest that letters are more authentic or sincere, but rather that notions of authenticity and sincerity are fundamentally different for letter writing, since the perception of security and secrecy alters the exchange of information. Epistolary relations capture a world of the self believed to be safeguarded by the inviolability of correspondence and the sealed cover of an envelope. To read another's letter is, in effect, to violate the intimacy and confidentiality shared by the correspondents (Bou 128).

There is, of course, a difference between authentic letters and epistolary fiction: to speak of reading epistolary fiction as a violation of privacy makes little sense given that epistolary fiction is a *public* text. Reading someone's private letters is not the same activity as reading a fictional character's "private" letters. In epistolary studies, arguments for a distinction between authentic correspondence and letter fiction often focus on the lack of verisimilitude in literary works, emphasizing formal aspects that pertain only to letter fiction, such as the interruption of an editor who gathers the material for the reader or unrealistic amounts of time for writing and responding to letters. The conclusion is that epistolary literature does not accurately reflect real-life letter exchanges (Decker 23). In spite of their differences, this study maintains as one of its premises an equivalence between fictional and authentic letter writing: the letters of epistolary works share much in common with authentic ones, and the way we read real letters influences the way we approach epistolary fiction. Critics who perceive a close proximity between the two types of epistolarity draw attention to how authentic letter writing often courts "literariness," thus assimilating the real letter to the fictional one. The act of composing a letter leads writers to invent and fantasize, to produce a document that borders on fiction (Guillén, "On the Edge" 4; Salinas 43; Bou 134).

While such an argument renders the authentic letter "literary," the genre also implies that fictional letters replicate the real-life activity of reading letters. In "Introduction to the Structuralist Analysis of Narratives," Roland Barthes writes that "there is no counting the number of narrational devices which seek to naturalize the subsequent narrative by feigning to make it the outcome of some natural circumstance and thus, as it were, 'disinaugurating' it: epistolary novels, supposedly re-discovered manuscript, author who met the narrator" (116). Epistolary fiction "naturalizes" the act of reading fictional letters by aligning the reading of fiction with the real-life practice of reading someone else's letters. The genre depends upon a mimetic relationship between senders and receivers that appears in actual correspondence, but it does so by underscoring the principle that we are reading letters not destined for us. The formal dimensions of the genre depend on the notion that the letters we read have been purloined, that they belong to someone else and have been collected for the reader; Perry notes that booksellers in eighteenth-century England often deliberately blurred the line between real and fictional letters (79). Epistolarity is a broad category that en-compasses both a literary genre, a set of formal characteristics shared by particular texts, and a mode, in which the literary form has an exter-nal model with its own characteristics. Epistolary writing refers to the concrete act of composing a letter as well as the array of discourses and functions that support letter writing as a social practice. By virtue of its equation of fictional letters with real ones, the epistolary genre com-pels us to address its social and historical context and to explore, in the words of Mary Favret, "the envelope of contingency" that surrounds all letters (56). *Confessions of the Letter Closet* thus maintains that epistolary fiction develops in relation to the authentic correspondence of its time (i.e., the discursive function of letter writing occurs within a specific social and political context) and the historicity of the literary genre (i.e., the formal constraints and evolution of aesthetic trends guide the letter's fictional deployment).

Let us turn to the historical evolution of the letter form in the nineteenth century. The discursive function of letter writing is crucial for understanding how letter correspondence becomes a vehicle for the expression of queer desire. The letter as a historically specific mani-festation of the closet remains closely tied to the discourses of privacy that emerge most saliently in the era of the postal system and to the discourses of sexuality in the late nineteenth century. Thomas Beebee cogently summarizes: "Fictional uses of the letter appropriated the status and power the letter had acquired from its established functions within other discursive practices" (3–4). As a result, scholars often remark on the "porous" boundaries between the letter, letter-writing manuals, and the development of the epistolary novel (Gilroy and Verhoeven 2). Critics of epistolary fiction who adhere to this discursive view of fiction and correspondence tend to conceive of the letter in terms of containment by and resistance to social power, surveillance, and gender roles. In her study of the French novel, English Showalter condemns the epistolary genre as an antiquated form of literary bondage, a set of formal shackles to be removed so that narrative forms may evolve (192). In contrast with Showalter, for example, Terry Castle sees Richardson's use of the epistolary form in *Clarissa* as a means of disrupting univocal meaning and closure, perceiving the multiplicity of voices and perspectives inherent in much epistolary fiction as a mode of cultural contestation. The development of letter writing as a social practice, in conjunction with the shifting terrain of sexuality in the nineteenth century, points to how the letter was a disciplinary tool whose function dovetailed social norms, including, as we will see, the increased concern with sexuality as a discrete category of knowledge.

Nowhere is the disciplinary function of letters more apparent than in the numerous manuals and handbooks that codified proper formal models to be copied by letter writers. In his study of *sécretaires* and letter-writing manuals in eighteenth-century France, Roger Chartier asserts that such guidebooks served both a literary and social purpose: they became the nucleus for the epistolary novel, and moreover they codified idealized models of behavior and social arrangements (15, 95, 98). Beebee also notes, following Janet Altman's cue, that letter-writing manuals were part of a "letter-writing machine" whose overarching function was to establish a system of roles for literate classes and to exercise control of language (47). Guides from nineteenth-century Spain, for example, offer ample evidence of the formal and social norms that "correct" letter writing entailed. The *Repertorio epistolar* (Epistolary Repertoire, 1878) provides models for all possible cases of epistolary exchanges. Everything from the proper use of envelopes to the use of stamps or wax is a subject of the manual, and the function of letters as a mode of signaling class continued to be at the forefront of such instructions. Letter writing, beginning with the *ars dictaminis*, has long been pressed into the service of didactic instruction. Perry similarly argues that letter writing in eighteenth-century England played a substantial role in the moral education of the literate class, with letter manuals instructing readers in "morally correct responses to life" (86). Gender and sexual relations stand out in particular as one of the primary domains of control for letter-writing manuals. Not only did letter manuals codify proper forms of expression but they also offered strict guidelines for what sentiments should be expressed and to whom. This impulse is reflected in epistolary novels such as *Pamela* and *Clarissa,* which underscore the transgressions and dangers that may befall female protagonists when epistolary and gender norms are not properly followed. These two examples also serve as a reminder that letter-writing manuals have often focused primarily on women as explicit addressees, encouraging them to adhere to proper notions of decorum.

So too in the case of Spain, where the *Ramillete de amantes* (Lover's Bouquet, included in the *Repertorio*) and Pilar Pascual de Sanjuán's *Manual epistolar, para las señoritas* (Epistolary Manual for Young Ladies, 1877) offer instructions for women letter writers. The author of the preface to the *Ramillete de amantes* advises: "A woman should write with care what she wants to express, since at times she does not think carefully about what she writes, and writes what she does not think" (14). Pascual de Sanjuán's text recommends that women should limit their writing to letters, and even then to writing them occasionally (6). These texts establish rigid guidelines for women letter writers, but their effect is to make the rules for letter writing prescriptive for women's roles in general. The *Ramillete* advises the woman writer to remain discreet and only reveal her emotions in part, and only once she is familiar with the male writer with whom she is corresponding. The *Epistolario moral literario* (Literary Collection of Moral Letters, which follows the *Ramillete de amantes*), to offer a final example, takes the form of a letter from one woman to another to offer moral and religious lessons; the authorial voice advises women to stay home and take care of the family.

The formal guidelines prescribed in letter-writing manuals are ideals. Undoubtedly letter writers failed to live up to those norms and used formulas improperly. The need to codify and exemplify the proper modes of address and the correct use of language implies that there are improper modes of address or epistolary relations for which the guides offer no examples. Letter correspondence remains open to the possibility of libidinal relations that do not adhere to the normative gender roles prescribed for senders and receivers. Chartier remarks in his discussion of the Troyes edition of *Sécretaire à la Mode* from 1730 that the section of "amorous letters of all sorts of subjects" includes three letters penned by men addressed to other men "by mistake" (80). The letters themselves do not contain any amorous content, but the location of those letters within the collection draws attention to the absence of homoerotic desire within the capacious section of "all sorts of subjects"; "all sorts" does not in fact include all sorts. The prescriptive function of the letter-writing manual revealed one of the elements that had been eliminated in the process of (mis)categorizing the model letters. The possibility that male letter writers might send missives to other men reveals the extent to which homoeroticism appears only by means of its absence.

The letter is initially subject to control in the form of writing manuals that detail the appropriate modes of expression. But there is perhaps no other change in the history of letter writing more significant than the development of the penny post for understanding the link between letters and sexuality. Chief among the discursive shifts in letter writing is the transformation of the letter as a legal document or formulaic mode of prose composition into a highly individuated form of writing. A topos of seventeenth- and eighteenth-century epistolary fiction is that letters are "windows to the soul," transparent fragments of an individual's psyche. In a compelling analysis of letters, literature, and the postal system, Bernhard Siegert argues that the eighteenth-century concept of the letter as the repository of individual consciousness was part of a confessional matrix of writing. The interpretation of one's letter writing was meant "to tease a confession of truth from the letter's text—a confession by means of which an individual had to prove his or her identity" (75). Siegert's novel claim is that this concept of the letter was achieved through the extension of the postal system and later consolidated through the concept of postage as a form of prepayment. The Penny Post Bill was passed in England on July 29, 1839, influenced in large part by Rowland Hill's 1837 treatise *Post Office Reform*. Hill called for penny postage, or prepayment, to replace the traditional system of payment upon delivery. Consequently, everyone could have access to the mail with a standard rate, and the post was no longer exclusively at the service of the crown nor for a privileged, literate social class. While the postal system had limited its access to an elite class, Siegert argues that the use of the postage stamp was designed to intercept "the people's noise," to regulate and redirect communication among all levels of society (105). Hence, the use of the stamp allowed all classes to be enmeshed in the system, absorbing them into the postal web so that "even the illiterate could not slip through the gaps in the postal net" (106). The postal system was thus transformed into a commercial and ideological enterprise for the "interpellation" of subjects: "The State produced 'subjects' in both senses of the word by inventing the general post, the postal monopoly, and the usefulness of the postal system" (8).

The postal system depended upon the ideological charade that the letter was both universal (anyone could write a letter) and singular (each letter was the unique expression of a unique individual). "As long as letters had a personal history at the post offices, they could serve as metaphors for the individuality of the people who wrote them" (28). The consequence of the metaphorical substitution of the letter for the person was that the letter took over the act of confession, as people wrote to each other confiding their intimate thoughts and secrets, all contained within and delivered by the post (38). The letter allowed for the transmission of secrets hidden beneath the seal of the envelope. One of the key functions of the postal system, Siegert argues, was to *expand* the domain of confession: "The postman's satchel thus holds more secrets, and no less securely under proper administration, than the seal of confession, and the symbol of discretion is none other than that of the postal service" (38).[10]

The rise of the postal system also explains the prevalence of epistolary terminology in our concepts of subjectivity: postage stamps and mailboxes would provide poststructuralism and psychoanalysis with a language for describing subjectivity. Indeed, Siegert goes so far as to attribute the concept of the unconscious to the postal system, as Freud would make various references to posting letters and misaddressing envelopes in his *Psychopathology of Everyday Life* (71).[11] As a result, letters became portals into the opaque psychic inner workings of their writers:

The letter's text came to be a symptom—the symptom of a measurable and potentially individualized deviance from the reference input or the norm, and *therefore a semiotic prerequisite for the medical-moral knowledge of sex*. The (at least theoretical) tendency of postage to disappear was the prerequisite for a hermeneutics of the private letter that effected the psychologization of its author. The possibility of confirming a soul (an unconscious) for the letter writer was determined by postage. Once this possibility had set the psychological machine of interpretation in motion, it became impossible for any letter not to reveal its secrets—or those of the soul—to the disciplined eye of its pedagogical recipients. (77, my emphasis)

This view of development of the postal system can easily be seen as an extension of power: postage stamps, mailboxes and slots, and postal workers all reduce the individual to names and addresses. While previous postal systems depended upon the presence of the addressee for the letter's receipt, the creation of mailboxes and mailslots eliminated the need for the recipient to be available for delivery or even aware of the delivery which "could slip under the threshold of consciousness" (111). The postage stamp and the mailbox catalyzed a shift in concepts of identity. The name became the street number and the body the mailbox, and individuals became subjects of addressability: "We exist in the eyes of the law as long as only one mail slot is to be found at the address recorded by power [. . .] Letters sniff out the addresses we owe to power, which has taken up residence in the technology of communication, in order to confine us to an identity" (116). Siegert thus links Hill's development of penny postage to Jeremy Bentham, who visited Hill's school in 1827. Bentham's creation of the panopticon, the basis of Foucault's theory of power and discipline, operates like the postal system in which the individuals who send mail are not unique creations but rather functions of the postal system, or relays, as Siegert dubs them. The individual as the site of consciousness is merely a fiction and the subject simply a relay between postings.

Siegert only alludes briefly to the consequences of his argument for thinking about letter writing, subjectivity, and sexuality. Insightfully, he notes that, with the exception of the signature and handwriting, nothing in letters could guarantee the gender of the author, thus allowing for "hommo-sexual" correspondents (134). The perception of the letter as an instrument of disciplinary power resonates strongly with Foucault's well-known arguments about the expansion of confession in the nineteenth century as an epistemic shift that, through an incitement to speak about sex, produced sexuality as the secret truth of the subject. It is not difficult to extend Siegert's line of thinking in the lengthy quotation about the "medical-moral knowledge of sex" to Foucault's arguments in the first volume of *The History of Sexuality* about the transformation of the discourses around sexuality and the subject. Confession was made obligatory by the Roman Catholic Church in 1215 in the Fourth Lateran Council. The obligation to confess led Foucault to argue that confession transcends its specific religious domain, becoming a technique of subjection that compels the self to fashion a discourse of truth. The expansion of confession as a disciplinary tool shifted sexuality from a list of acceptable or forbidden acts to accord sexuality a central place in the development of the subject. The result was the creation of the category of the homosexual. It is not surprising to find that Foucault specifically mentions letter writing in describing the many forms that confession has taken (63). The function of letter correspondence was, according to Siegert, not only to produce communication but also to assign positions to the sexes, positions inside an organization of knowledge (75). The norms of letter writing subject writers to a confessional machinery that locates truth in one's sexuality and attempts to control the forms of that truth according to rigid guidelines that reflect social norms. As the queer potential of letter writing came into view and entered discourse, the assumption that a letter could express or contain references to homosexuality increased. If sexuality is tied to a confessional matrix, a historically specific apparatus for producing forms of subjectivity rooted in the objects of one's desire, then letter writing as a confessional practice would logically become a key site for the expression of homosexuality.

The preceding argument is not meant to suggest that evidence of homosexuality is to be found only beginning in the nineteenth century, that no evidence of expressions of desire can be found in letters prior to that century, nor is it to reject the historical recuperative project of finding evidence of homoerotic relations prior to the nineteenth century.

Numerous letter collections prior to the epistemic shift that Foucault traces attest to profound emotional attachments between members of the same sex, although the expressions of homoerotic desire invariably present the historical dilemma of categorization according to modern conceptions of sexuality that appeared a posteriori. For example, the Spanish painter Francisco de Goya's letters to Martín Zapater, written between 1771 and 1792, evince a rhetoric of passionate friendship, so imbued with eroticism as to discomfit many of Goya's more contemporary readers: "with your image in front of me I have the sweetness of being with you, oh man of my soul, I didn't believe that friendship could reach the stage that I am experiencing" (qtd. in Pagés-Rangel 179). As Roxana Pagés-Rangel aptly notes, the correspondence is not easily deciphered, as specific turns of phrase and words allude to a private jargon shared with Zapater. She deftly addresses the editorial attempts to link such passionate discourse to Goya's developing illness, to downplay such language as mere rhetoric, or to ignore the implications altogether for the sake of maintaining a coherent authorial figure for Goya. She is careful not to assert a gay identity for Goya, but neither does she shy away from the homoerotic dimension of the relationship. My point is not to deny the eroticism of such exchanges prior to the invention of the category of homosexuality. Rather, I claim that as homosexuality increasingly becomes part of public discourse as a discrete category, it similarly infiltrates the discursive space of letter correspondence and, in turn, the literary domain of the epistolary novel.

In what ways did the discourses around epistolarity, confession, and sexuality leave their mark on epistolary fiction in Spain? Janet Altman has argued that the national traditions of epistolary fiction differ according to their uses of the letter: the German epistolary novel uses the letter as a form of diary, the English as a form of witnessing or testimony, and the French as a weapon (194). Although Altman presents these uses of the letter as if they were discrete categories, I understand her division of epistolary practices along national differences as an attempt to underscore the contingent nature of the impact that social transformations in the letter had on epistolary fiction. The letter in Spain bears a strong correspondence with the letter as confession, not unlike the German and English use of letters as confidential modes of communicating with others (that border is blurred, however, when confidential letters are sometimes used in epistolary works as weapons that reveal the secrets of other correspondents). By using the letter as the individual expression of private thoughts, canonical works of the genre such as Samuel Richardson's *Pamela* (1740–41) and *Clarissa* (1747–48), Jean-Jacques Rousseau's *Julie, ou La Nouvelle Héloïse* (1761), Choderlos de Laclos's *Les liaisons dangereuses* (*Dangerous Liaisons,* 1782), and Johann Wolfgang von Goethe's *The Sorrows of Young Werther* (1774) bear witness to what may be called the confessional function of letter writing. In all of them, the protagonists put thoughts to paper that are meant to be confidential, that would only be conveyed to certain parties under certain circumstances. As is well known, the respective denouements of these works bespeak the dangers that confessional letter writing courts; as Perry notes, eighteenth-century publishers of English epistolary fiction underscored the "revelatory possibilities of private letters" (74). In his 1850 introduction to a collection of Spanish letters, Eugenio de Ochoa defines them as "types of intimate expansions, in which one alone spills the entire contents of the heart onto paper, in the security of an inviolable secret and with even more freedom than in a private conversation" (v). Fictional works such as Juan Valera's *Pepita Jiménez* (1874), in which the young priest Luis writes to the *Deán* confessing his burgeoning love for the widow Pepita, draw heavily on the rhetoric of confession. With some exceptions—such as the Spanish realist author Benito Pérez Galdós's *La estafeta romántica* (The Romantic Post Office, 1899), which uses multiple correspondents—the single-voiced confidential mode of letter writing predominates in Spanish epistolary fiction.

In comparison to the French and English canons, Spain cannot lay claim to a quantitatively rich epistolary history. Critics of epistolary fiction in Spain continually point up the relatively weak tradition of the genre vis-à-vis French and English literature, in spite of evidence to the contrary (Reyes xxi).[12] As Ochoa writes: "It is not possible to ignore that our literature, rich in all genres, is not so in the epistolary genre as much as it could and should be" (vii). The epistle in Spain has a profound history—beginning with the *cartas de relación* (accounts of service provided to the monarchs) and thriving through the seventeenth century, then declining to a low point in the nineteenth century—that has long been overlooked. A comparable use of the private letter for literary purposes was decidedly less popular. Hazel Gold persuasively argues that epistolary novels were published in Spain throughout the nineteenth century, but that most of them were not written by major novelists nor did they make up a significant percentage of the novelistic production (134). More recently, in her study of epistolary fiction in the late eighteenth and early nineteenth centuries, Ana Rueda has argued for a revision of current literary histories by unearthing a number of epistolary works between 1789 and 1840. Where the French and English traditions supposedly decline after 1789, Rueda asserts that at this time the genre began to flourish, confirming Gold's arguments for the presence of the epistolary novel in the nineteenth century (*Cartas* 45).

In spite of the letter form's popularity in the eighteenth century in Europe, it is difficult to ignore that its influence on Spanish letters at the end of the eighteenth and beginning of the nineteenth centuries, while considerably stronger than previously thought, never reached the vigor displayed in English or French traditions. The reasons for the lack of an epistolary tradition are more difficult to ascertain. Ricardo Senabre argues that the translation of *Clarissa* in 1751 into French and the advent of circulating libraries that allowed for people to read at home generated considerable interest in the epistolary form among French readers (68–69). In contrast, he maintains, the epistolary form suffered in Spain due to the belated translations of letter novels and the absence of a large reading public (71). Spanish translations of *Pamela* and *Clarissa* were published in 1794, *Werther* in 1803, *Julie* in 1814, and *Les liaisons dangereuses* in 1822.[13] The Castilian version of *Clarissa* was "corrected and adjusted to the customs of the Spanish reading public by the translator," and a complete, unaltered version of *Julie* would not appear until 1820 (71). As Senabre points out, over a half-century passes by the time the works of Richardson and Rousseau reach the Spanish public. While Juan Valera may have been influenced by *Werther* (mention is also made in Galdós's *La incógnita* [*The Unknown*, 1889]), there is little doubt that foreign models of epistolary fiction did not establish strong roots.

In contrast with Senabre, Gold speculates that the paucity of letter novels may be owed to hostile attitudes toward foreign models of literature, to the association of letter writing with women, and with the form's close ties with confession as both a religious speech act that focuses on the moral nature of one's actions and a secular, psychological process that emphasizes introspection as a mode of understanding oneself. For Gold, the discretion that suppressed the publication of real-life letters in Spain extended to the novelistic treatment of the form: "these same taboos were undoubtedly strong enough to have discredited the epistolary novel's pretensions to the mimetic representation of confession and other revelations of intimate, daily experience" (137).[14] The association of letter writing with confession, in the context of Catholic-dominated Spain, debilitated its uptake by authors for literary purposes: the private letter made public was likely seen as an invasion of privacy and a violation of the secrecy of confession.[15] Beebee similarly claims that "the Catholic practice of confession made intimist letters such as formed the basis of epistolary literature seem a sacrilegious invasion of privacy" (188). The concerns around secrecy and intimacy also explain why epistolary fiction, with its focus on private correspondence, suffered at the same time that numerous essays and moral treatises modeled themselves on the epistolary form (Gold 137). In other words, where the *letter* was a private and confessional mode of writing, the *epistle* functioned as a public mode of address.[16]

The suspicion of and concern with surveillance in the era of the postal system may have also contributed to the paucity of published correspondences, to the degree that there was a clear equivalence between the authentic and fictional letters. The history of the post reveals a marked concern with state surveillance and privacy. In England, the first one-penny stamps were issued only months after the official launch date of the penny post on May 6, 1840. Although decreed in Spain on August 17, 1843, the postal stamp did not take effect until January 1, 1850. (He does not offer a precise date, but Eduardo Verdegay y Fiscowich asserts that D. Fermín Caballero proposed a postage stamp for envelopes before Rowland Hill's 1837 innovation [278].) In 1856 it became standard practice, leaving behind the former system of allowing the recipient to pay upon delivery (Verdegay y Fiscowich 286). As a state institution, the post inspired a great deal of suspicion on the part of the public. Throughout the latter half of the nineteenth century and the early part of the twentieth, Spaniards consistently complained about the lack of a well-organized mail service.[17] In "El servicio de correos y la opinión" (Postal Service and Public Opinion), for example, Mariano Pardo de Figueroa discusses how people send money via the post: they seal, open, and then reseal the letter without including any money so that it appears as if a postal employee had stolen it (5). People also abused the less expensive charge for sending newspapers by writing notes in the margins of the papers rather than mailing letters; the abuse was apparently so great that the postal service devoted significant resources to tracking down contraband, delaying mail delivery (9–10). A final example serves to demonstrate the public's lack of faith in the system. In a letter to Galdós dated January 26, 1895, Paco Navarro y Ledesma writes: "As you have so much interest in safeguarding the letter from Clarín, I don't want to send it by mail. Within three or four days, a friend of mine going to Madrid will hand deliver it to you" (Ortega 322).

The legal discourses around letter correspondence and the postal system reflected the social concern for secrecy and rights of privacy. In Spain, the constitutions of 1869 and 1876 guaranteed inviolability of correspondence, and in article 55 of the Reglamento Orgánico de Correos from July 11, 1909, violation of correspondence was among the worst offenses (Castán Vázquez 20).[18] Lorenzo Benito notes that while the material letter itself was protected by property rights (*el derecho a la propiedad*), the ideas contained in the letter were not, not even under intellectual property law, as no mention of correspondence and intellectual property is made in the various decrees from 1813 to 1879 (Ramella 562). The Ordenanzas de Correos of June 8, 1794, declared that the state only recognizes the ownership of the addressee; upon mailing the letter, the author ("remitente") has given up rights. The Tratado de Berna of October 9, 1874, which established the Union General de Correos, forced Spanish law to align itself with European law, giving some rights to the author. Beginning in 1889, in conformity with European law, all correspondence belonged to the sender until it had reached the addressee (565). But Benito is quick to point out that the rights of publication within Spanish jurisprudence had not been worked out, leaving open the question of who could publish private correspondence (584).

Elizabeth MacArthur claims in her study of seventeenth- and eighteenth-century French epistolary writing that the genre becomes "extravagant" in the sense of being beyond the norm, or excessive—a term whose inflections of deviance, transgression, and abnormality cannot go unnoticed. The result, she argues, is that the loss of popularity of the epistolary form in the eighteenth and nineteenth centuries can be linked to a perceived need to control deviance and a strong desire for narrative closure. The epistolary form may not disappear entirely, but MacArthur's point is that the social perception of letter writing as a genre steeped in secrets and transgression may have had a deleterious effect on the novelistic genre. Certainly that may be true in the Spanish context, since there is a short conceptual distance from desire and deviance (and the desire to control deviance) to the categories of homosexuality and heterosexuality that develop in the nineteenth century. Although the concerns with confession, privacy, and the revelation of secrets may have suppressed the development of the epistolary novel, they did not foreclose the genre altogether. Instead, those anxieties became part and parcel of the genre's narrative plots. Luis Gutiérrez's *Cornelia Bororquia o la víctima de la Inquisición* (Cornelia Bororquia, or the Inquisition's Victim, 1799–1800), Valera's *Pepita Jiménez,* and Galdós's *La incógnita* and *La estafeta romántica* employ the letter form as a confessional mode of writing or for amorous connection. Gold notes that in many of these works the narrative plot centers on sexual transgression. Nevertheless, where the letters of Lovelace to Clarissa or of Valmont to Madame de Tourvel achieve seduction through letters, Spanish novels recount the seductions in letters to another party (138). In *Cornelia Bororquia* the titular character is kidnapped by the Archibishop of Seville under pretenses of blasphemy so that he might seduce her. She is eventually interrogated by the Inquisition after she stabs him to death, and she herself is put to death by being burned alive. Published in Paris, the book's strong condemnation of the abuses of power by the Inquisition led to its censorship in Spain until 1831. *Pepita Jiménez* is composed of confessional letters in which Luis, a seminarian, struggles with his faith in God and sexual interest in Pepita Jiménez and conveys his "impure" thoughts to his uncle, the *Deán*. In *La incógnita*, Manolo Infante writes to Equis about the Madrilenian society that the latter has abandoned for Orbajosa. In the process, the letters shift in tone from a representation of social relations to the romantic love that he feels for his cousin Augusta. While Manolo Infante's letters reveal his lack of maturity in romantic matters, the letters of *La estafeta romántica* are a collective rejection of romantic passion in favor of a more pragmatic, grounded approach to relationships, as the main character Calpena is dissuaded from pursuing a frustrated romance by his mother and her friend Valvarena, who successfully steer him toward marriage with Demetria.[19]

If sexual desire appears as the topic of confession in these epistolary works, the representation and function of desire does not remain static. A brief overview of three works—*Pepita Jiménez*, *La incógnita*, and Juan Francisco Muñoz y Pabón's *Amor postal* (Postal Love, 1903)—will establish a number of the fundamental characteristics that persist in epistolary fiction in the twentieth century. At the same time, these works bear witness to an increasing awareness of homoeroticism as a desire that may be communicated via letter writing. Whereas *Pepita Jiménez* opens up the epistolary form by refusing to condemn the "illicit" desires of the young priest for his father's female love interest, *La incógnita* focuses on opaque areas of desire that resist categorization. Finally, *Amor postal*, published at the turn of the century, raises in an explicit manner the exchange of desire between letter correspondents of the same sex in order to expel such desire through the act of confession itself. These epistolary works reveal an increased concern in the second half of the nineteenth century around homoeroticism as potential sexual transgression. This is, it must be noted, a concern with homoeroticism among men. Lesbianism remains all too absent from these remarks and these works. While epistolarity is linked to women in nineteenth-century Spain, the anxieties around male sexuality do not produce a comparable body of works concerned with queer desire among women. Female desire—whether in epistolary fiction or in letter-writing manuals—remains circumscribed by men; in Galdós's *Tristana*, for example, the narrator-editor of the novel publishes fragments of the eponymous protagonist's letters to Horacio.

First published in three installments in *Revista de España* in 1874,

Pepita Jiménez draws on a literary form in disuse but whose public circulation had been increasing since the introduction of the stamp in 1850. Whether or not "the post-office window replaced the ears of the priest," as Siegert asserts (28), in Valera's text the confessional function of the letter plays a significant role. The novel engages with the dynamics of confession, interpretation, and pedagogy through the tripartite structure of the letters of the young seminarian Luis de Vargas written to the *Deán,* the third-person narration entitled *Paralipómenos* that describes the events during the month after Luis's correspondence, and the Epilogue composed of letters from Luis's father to the *Deán.* The novel begins with the topos of the found manuscript, which the anonymous narrator claims to have received after it passed through several hands. The names have been changed, and the anonymous narrator affirms that the letters were real; the *Deán* burned the originals or returned them to their owners. In this manner, the narrator avoids the thorny issue of violating the sanctity of confession and the public revelation of secrets—"changing only the names so that if their bearers are living, they may not wish to find themselves in a novel without their wish or consent" (2).[20] Valera, in asserting the veracity of the letters but hiding the author's identity, circumvents the concern about the right to secrecy.

The novel is a struggle between two forms of love—divine and profane—and between two objects of desire—God and Pepita. The political context and Valera's ideas on the novel undoubtedly influenced the narrative plot. The emphasis on Catholicism in the novel emerged, in part, from the ideological clash between the secularist strain of liberalism that led to the Revolution of 1868 and the traditional Catholicism of the Carlists who launched the Second Carlist War in 1872. James Whiston argues that the novel's treatment of Catholicism, mysticism, and secular love reflected Valera's desire to produce a "view of life that could encompass both religious and worldly values" (78). At the same time, Valera was something of an anomaly in nineteenth-century Spain, and his aestheticist tendencies—his treatment of the novel as a form of poetry, his desire to use literature to create objects of beauty—placed him in opposition to the dominant realist and naturalist trends of his time. Valera's use of the epistolary mode reflects his profound interest in the affective dimension of his characters and the influence, as Leonardo Romero asserts, of epistolary predecessors such as Goethe's *Werther* that focus on the psychological struggles of the letter writers (67).

In this respect, Valera's use of the letter moves between the moralizing dimension of letter writing rooted in religious confession and the sentimental, psychological mode of writing tied to secular notions of confidentiality. At one point, Luis self-consciously characterizes his letters as a form of confession: "I always write to you as if I were on my knees in the confessional before you" (66).[21] In the letter exchange, the *Deán* reads between the lines and sees that, in spite of Luis's protests to the contrary, his feelings for Pepita are more amorous than he admits; in the end, the female object of desire wins over religious devotion. Valera's novel thus deploys the letter form, at least initially, as an instrument of psychological analysis and as a pedagogical tool of reading that wrests the letter from the confines of confession as the revelation of secrets that, in turn, leads to an act of atonement for one's sins. Ruth Hoff makes a similar argument, tracing the relationship between confession and sexuality in Luis's letters, to point to how his letter-writing activity, while adopting a confessional tone, is also an act of interpretation of both his truth and of Pepita's (217). Luis writes: "[H]ow can one fathom the intimacies of the heart, the secrets hidden in the mind of a maiden, reared perhaps in an overly sheltered manner and ignorant of everything?" (9).[22] As if the confessional direction of the letter were somehow being twisted by veering outward from his own mind, he quickly reverses course: "Be that as it may, and laying aside these psychological probings which I have no right to make, for I do not know Pepita Jiménez" (9).[23] His narration returns to the confession of his own thoughts and feelings, all in the service of receiving guidance: "You have taught me to analyze all that my soul experiences, to seek its origin, good or evil, to plumb the innermost depths of my heart—in short to make a scrupulous examination of conscience" (12).[24] In many respects, Luis's statement is a summary of confession, and as such his letters become a mode of self-analysis in which he returns to his own writing for additional interpretation.

Over the course of the novel, letter writing increasingly emphasizes the role of psychological insight over the need to expel one's sins, although confession as a religious practice never entirely goes by the wayside. In the third section, Don Pedro's letter provides the reader with the remainder of the story, since logically he would have had access to the events that he narrates. In it, Don Pedro performs something like a confession on Luis's behalf, and Valera balances his critique of Catholic confession. While the two priests in the novel—the Vicar and the *Deán*—are portrayed, Whiston argues, as "ineffectual" except in their unwitting assistance in the evolution of Pepita and Luis's relationship (45), religion finds its place in the home in the novel's conclusion: the happiness of the newlyweds' home is balanced by Luis's continued love for God. "You must not think, however, that Luis's and Pepita's fondness for material goods has cooled their religious feeling in the least. [. . .] Amidst his present good fortune, Luis has never forgotten the collapse of the ideal he had dreamed of" (179).[25] Although the confessional element has been excised from the letter writing, the letter still functions as a mode of psychological insight: Luis is not the author, but his heart—now opened by virtue of his earlier epistolary activities—remains an open text for Don Pedro to interpret and share with his readers.

Pepita Jiménez reflects a shift away from the letter as a moralistic tool of confession: the novel employs the letter form less as a means to admit one's guilt and more as a window into an inconsistent and shifting consciousness. Whether about oneself (Luis) or others (Don Pedro), the letter becomes a repository of psychological content open to the reader's interpretation. It is here that Galdós's *La incógnita*, undoubtedly influenced by Valera's work, offers additional insight into the genre. As Thomas Franz astutely observes, there are a number of important parallels between *Pepita Jiménez* and *La incógnita*: the singular, first-person epistolary form; the addressee who is able to see into the revelations more than the letter writers intend; the use of the letter form as a confessional document; the similarity of the amorous desire that the protagonists feel toward a woman and the reasons given to justify their feelings. Foremost among the shared attributes for our purposes is the way in which the revelations offered by Luis and Manolo, respectively, reveal more than intended (Franz 40). At the same time, *La incógnita* also stresses the impenetrable quality of certain types of desire that remain all too enigmatic to observers. Whereas *Pepita Jiménez* portrays the unveiling of a false consciousness that is readily apparent to the reader of Luis's letters, *La incógnita*'s use of the letter as a mode of psychological illumination underscores the opacity of the mind. In Galdós's work confession as a verbalization of past desires and secrets in search of absolution from moral condemnation evolves toward a psychological approach that emphasizes the limits of introspection and self-knowledge.

La incógnita is not Galdós's first use of the epistolary form. He included letter writing in *Doña Perfecta* (1876), and later in *Tristana* (1902). His use of it in 1889, followed by the use of dialogue in *Realidad* (*Reality*, 1889), reflects a shift in the narrative trends at the time. Leopoldo Alas (Clarín) argued that the turn toward a psychological narrative mode was, for Galdós, a new phase that emulated foreign writers who were surpassing naturalism (246–47); Senabre notes that Galdós was sensitive to literary trends and the translation of Paul Bourget's work was a decisive influence (74). *La incógnita* is a psychological novel in many respects. The protagonist of the novel, Manolo Infante, writes letters to D. Equis X to entertain him with tales of events and people of Madrilenian high society known to both of them. Infante is a young politician whose lack of experience troubles him, and his interlocutor, who resides in the town of Orbajosa, occupies the privileged position of being something of an advisor or figure of authority. Manolo's letters are concerned on the whole with a series of enigmas that emerge from his desire for his cousin, Augusta, and the unexplained death of another character, Federico Viera. The first half of the novel is concerned primarily with scrutinizing Augusta's actions and comments for evidence of adultery. His letters reveal his shifting opinions of his cousin, as well as the various other figures who mediate his connection with her. At various moments he evokes the confidential aspect of a confession to characterize his activity and relationship with Equis: "I'm telling you all the phenomena taking place in my soul because you're my confessor and I should conceal nothing from you" (95).[26] At another point he calls into question Augusta and her husband Orozco's religious devotion, pointing out that they occasionally attend mass but do not go to confession (109–10); confession appears as a much more secular investigation into the minds of others rather than a religious act of penitence. Given the confessional nature of their correspondence, Infante expects absolute confidentiality from the outset, in exchange for which he will relay everything (5), and then bristles at the novel's close when he realizes that Equis's whimsical suggestion to publish the letters in a local newspaper has become all too real. In the end, Equis does not choose such a small venue, however, as the text is transformed magically into *Realidad,* whose purpose is to resolve the enigmas of the first text.[27]

As a psychological and detective epistolary work, *La incógnita* uses the epistolary form in two principal ways: to offer psychological insight into Infante and to draw attention to the way language not only reflects reality but also creates it. Infante's letters attempt to convey the reality of life in Madrid to Equis, but he is aware that his writing *produces* that image of society. As Akiko Tsuchiya notes, Infante "constantly struggles to reconcile two contradictory visions of language: his search for a referent behind the sign (that is, his search for a solution to the various enigmas of the novel) inevitably comes into conflict with his role as inventor of the autonomous language of fiction" ("*La incógnita*" 337). Infante's awareness of language's capacity to create meaning thus obscures his capacity to interpret the enigmas of subjectivity. Indeed, over the course of the novel it becomes apparent that the explorations for such enigmas as Augusta's adultery and Viera's death reside in the characters' consciences, not in facts. Federico Viera's personality is one of those enigmas. His reputation oscillates between virtue and decadence, and his gentlemanly honor is smeared by *pecadillos.* Viera is besotted by his "grave defects" and "the permanent obstacles of his character— a problem which admits no easy solution" (77).[28] The character problem that afflicts him is never clarified (gambling is one of his vices), and Infante ultimately accepts that Viera will never confide the "vice" that plagues him. To some extent, his investigations prove fruitless, and he never confronts Viera directly; Viera's death, of course, prevents Infante from doing so. Nevertheless, Infante does not adopt the same perspective with Augusta. He suspects that she and Viera were involved in an affair, which he speculates contributed to Viera's demise. Infante urges her to confess, or at least, to confide in him on several occasions—"She could therefore feel quite free to reveal it to me, for I'd hear her out like a confessor and then bury it within myself as within a grave" (204)— but she unfailingly rebuffs him.[29]

Infante's inability to penetrate people's minds and accurately discern the psychic workings of desire leaves the enigmas of *La incógnita* unresolved. The sequel, *Realidad,* supposedly offers answers that the first text does not provide. Often read together, the two novels conjure a hermeneutical question for critics who use the latter either to explain the former or to secure the former's difference from the latter. The limits imposed by the subjectivity of letter writing and Infante's access to information are ostensibly surpassed through the use of dialogue. As Tsuchiya observes, some critics have viewed the passage from the epistolary form to dialogue as an attempt to complete the vision of reality that Infante failed to produce in his letters; others have focused on how the play between the two works produces an even more ambiguous version of reality (336). Like Infante at the end of *La incógnita,* the reader of *Realidad* approaches the text seeking answers to the enigmas that were left unanswered. Yet those intimate conversations are nevertheless subject to the vagaries of language and interpretation, never providing wholly satisfactory answers. Opaque and resistant to reading, the "reality" of Viera's truth is still encased within language. In the end Viera's moral dilemma—that inner struggle that motivates much of the story—is hardly clarified.

Infante writes in *La incógnita:* "but I'm beginning to believe that fate actually exists in this instance, and that Federico doesn't get ahead because of some insurmountable inner obstacle, as well as because of external circumstances beyond his control" (77).[30] Viera may be a mystery, but Infante manages to identify, at least in general terms, the forces at play: some unknown, unconquerable internal force and external pressures beyond his control are the source of his dilemma. Put otherwise, Viera is trapped between his own psychic desires and the pressures of his society, which apparently are at odds. Given the web of secrecy that surrounds Viera and the characterization of his struggle, it is not surprising that critics have appealed to homoerotic desire as one solution. One of the hypotheses that emerges in the novel is that Viera was engaged in a love triangle with Augusta and her husband Orozco, and therefore his murder was the result of a love affair gone sour. For example, in his introduction to *Realidad,* Ricardo Gullón claims that Orozco is the figure who truly motivates Viera's desire for Augusta; Viera's cousin is simply a relay that allows for the mediation of desire between the two men. "Orozco, then, would be the determining factor of Viera's conduct, and in order to accept this hypothesis it is not necessary to turn to insinuations of a latent homosexuality. The issue is more complicated than all of that, and all things considered, the important thing is the structural function of the mediator" (17).

Much could be made of the way that Gullón assumes that homosexuality is "simple" and that "complicated" sexual and social relations are empty of homosexual desire. But the more important element is the way in which homosexuality appears *already* to function as the answer. Gullón does not cite any particular sources, but the rhetorical structure of his argument is designed to foreclose homosexuality as a solution that was already in circulation. Taking the opposite stance, John Sinnigen has recently argued that homosexual desire is explicit in both *La incógnita* and *Realidad* and that Viera's suicide may be explained by a need to repress homosexual desires. For Sinnigen, Augusta is simply a means of channeling sexual desire through a heterosexual object to reach the true object of desire: her husband. Gullón may be right that the structural relationship is more important than marshaling sufficient evidence to claim that Viera really desired Orozco and that Augusta was merely a means to appease that desire. But the possibility—the suspicion, if you will—of homoeroticism as a solution is important for what it suggests about Galdós's use of the epistolary form. The letter form in *La incógnita* opens up the possibility of a psychological examination in which the categories used to explain desire become unstable. But letters are not a transparent window into the mind. The instability around desire—as a vice, as an intolerable internal force—remains a mystery of the psyche. The sexual transgressions of the novel, whether homosexual or heterosexual, are not fully explained, and language—in letter form—cannot offer a mimetic, accurate reflection of reality since it participates in the production of that reality.[31]

Muñoz y Pabón's *Amor postal* continues the use of amorous epistolary correspondence in the service of a confessional mode that recalls early works such as Pablo de Olavide's *El Evangelio en triunfo ó Historia de un filósofo desengañado* (The Triumphant Gospel, or the Story of a Disillusioned Philosopher, 1797–99) in which the letter writer offers a public confession of his errors in the face of the Inquistion (see Rueda, *Cartas* 297–300). In spite, or perhaps even because, of its heavy-handed moral treatment of desire, *Amor postal* is a remarkable text for understanding the evolution of the epistolary genre for the representation of sexuality. The very concept of the postal system is already present in the title, and the novel is composed of a series of postcards between two interlocutors. The use of the postcard, rather than the private missive, distinguishes the novel from its epistolary predecessors, but it also highlights that which remained latent in them: the role of the postal service as an intrusive entity of the state. Postcards are open to the prying eyes of the postal system and its workers, and indeed Concha remarks that the postal carrier has been giving her quizzical looks upon delivering her mail, thus reiterating the anxieties around surveillance that characterize the public perception of the Spanish postal system. The advent of the postcard—the Spanish version was created on May 10, 1871, and began to circulate in July—provoked concern about the dissemination of private information. As one writer put it: "The public has no qualms about using the little cardboard that reaches our hands stark naked, and violated by the eyes of almost everyone whose hands it has touched" (Thebussem, "Más datos" 70). The private letter, hidden in an envelope and protected by the inviolability of correspondence, finds itself rendered "nude" and thus "violated" by the post. At the time, recommendations for avoiding an invasion of privacy included obtaining a mailbox with a lock, so as to foil the curious gazes of domestic servants, or using a private code that only the sender and receiver would know (Thebussem, "Las cartas tarjetas" 766). *Amor postal* dramatizes the conjunction of personal matters and public communication via the postcard.

In the brief novel, Carlos Vergara writes to Concha in order to establish a friendship, which he hopes will develop into an amorous relationship. The exchange of postcards is highly predictable: Carlos presses to meet Concha, while, as a discreet lady, she postpones any direct contact. The majority of the postcards read as if from a letter-writing manual, often formal to an extreme, and there is little to no plot development other than the increasing passion that Carlos expresses openly and ever more fervently, in contradistinction to Concha's reservation about her feelings for a man she has never met. The bulk of Concha's postcards beg Carlos to accept her friendship and desist in pursuing a love affair. The only information we learn is that Carlos does not go to confession (he does not like the idea of kneeling before another man and revealing his secrets). This horrifies Concha, and she compels him to do so if any love were to ever flourish between them.

In the final pages, the plot takes an unexpected twist as Carlos threatens to travel to Villacualquiera ("Anytown") to meet Concha in person. The final postcard that Carlos receives reveals that his interlocutor was never in fact a woman but a man, and furthermore a priest, Pedro Lasso, who turns out to be Concha's uncle. In his letter he asks for forgiveness for the "generous love" ("generoso amor") that Carlos has offered him and offers to fulfill the penitence Carlos deems appropriate for his masquerade. He pleads: "Be merciful and grant me the honor of accepting forever the frank, pure, disinterested, although useless, friendship from your humble servant, and friend, and brother, and father, and . . . anything you want, except *novio*" (91–92).[32] The priest's missive oddly situates him on the opposite side of the confessional as he asks for forgiveness and even penance for his transgression. The list of possibilities moves from a straightforward pardon to the establishment of a fraternal bond—to the final line in which the specter of same-sex desire is named as *novio* ("boyfriend" or "fiancé"). An ostensibly heterosexual relationship, once revealed to be founded on an invisible homoerotism, is now recuperated as a homosocial male bonding that comes into being as a disavowal of the prior, unstated homoerotic connection.

In a sense, *Amor postal* reflects an early awareness of the radical instability of gender within letter writing, gesturing toward the work of Barthes and Derrida, both of whom expose in different ways how letter writing operates under the fiction that gender is stable. Rather than seeking to find identity in epistolarity, Barthes and Derrida explore the inherent instability of identity in letter correspondence: because gender is a linguistic function in letter writing, gender is always capable of being manipulated or misinterpreted. Consequently, the epistolary performance enacted in both authors' works wavers between homosexuality and heterosexuality, between male and female addressees (Kauffman, *Special Delivery* 111). While in *A Lover's Discourse* Barthes deliberately addresses a male beloved at times, Derrida uses the pronoun "lui" ambiguously: "To reach the conclusion . . . that I am certainly writing to a woman . . . would be as daring, in your case, as using it to infer the color of your hair" (*The Post Card* 79). Given the inherent instability of senders and receivers in epistolary relations, Barthes's and Derrida's writing, in Kauffman's words, "oscillates between male and female, heterosexuality and homosexuality" (*Special Delivery* 111). Derrida writes: "What can this ciphered letter signify, my very sweet destiny, my immense, my very near unknown one? Perhaps this: even if it is still more mysterious, I owe it to you to have discovered homosexuality, and ours is indestructible" (*The Post Card* 53). Barthes's and Derrida's respective formulations underscore the ways in which the thematic traditions of amorous epistolary works establish specific hermeneutical expectations in the reader, particularly in terms of the beloved's (gender and sexual) identity. In contrast with the recuperative project of finding homosexual relationships, Barthes and Derrida emphasize the instability of both sender and receiver as signifiers in order to interrogate the presumed heterosexuality on which the tradition of love letters is founded.

The instability of gender is hardly celebrated in *Amor postal,* however, and in his letter of response, Carlos offers an anxious response that reveals his homophobic reaction to the preceeding epistolary exchange: "Mr. Don Pedro Lasso, my frustrated love: Let's end it, man, let's end it! . . . No more! The joke I've suffered from with my postal love shames me, and I don't know if I should commit suicide or break out in laughter" (93).[33] Knowing that his postcards have been read by the postal worker, and anyone else who comes across them in Villacualquiera, Carlos immediately breaks off the exchange at the novel's close. Love is now replaced by shame—the shame produced not only by being duped but also by the implication that this was, in some fashion, a homoerotic relationship. The plaintive cry to end the letter exchange is itself a paradoxical gesture: the only way to say no to letter writing is to write a letter that says "no more writing." Carlos's reaction, bolstering his sense of heterosexuality, is exaggerated, for it is obvious that he has not engaged in any physical same-sex behavior. The pair of choices he offers designate two opposing perspectives: either he laughs it off (it was nothing more than a trick) or commits suicide (although a trick, it has revealed a truth he would have preferred never to confront). Although

Carlos adopts the first choice, the second is particularly noteworthy in that it would appear that the mortal sin of suicide is of a lesser degree than a potential homoerotic relationship. The excessive quality of the response reflects the novel's anxious determination to reassert a proper gendered relationship.

Amor postal thus adheres more closely to the earlier epistolary narratives of the nineteenth century in its use of confession as a form of moral opprobrium. Only upon learning that Concha is really a man does Carlos take the moral lesson to heart. Until that moment, the reader suspects that he has merely followed Concha's entreaties to go to confession in order to win her love. Confession is not about an intimate conversation between two men, the novel tells us, but a relationship to God. Nevertheless, Carlos's earlier discomfort with the idea of confession—of kneeling before a man and telling his intimate thoughts—already suggests that an underlying homophobia is at play. As a result, the priest's final words—"anything you want, except *novio*"—are an excessive supplement that reveals the extent to which the homoerotic posting has put into circulation the very desire it was meant to contain. Even when the verbal masquerade has been stripped away, the rhetoric of love persists, somewhat ironically, in their respective postcards. The priest refers to Carlos's "generous love" for him, and by ending with "my failed love" Carlos's final letter deploys the conventional phrases that marked their earlier correspondence. This is not to suggest that there really was a burgeoning same-sex love here: although the priest may have enjoyed the game, his use of feminine epistolary codes was a rhetorical strategy designed to inculcate Carlos with Catholic values. Nevertheless, the novel allows for a queer desire to be posted and put into circulation, one that confession itself generates in its very attempt to expel it.

In contrast with Derrida's deconstructive play of epistolarity, *Amor postal* exploits the capacity for gender to be manipulated in epistolary relationships in an attempt to strengthen proper gender and sexual hierarchies. Heteronormativity is reestablished in the end through an abjected homoeroticism. The very act of naming it obliquely through the word *novio,* while calling attention to homosexuality, can only name it through prohibition, as something to be rejected. It is not insignificant that this relationship be out in the open, rather than in secret through the use of envelopes: it underscores the possibility that someone else might be privy to your most intimate desires expressed via the post. The novel's moral strategy is all too apparent, for it redoubles the confessional relationship between confessant and priest by making the postal system itself an all-seeing disciplinary agent. The basic message of the novel is a rather obvious moral lesson about romantic entanglements via the post: you never know who might be receiving and responding to your letters.

Pepita Jiménez, La incógnita, and *Amor postal* outline collectively a number of the generic parameters that epistolary works in the twentieth century will continue to exploit in their explorations of sexuality, be they concerns with psychological self-examination (Valera), the sexual enigmas of others (Galdós), or the possiblity of unforeseen sexual relations (Muñoz y Pabón). Likewise, these novels underscore the association of letter writing with confession and secrecy, blurring the boundaries between religious acts of contrition and psychological self-examinations. In the process, they dramatize the vicissitudes of putting one's most private thoughts to paper and facing the possibility of seeing one's intimacy made public. Valera's and Galdós's efforts to distance the epistolary genre from the explicit moralizing that characterizes works of the first half of the nineteenth century do not dissolve the link between letters and illicit desire. Their works recast the view of desire, treating it either as a desire that emerges in confession in spite of the confessant or as a desire whose opacity becomes a topic of the letter exchange. From the privacy of a letter exchange to the less concealed nature of postcards, *Amor postal* bears witness to how confession expands its domain over sexuality in an attempt to regulate behavior. Homosexuality can appear in letters because they remain hidden from view, passing through the postal system undetected. The specific use of the postcard reflects the increased will to knowledge around sexuality—a means to expose the sexual dangers that epistolarity's inherent instability can generate—as well as a sign of the proliferation and dissemination of queer desire in the larger domain of Spanish public discourse. The evolution of the epistolary novel in the latter half of the nineteenth century thus sets the stage for a critical analysis of the directions that queer mail will take in twentieth-century Spanish epistolary fiction.

PART I

❦

QUEER TRACES

CHAPTER I

Archival Resurrections of Queer Desire in Miguel de Unamuno

Writing is that neutral, composite, oblique space where our subject slips away, the negative where all identity is lost, starting with the very identity of the body writing.
—ROLAND BARTHES, "The Death of the Author"

La novela de Don Sandalio, jugador de ajedrez (*The Novel of Don Sandalio, Chess Player,* 1933) is a curious text with a deceptively simple plot. An unnamed protagonist suffers from a mental crisis about humanity and his place in the world, which leads him to take refuge in an undisclosed location. In spite of his fear of fellow men and a desire for solitude, he joins a local club where he begins to play chess with Don Sandalio. The bulk of the text consists of twenty-three letters, addressed to his friend Felipe, which relate his impressions of and shifting attitudes toward Don Sandalio as narrative events unfold. The chess games are interrupted several times, first by the death of Don Sandalio's son, a second time by the letter writer's own infirmity, and on a third occasion by Don Sandalio's imprisonment and sudden death. The entire episode lasts two months, and yet by the close of the correspondence their relationship still remains something of a mystery. Unamuno's short novel is so rife with unresolved ambiguity that there is little wonder why critics have considered it one of his most enigmatic works (Nicholas 117; Gullón 316).

The novel is enigmatic in part because Unamuno's use of the letter form appears to obey a traditional approach to letter writing as the expression of a coherent authorial identity or single consciousness. The univocal epistolary text, composed either of a single letter or a series of letters by the same person—Goethe's *The Sorrows of Young Werther* and Guilleragues's *Lettres portugaises* (*The Portuguese Letters,* 1669) are two canonical examples—is particularly adept at representing a single voice. The collected letters of one individual ostensibly provide the reader a privileged insight into the writer's personality or into the writer's perception of someone else's psychological profile. Unamuno's letter correspondents depend upon the so-called epistolary pact, the notion that there is no difference between the written "I" and the "I" of the hand that writes, that the words of the writer are a sincere expression of the individual's mind (Guillén, "El pacto epistolar" 87–88). Yet Unamuno does not present the narrative's letters as the product of a coherent subject but rather as the search for coherence in spite of its fragmentation and internal strife. The details of the narrator's life are left out of the correspondence, presumably because Felipe would already know them: he has lost his family and home, is solitary and struggling with a psychic burden that afflicts him, and he forges a strong yet mysterious attachment to the chess player that helps to assuage his tormented state. In his prologue to *San Manuel Bueno, mártir* (*Saint Manuel Bueno, Martyr,* 1933), Unamuno focuses our attention on the psychic life of Don Sandalio when he writes: "Don Sandalio is a character seen from the outside, whose interior life escapes us, perhaps he doesn't have one . . . But is it that my Don Sandalio doesn't have an inner life, he has no conscience, or rather knowledge of himself, does he not dialogue with himself?" (13, my translation).[1] Nevertheless, Unamuno later affirms that the character does have an inner life, a conscience, which the reader can discern in the letters (13). Don Sandalio's silence, his "enigmatic shadow" ("sombra enigmática"), his lack of disclosure about his personal life: all become ciphers of an enigma to be decoded.

But Unamuno is not content to leave the interpretive task in the hands of his readers. At the end of the story, he returns to offer his own exegesis. The introspective nature of the letter writing leads him to claim that the true author of the letters is Don Sandalio himself, whose death was just a novelistic trick "the better to represent as well as disguise himself and conceal his own truth" (224).[2] Hence Don Sandalio was writing about his own life; the pair of correspondents was actually the product of a single mind. Unamuno's intervention effectively unmasks the letter writer, calling attention to the writer's rhetorical strategy of displacing his own voice onto a third person. His interpretation in effect undermines the epistolary pact since it refuses to accept the letter writer's authorial identity at face value. The letters reflect instead the transformation of the writer into a figure of discourse, a rhetorical visage for the addressee. The epistolary form, we might say, generates the *figure* of a singular, coherent consciousness in order to suppress the linguistic mediation that perforce disturbs that coherence: something like the "death of the letter writer" emerges in epistolarity.[3] It is precisely this instability that allows Unamuno to engage in his rhetorical unmasking of the letter writer, exposing the "truth" of his authorial identity. Nevertheless, Unamuno's exposure of this identity still leaves the enigma in question unresolved; he does not say what that "truth" might be or why the letter writer felt compelled to represent himself in the third person. His epilogue, rather than offering an answer, reiterates the call for interpretation.

François Meyer has insightfully argued that "Unamuno's entire oeuvre is inspired by a sharp and irreducible feeling of the 'mystery' and the 'secret' that reposes beneath his conscience, ideas, and knowledge" (102). An avid reader of theology, philosophy, psychology, and ancient and modern history, Unamuno was an eclectic thinker who displayed in his prolific writings a remarkable concern with the vicissitudes of the self. In particular, he was acutely sensitive to the psychic conflicts that individuals face in their social relations with others. Profoundly influenced by Catholicism, Unamuno's interest in metaphysics and human subjectivity was also intertwined with religious doubts. He confronted his fear of death and yearning for immortality in works such as *La agonía del cristianismo* (*The Agony of Christianity*), written in 1924 while he was exiled in Paris. In that text he views life as a constant bodily struggle against death: "psychical or spiritual life is, in turn, a fight against eternal oblivion" (368–69). Unamuno's preoccupation with the mysteries of the psyche and religious faith appear, for example, in what is considered one of his finest works, *San Manuel Bueno, mártir,* composed in

1930. The narrator, Ángela Carballino, relates the struggle of the town priest, Don Manuel, to reconcile his lack of faith in the afterlife with his duty to his parishioners who place their faith in his spiritual guidance. He harbors his lack of faith as a burdensome secret. Following shortly on the heels of *San Manuel Bueno, Don Sandalio* shares with its predecessor the emphasis on the personal vision of a narrator who relates a subjective impression of the story's events as well as the enigmatic nature of a character who suffers a secret in silence. At first glance, *Don Sandalio* rests comfortably within the canonical framework of Unamuno's fiction.[4]

But in spite of their proximity, the two novels differ substantially in their critical reception. As both D. L. Shaw and Robert L. Nicholas note, criticism of *Don Sandalio* has been less than abundant or enthusiastic (115; 152n). Any number of hypothetical reasons could be advanced to explain the novel's relative lack of interest for scholars—its univocal epistolary technique, its brevity in comparison to other literary texts, its attenuated plot—yet none is particularly convincing. A more plausible answer may be that the thematic focus on San Manuel's spiritual crisis in the face of death resonates strongly with Unamuno's writings on the subject, more so than in the case of *Don Sandalio*. Critics have struggled with *Don Sandalio*'s enigmatic resolution, and as a result have generally interpreted the text as a reflection of Unamuno's personal struggle with identity. Shaw's reading, for example, examines the novel in light of Unamuno's essays on the struggle of the self to achieve a coherent identity—what Unamuno referred to as *serse* or "being oneself"—in the face of the "diversity behind the apparent unity of the individual personality" (115). Similarly, José Luis Abellán has argued that the novel addresses the struggle between the private self and the public image of the main character and the difficulty of ascertaining which self is the authentic one (58).

More recently, critics have examined this same struggle through the lens of contemporary theories of subjectivity. Taking a Foucauldian approach, Francisco La Rubia Prado reads *Don Sandalio* as a form of self-creation, a search for authenticity in the face of the inauthentic social traps that attempt to coerce individuals to conform to certain norms.

Don Sandalio and the unnamed letter writer are "enigmatic" beings who refuse to conform to the superficial and inauthentic world of the casino. The relationship between the two men offers the narrator a mode of authentic communication. Drawing on various psychoanalytic theorists, Freud and Lacan among them, Alison Sinclair interprets the struggle in *Don Sandalio* as one in which the pre-Oedipal self faces a terrifying other. The letter writer struggles with a "terrifying attraction" that will draw him to Don Sandalio (195). For Sinclair, the attraction and repulsion to Don Sandalio is the struggle of a man who seeks out some sort of security, yet that security is fraught with the danger of ceasing to exist as himself out of fear that "he will be subsumed in Sandalio" (205).

Don Sandalio is indeed about the struggle of the self with its own incoherency, of the conflict between one's self-perception and one's public image, of a search for authenticity in the face of social norms. But the letter writer's struggle to understand the internal splitting of the self is also a confrontation with the profound role that sexuality plays in organizing social relationships and, in particular, the normative social arrangements of heterosexuality. Wives are never mentioned, family relations are deliberately ignored, sons and sons-in-law are dismissed out of hand. The novel's use of the epistolary form to shed light on an individual's private thoughts allows the reader a glimpse into the world of a man whose most profound emotional attachment is not to his wife or family but to another man. No other text by Unamuno emphasizes so passionately the interpersonal dynamics between two men. Expanding upon the interpretive paths traversed by La Rubia Prado and Sinclair, I propose to read the letter writer's attraction to Don Sandalio *as a form of attraction,* one that is never quite consummated nor named, but nonetheless troubles his own sense of self. The language used by the letter writer to describe Don Sandalio (at moments suggestive of homoeroticism), an oblique allusion to Oscar Wilde, and the explicit rejection of a female object of desire collectively call attention to the diffuse presence of a homoerotic charge between the two men. The letter writer, near the end of his correspondence, recognizes the possible homoerotic interpretation of the intimacy shared by the two characters and moves to disavow it by downplaying the importance of sexuality altogether. The door to the letter closet, opening ever so slightly in Unamuno's text, will suddenly be closed shut.

That Unamuno should use the epistolary form to explore a fictional character's existential crisis is hardly surprising since he perceived letter correspondence as a mode of confession, a "communion between solitary beings" (11: 942). Juan Marichal has argued persuasively that Unamuno's predilection for confession made him the first of his kind in Spanish letters (53–54). The nineteenth century, he asserts, saw the rise of autobiographical genres that serve as a confessional for the writer, through which he bears his soul and confesses his intimacy to an unseen and unknown reader (51). Although certainly others before him have confessed in writing, Unamuno's originality lies in his use of confession for a social and moral function. As a result, Unamuno transformed his essays, fiction, and personal correspondence into an all-consuming confessional project. In an essay from 1905, "Soledad" (Solitude), he espoused the value of confession in overturning the social pressure to hide one's "impure desires" for fear of retribution. Anticipating a future age of public confession, Unamuno foresaw a society in which the lack of secrets would allow for everyone to move beyond guilt and to forgive one another for past sins: "the great social institution of that [future] era will be that of public confession, and then there will be no secrets" (3: 897). Unamuno's cultivation of the intimate genre of literary confession served the purpose of a spiritual development. Unamuno thus moves his confession from the private sphere to the public domain: "Our journal should be our words, our writings, our letters, thrown to the wind, with gusts of our soul" (Marichal 58).

Unamuno was an avid letter writer: "I will never see myself free from the other vices of which Spaniards complain, but yes, of epistolophobia. I suffer, rather, from epistolomania" ("El morillo al rojo" 10: 374). In "La intimidad de los escritos" (The Intimacy of Writing) he defended his penchant for letter writing, diagnosing Spain with a debilitating *epistolofobia* (11: 939), and in "Sobre mí mismo" (About Myself) he reiterated his love of confessional genres such as autobiographies and epistolary correspondence (10: 244). Nevertheless, Unamuno's confessional project had its limits. As Marichal details, Unamuno believed that there should be a limit, a barrier of discretion, that represses certain aspects of one's confession. In this respect, Unamuno's cultivation of confessional forms remains strongly tied to religious confession as established by the Catholic Church. In "Cartas" (Letters), he admits that the more he became a public figure, his private letters became less personal and intimate (10: 521–22). He attributes this shift in part to the lack of time he had to correspond with others, but he was also aware that the public interest in private correspondence necessarily influenced what he wrote in his letters, and as such, he exercised discretion. In his 1899 "Carta abierta" (Open Letter) to Casimiro Muñoz, for example, he notes that letter writers scrutinize what they write knowing that their letters may be published at a later date (8: 69). Sinclair argues that Unamuno was concerned with his public image in his letters and thus often retreated from difficulties arising from differences of opinion with his correspondents (19–20). Abellán similarly remarks that in Unamuno's epistolary correspondence with Clarín, he oscillates between sincerity and vanity, between telling the truth and presenting an image for the public, given his awareness that the letters would eventually reach a wider audience (76). Unamuno perhaps summarized it best when he wrote that famous writers did not have "private" correspondence, for they were always aware of the public's scrutinizing gaze ("La moralidad artística" 8: 1167).

As much as his prolific letter writing and critical stance regarding Spaniards' alleged *epistolofobia* distinguish him from the norm, Unamuno's wariness about the public interest in one's correspondence is not exceptional. Published letter collections, or *epistolarios,* were rather scarce in Spain, a problem that Eugenio de Ochoa has attributed to editors' reservations about publishing such collections (vii). In the Spanish context, all evidence concerning epistolary writing points toward a history of privacy, reservation, and suspicion. Alfonso Reyes notes, for example, that while letters may provide ample biographical evidence for historians, their diffusion is considered a violation of someone's intimacy (xi). The debates around inviolability of correspondence and the right to property offer further evidence that the reading of others' letters was generally perceived as an invasion of privacy. Juan Ortiz del Barco's polemically argued *Propiedad de la correspondencia privada* (Ownership of

Private Correspondence, 1909) adopts the opposite position, rejecting the argument that letters should not be published for fear that they would tarnish the writer's public image. Ortiz del Barco claims that there should be no concern about publishing private letters because writers should exercise discretion. He thus argues for the right to publish the letters of the Spanish essayist Ángel Ganivet "because it is absolutely the only way to study the figure of Ganivet and to be able to discover or clarify what appears mysterious" (19). Letters, as biographical documents, illuminate the mysteries of a given subject's personality. By implication, Ortiz del Barco argues, not unlike Unamuno, that confession by letter is good for the soul, and thus for the reading public, since letters expose the truth (even if that truth is carefully crafted by the author).

Perhaps no other figure dramatizes the public's profound interest in others' private lives and the generalized fear of one's own intimacy being disseminated through letters during this period than Federico García Lorca. Lorca's correspondence from the 1920s and '30s reveals an increasing reticence to put his struggles with homosexuality into writing, even if only through veiled references. In his earliest extant letters, Lorca addressed his conflict with desire more directly. One of his letters from 1918 to Adriano del Valle has become a key archival document for evidence of his sexual anxieties:

> I see before me many problems, many eyes that imprison me. The spirit that lives in us and hates us pushes me down the path. I have to walk because we have to grow old and die, but I don't want to obey [. . .] and yet every day that passes my doubts and sadness increase. Sadness from the enigma that is myself![5] (*Epistolario* 48)

But from 1918 to 1928, just before his trip to New York in 1929, Lorca referred time and again to his inability to express his inner feelings, fearful of what others would think. In a letter to Jorge Zalamea from 1928, he reiterated his desire for privacy: "this letter contains unpublished verses of mine, feelings of a friend and a man that I would not want divulged. I very much want my intimacy" (577). The fragment of the letter to Zalamea suggests that it was Lorca's awareness of the risks of putting his desires into written circulation that led him to compose letters in such a way as to avoid the peering glances of other readers. Nor would Lorca's later letter correspondence break this silence to offer a more intimate portrait. Although he conceived his trip to New York in therapeutic terms (he wrote of a "sentimental crisis" in his letters), this venture did not spark greater openness. Andrew A. Anderson, for example, notes that in other letters Lorca reiterated: "Keep this letter; Don't read my letters to anyone, for a letter that is read [to another] is an intimacy that is broken" (García Lorca, *Epistolario* 402). The end result, as Miguel García-Posada argues, is that the earlier confessional tone of Lorca's letters gives way to reservation and modesty in his later writings, and as a result, "the writer's inner 'I' is only insituated at particular and in rare instances. That is the secret that the letters to Salvador Dalí, to Emilio Aladrén, and to Rafael Rodríguez Rapún contain, or contained" (García Lorca, *Obras* 4: 14).

Lorca's increasing reticence to disclose private information may have prevented future readers from gaining access to his most intimate thoughts, but it certainly did not prevent future scholars from amassing his epistolary writings in order to present an avowedly accurate portrait of the poet. The importance of Lorca's letters in the context of Unamuno's narrative is not whether his correspondence actually provides clear evidence of his homosexuality, even though scholars have read them for such. It is, rather, the very impulse to collect and read his letters because they supposedly contain sexual secrets that concerns us. To put this in psychoanalytic terms, the private, familiar letter, hidden from view by an envelope, reflects a concept of desire as an unconscious secret, an enigma, that becomes the source of attraction for others. Shaped by their association with confession, letters are perceived to contain secrets to which we are denied access, and therefore our interest in reading others' correspondence is often linked to the desire to gain access to that information.[6]

As a collection of letters written, sent, and resent—only then to be edited and published by Unamuno—the correspondence in *Don Sandalio* echoes the actual practice of publishing authentic letter collections and reflects the conceptual shifts around letters as repositories of a subject's identity (e.g., Lorca's sexuality, Ganivet's personal life). In *Don Sandalio,* the enigmatic dimension of the writer's identity in the novel appears from the outset. In the first letter, the reader quickly ascertains that the letter writer is a man afflicted with an unbearable sense of solitude. To be alone, he discovers, is to submit himself to an interminable self-analysis: a painful predicament in which the mysteries of the self cannot be pushed aside, since they impose themselves at every turn for explanation and resolution. The symbols of his existential crisis thus come swiftly in his letters, as he discovers in his explorations of a local forest an old oak tree whose heart has been exposed by a profound wound. When he remarks that the tree is comforted by the protective embrace of ivy, he realizes that he too is in search of companionship.

Enter Don Sandalio. The initial description is of a somewhat pathetic man whose appearance elicits pity in others. The narrator's interest turns on an identification with Don Sandalio as someone who is completely alone in the company of other men, isolated from the conversations and activities of the fellow members of the casino. The letter writer is attracted to Don Sandalio, for he believes that they both share the same sense of solitude in the world: the images of the hollowed-out oak tree and the burnt house serve to reinforce their common connection, based on what he describes as an inner wound that isolates them from the rest of humanity; the emptiness of the oak tree becomes emblematic of the letter writer's own psychic emptiness and search for fulfillment in the figure of the chess player. Yet this chance encounter also inspires a response in the letter writer that reflects a deeper connection than identification. His consternation is such that he avoids the casino for two days as "the image of Don Sandalio follows me everywhere" (191).[7]

While the exact nature of the letter writer's obsession is still not clear, at the end of the fifth letter he exclaims in a rather melodramatic tone: "It's obvious that I need Don Sandalio, that I can no longer live without him" (192).[8] Through his letters, he narrates a fantasy life in which he divides the chess player into two separate entities: the real Don Sandalio and an idealized fantasy figure. The rhetoric that the letter writer employs to describe the idealized figure has such passionate overtones that it borders on amorous: his repeated use of the possessive "mi" or "el mío," his description of their relationship in terms of suffering—"I even dream of him, and almost suffer with him" (197)—and his desire to know nothing of Don Sandalio's personal life in order to maintain his fantasy are all examples of his growing attachment.[9] Drawing a parallel between himself and Robinson Crusoe, he uses the metaphor of the trace of a naked footprint on the sand of a beach to describe the emotional impact Don Sandalio has had on him (194; 71).

This is not the first reference to Crusoe, but rather the second, and it is a repetition worth exploring further. In his first letter, the writer likens himself to Crusoe as he flees from other men, the sight of a footprint in the sand the intolerable sign of the presence of others. Now that Don Sandalio has entered his life, the reference to Crusoe no longer conveys the fear of others but rather the solace that company may bring. The reference to Crusoe can also be read as an allusion to José Ortega y Gasset's 1911 essay "Psicoanálisis, ciencia problemática," in which he characterizes Freud as a *robinsón* whose psychoanalytic method allows him to recognize footprints as entry points in the murky space of the psyche. In Spain, Freudian psychoanalysis was amply debated during the 1920s and into the '30s (Glick 7), but Unamuno's relationship to Freud's writings is not well known. To answer the question of his knowledge of Freud, critics have noted the slim presence of Freud in Unamuno's library (the Spanish translation of *Psychopathology of Everyday Life*) and the broader cultural milieu in which Freud exercised considerable influence, primarily in the fields of medicine and law (Glick 8–10; Sinclair 34). The explicit presence of Freud in Unamuno's writings is rather negligible; Unamuno briefly alludes, for example, to *The Interpretation of Dreams* in a 1918 essay, "El contra-mismo" (The Counter-Self) (9: 76). More recently, Sinclair has shown that Unamuno had read numerous works in the field of psychology, some of which were derived from Freudian psychoanalysis (38–41). While it may be impossible to ascertain if Unamuno had read Ortega's essay (the two writers corresponded, but no mention of the essay is made in their letters), the connection between Crusoe and Freud nonetheless finds an uncanny link in Unamuno's narrative. The letter writer is also a Crusoe in the Freudian sense that Ortega gives the term: his entire narrative is a sort of private psychoanalytic session to work through his self-imposed solitude, with Felipe functioning as the absent analyst. Hence, in the remainder of the correspondence, the letter writer not only relates further developments in their relationship but also attempts to make sense of his connection to Don Sandalio by analyzing the subsequent events that transform their interpersonal dynamic.

"Don Sandalio is driving me mad, Felipe" (201): these words end letter XII.[10] Nine days later, in letter XIII, the letter writer is in bed, suffering from a strange illness induced by his relationship with Don Sandalio and to whom he specifically attributes the cause (202; 77). Yet the sojourn in bed is hardly debilitating, as the letter writer appears to enjoy his infirmity. "And besides, I've been enjoying the pleasures of bed, the sheets sticking to me ever so amorously!" (201, trans. mod.).[11] The opportunity to daydream grants him time to continue his fantasy life with Don Sandalio, entertaining himself with the idealized fantasy that Don Sandalio "has imposed on my innermost soul" (197).[12] He wonders if Don Sandalio is thinking about him, if he misses him, if he has replaced the letter writer with someone else. He even goes so far as to wonder if he exists at all for the chess player (202–3; 77). His anxious string of questions not only affirms his mental desire to maintain control of the chess player but his concern for the other's indifference to his absence highlights the desire for reciprocity in the relationship.

His self-interrogation echoes the Lacanian version of desire in which the subject wonders what the other wants from him and what he means to the other (*Seminar* 11: 214), and in this respect, the letter writer remains utterly tied to the real Don Sandalio, whose actions demonstrably affect the letter writer's perception of their relationship. Throughout the correspondence reality imposes itself upon the fantasy as Don Sandalio's absences cause the narrator additional emotional turmoil. The first time Don Sandalio fails to appear, he reluctantly accepts an offer from another casino member to play chess, fearful that his actions may be read as a betrayal (205; 79). The news of Don Sandalio's imprisonment, recounted in letter XV, plunges the letter writer back into his melancholic solitude, an "unforeseen event that," as he puts it, "totally changed the meaning of my personal life" (207, trans. mod.).[13] The chess player's mysterious death while still in prison only furthers his anguish: "And then . . . I found myself crying. I was overcome by a black anguish and cried, Felipe, for the death of my Don Sandalio. Why? I felt a great void within me" (212).[14]

The role of the law adds another layer of ambiguity to the narrative, for it appears that the letter writer is implicated in the motive behind Don Sandalio's incarceration. Little information is given to Felipe: the reader learns that the letter writer is forced to testify before a judge, but cannot, or will not, answer any of the questions; and that it was Don Sandalio's son-in-law who turned him in and who asks that the letter writer testify in court. During a subsequent visit to the casino, the son-in-law reveals that Don Sandalio spoke often of the letter writer at home: "'I had thought, Sir,' the youth said then, 'that you had formed some attachment, perhaps had even felt some affection for Don Sandalio'" (217).[15] The letter writer is disturbed by this information, believing himself to have been almost nonexistent to Don Sandalio, but responds affirmatively that he was attached to him, though only to his fantasy of the chess player. In the end, the motive behind the incarceration, and the letter writer's role in it, are left unexplained. Nevertheless, the episode as a whole underscores the conflict between private and public perceptions of relationships, as Abellán has suggested. The disjuncture between the narrator's own point of view and that of the son-in-law produces the conflicting perspectives on the nature of the relationship between the two men.

What is the nature of Don Sandalio's and the letter writer's attachment, of their "affection," as the son-in-law puts it? The narrative setting of the casino implies a male heterosexual atmosphere where conversation and gaming take place without homosexual inflections. Yet the letter writer's presence in the casino is an uncomfortable one, given his self-imposed exile and general hatred for the rest of humanity. The son-in-law's testimony has suggested that, at least from the perspective of outsiders, the bond between Don Sandalio and the letter writer was quite strong in contrast to his connection with the other members. The intensity of the relationship between the letter writer and Don Sandalio sets them apart from the rest of those who frequent the casino. In his initial letters, the letter writer invokes Flaubert's *Bouvard and Pécuchet,* already announced in the novel's epigraph, whose characters share the inability to tolerate stupidity. Based on the information in his correspondence, the letter writer and Don Sandalio form a sort of "odd couple" similar to that of Bouvard and Pécuchet: while the former are invested in chess as a form of leisure and the latter in accumulating knowledge after retiring from their posts, they have a shared disdain for others.[16]

The hatred of one's *prójimos,* or fellow men, and the need to be with them was a question that Freud raised in his discussion of male homosexuality and group identification. In *Group Psychology* (1921), he explored a significant link between an emotional tie to others that is at the same time shot through with "feelings of aversion and hostility" (42). Freud attempted to understand how homosexuality was structurally integral to group identification, but that in the process of identifying, homosexuality became something else, a "desexualized, sublimated homosexual love" (44). Freud claims that affectionate connections stem from original "'sensual' object-ties" whose sexual aim has been diverted, ties that may still persist unconsciously (90–91). Freud had earlier argued that homosexual desire could produce an identification, but the desire was not eliminated but rather transformed into "love instincts" and thus contributed "an erotic factor to friendship and comradeship, to *esprit de corps* and to the love of mankind in general" ("Psychoanalytic Notes" 61). Freud's account is plagued with inconsistencies, among them the distinction between the sexual and the social and between identification and desire. Still, his analysis is useful for pursuing the ambivalence around group identification and the potential passage of a repressed homosexual desire that founds such an identification to the open expression of homosexual desire. This ambivalence, as Christopher Lane argues, "produces a social body replete with eroticism on condition that homosexual desire be irreducible to a single object, and that the one who 'misreads' this desire—the homosexual—be pathologized" ("Freud" 161). Group ties and identifications may be haunted by the specter of homosexuality, which, although never fully explained by Freud, is linked to the antagonism and hatred that often operate in such group ties, even if they cannot be reducible to homosexual desire.[17] "The group's erotic composition is in fact *neither* social *nor* homosexual, but something else entirely" (Lane, "Freud" 156).

Freud's argument may help to explain the homosocial bonds that obtain between the casino-goers, and furthermore it suggests that the letter writer's anxiety stems, at least in part, from the perception that *his* identification and attachment to Don Sandalio are something more than the bonds the others share, that his hatred of the group is linked to the possibility that whatever homosexual attraction he might feel is not suppressed for the sake of a "general love of humanity." The distinction between eroticism and identification that lies at the heart of Freud's argument is that homosocial ties are stripped of their sexual content. In a volume published the same year as Unamuno's story, Emilio Donato y Prunera extends Freud's line of thinking by arguing against a concept of homosexual desire that does not necessarily find expression in a sexual *act*. Donato's *Homosexualismo (Frente a Gide)* (Homosexualism [Facing Gide]) is a vehement rejection of all of Gide's arguments in *Corydon* (1926) for not viewing homosexuality as a perversion. The text is a point-by-point rebuttal of the four dialogues in *Corydon,* to prove that homosexuality is in fact an aberration.[18] To be normal, he asserts, would require either that all men have homosexual tendencies, which he discards, or that even a majority of men have had homosexual experiences, a statistical possibility he denies. Donato does not deny, however, that men engage in sexual activity with other men. But the pleasure a man seeks from another man, he argues, is either a reflection of his lack of sexual satisfaction with women or a rational decision to seek out such pleasure (68). Its frequency, however, is such that it cannot be called normal. As much as he readily admits to the existence of homosexuality, his concern with labeling it "normal" or "natural" is that all male-male relationships suddenly become suspect. If "chaste love" does exist, he argues, then by extension any affection between two men without any physical expression would have to be called "homosexual chastity" ("castidad homosexual") (120). Donato claims that any sort of love without carnal contact is incomplete, and any relationship without such contact cannot be considered sexual:

> If the normal homosexual—Gide's expression—is the so-called chaste homosexual, then he is nothing more than a friend; all the friend you want, but only a friend. We don't dare see anything more than friendship between two men who love and help and even cannot live without each other, but who don't engage in homosexual practices. Nobody would even think to label as "normal homosexuals" two men who love each other dearly, like brothers, with nothing sinful between them.[19] (122–23)

Donato's text belies an anxiety about male-male relationships, and his argument is an attempt to shore up the boundaries between friendship and eroticism, thereby suppressing any sort of desire that may be foundational in a relationship between two members of the same sex. It is, in other words, a fear that homosociality will slip into homosexuality. Although writing in a different context and for a different purpose than Freud, Donato similarly confronts the ambivalence of group ties and identifications that may be haunted by the specter of homosexuality. His rhetoric is particularly significant, for it points to the ways in which the affective dimension of "those who cannot even live without each other," a phrase that appears almost verbatim in *Don Sandalio*, could be interpreted as indicating something more than friendship.

Donato is certainly not alone in recognizing that the border between friendship and eroticism is at times rather tenuous and thus needs, from a heteronormative point of view, to be reinforced. Aristotle argued in *Nicomachean Ethics* that lover and beloved did not find pleasure in the same objects and therefore could not be friends (221). Both Kant and Montaigne were careful to impose a limit on intimacy: for Montaigne, too great an intimacy between father and son would be inappropriate (136); for Kant, there is a proper distance that should be maintained—a "limitation on intimacy" that would prevent friends from being too familiar with each other (141). The philosophical tradition around friendship may exhibit a certain anxiety around eroticism, but Donato's condemnation of Gide's "non-practicing homosexual" underscores the ways in which homosexuality was complicating male-male relationships by rendering friendship much more ambiguous. Donato's text is also evidence that Gide's work, which first appeared in translation in 1929, and in a second edition in 1931 with a preface by Gregorio Marañón, had entered discourses of sexuality in Spain in the late 1920s and early '30s.[20] Alberto Mira further notes that it is Gide who would provide Spanish *decadentistas* a political model for early gay liberation, one that the Spanish civil war and Franco's rise to power would extinguish (Mira, "After Wilde" 44–45).

The thinning of the borders between friendship and homoeroticism at this historical juncture owes a great deal to the fundamental role that Oscar Wilde has played in the formation of the category of the modern homosexual. *De Profundis,* written between January and March 1897 while Wilde was still in prison, is a love letter and a letter of confession addressed to Lord Alfred Douglas in which he recalls their tempestuous relationship, by turns chastizing his younger lover's behavior and seeking to renew their contact. Although he does write the phrase "the love that dare not speak its name" at one point, Wilde consistently invokes friendship as the paradigm for their relationship. This association of friendship with homoeroticism is not limited to the British context. *De Profundis* was not translated into Spanish until 1925 (Unamuno had a copy in his personal library), but Unamuno confirms that he was aware of the fluctuating meaning of "friendship" in his short essay "La balada de la prisión de Reading," which addresses Oscar Wilde's publication of "The Ballad of Reading Gaol" upon his release from prison: in it Unamuno names Lord Queensbury as "the father of one of [Wilde's] *friends*" (8: 729). (Translations of Wilde's work entered Spain during the first decade of the twentieth century; "The Ballad of Reading Gaol," for example, was translated in 1909 by Ricardo Baeza.) In underscoring the fluctuating meaning of friendship, Wilde's *De Profundis* also draws attention to the ways in which the epistolary form itself functioned as evidence of homosexuality, the sealed envelope shepherding secret desires back and forth through the postal system. Wilde and Douglas exchanged numerous missives and telegrams, and Wilde's letters not only played a crucial role in his trial but have since served as biographical evidence of his sexuality. In *De Profundis* he makes numerous references to Douglas's abuse of his letters and at one point states that he has sole copyright of them (48). The letter, we might say, as a confessional document, increasingly became evidence of one's sexuality, and thus interpretations of friendship, of expressions of passion, affection, and the like could come under the scrutiny of readers as they undertook the interpretation of sentimental exchanges.

The ambiguity of the relationship between Don Sandalio and the letter writer is compounded by the fact that the latter does not attempt to clarify the border between friendship and eroticism. It is plausible to argue that their relationship is simply a friendship that fulfills a common solitude, in which emotions such as desire, passion, or even love would have no proper place. Of course, there is nothing simple about this friendship, especially when the letter writer does not in fact describe them as friends. The assumption of friendship, and hence the absence of any critical investigation of the potential homoeroticism between the two characters, follows from the notion that Unamuno's theoretical thoughts on and personal practice of sexuality would have necessarily inhibited the interpretation of homoeroticism in his literary works. Rafael Chabran summarizes this view when he observes: "It appears that [Unamuno] was never interested in nor involved in homoeroticism" (167).

The implicit assumption that underlies this argument is that Unamuno is Don Sandalio. Ricardo Gullón, for example, states unequivocally that Unamuno is the unnamed narrator, thus collapsing any distinction between author and text (323). The equation of Unamuno with Don Sandalio is problematic, for not only does it assume a simple correlation between his authorial figure and a single character that Unamuno would deny; it also ignores his own arguments about the relationship between an author's biography and his work. In "La moralidad artística" ("Artistic Morality"), for example, Unamuno claims that an author's biography impedes rather than assists in interpreting his or her aesthetic productions (8: 1166). For Unamuno works are autobiographical in that they are fictional creations that reflect the author's conceptual vision of the world depicted within them, not necessarily the specific facts of a writer's life (Longhurst xii). The presumption that Unamuno's work would not contain homoeroticism because he was heterosexual—in constrast with García Lorca, to offer one example, whose homosexuality has engendered considerable discussion about the possible homoerotic content of his poetry and theater—is a reminder of the extent to which the authorial figure and biographical information continue to exert considerable influence on queer readings in Hispanism.[21]

It would be more accurate to say that Unamuno's engagement with the topic of homosexuality remains to be elucidated. In addition to his apparent interest in the work of Gide (Sinclair 36), we note that he also engaged in an epistolary correspondence with the *decadentista* novelist Antonio de Hoyos y Vinent, well known at the time for being a dandy and homosexual. Unamuno also wrote a prologue for Hoyos's 1917 *El hombre que vendió su cuerpo al diablo* (The Man Who Sold His Body to the Devil).[22] Chabran's point that Unamuno was not interested in homosexuality is well taken, though, for there is indeed little reference to homosexuality in Unamuno's essays. According to Luis Fernández Cifuentes, Unamuno wrote a piece on Marcel Proust's *À la recherche du temps perdu* in 1925 that was lost and thus never published (291). The aforementioned "Balada" is the only text in which he explicitly engages with homosexuality. In that text Unamuno rejects a Wildean form of homosexuality—decadence, artifice, dandyism—by referring to it as "sterile games" ("juegos estériles").[23] By imputing a lack of or failed virility to homosexual men, Unamuno adopts a relatively common paradigm at that time.[24] Yet his explicit attack on the "Wildean" homosexuals in Spain is directed, at least in part, at the frivolous and artificial posing adopted from Wilde rather than at homosexuality itself. Hence Unamuno states that the Spanish homosexuals are, in fact, men, and thus can and do suffer. Unamuno seems drawn to the agonal discourse of Wilde's text, that is, the profound pain he expresses at his imprisonment. It may be that he endorses the text for its confessional element, for what appears to be a repentance from homosexuality on Wilde's part, but that interpretation is not clear. What is clear, nevertheless, is that Unamuno is drawn to the authenticity of feeling that he perceives in Wilde's text: his criticism of those who have modeled themselves on Wilde is directed at the deliberate cultivation of artificiality so associated with Wilde's aestheticism.

In this respect, one might consider that the homoerotic dimension of the relationship in *Don Sandalio* is in fact consonant with an amorous relationship as conceived in Unamuno's world. An amorous relationship between a man and a woman is rarely treated in erotic terms but rather in terms of shelter, comfort, and affection. It is commonplace to assert that for Unamuno a woman was always a mother.[25] In one of his more famous autobiographical anecdotes, Unamuno believed he was suffering from a heart attack one night in 1897 and began to cry. Concepción Lizárraga ("Concha"), his wife, called out "¡hijo mío!" ("my son!").[26] As much as his fictional works often involve the vicissitudes of familial arrangements, this anecdote underscores the fact that in his essays Unamuno tended to conceptualize love in spiritual rather than carnal terms. While it is true that no sexual act takes place nor any specific sexual reference is made in *Don Sandalio,* the chess player finds a form of comfort and solace in his relationship with Don Sandalio that is often associated with heterosexuality in Unamuno's work. Carlos Blanco Aguinaga, for example, reads the home and the wife as central figures for Unamuno: the home as a sanctuary of peace and within it, his Concha (112–13). In *Don Sandalio,* however, the letter writer, who has lost his home and seeks sanctuary, finds the emotional support and human connection not in a woman but in another man.

The substitution of a man for a woman may be, in fact, the "queerest" part of Unamuno's text. There are no mothers in *Don Sandalio;* the letter writer refuses to ask about the daughter-in-law and offers no information about Don Sandalio's wife; the letter writer's own family remains unidentified throughout the story. As much as he struggles with the meaning of his attachment to Don Sandalio, the letter writer reveals his own resistance to an explanatory model grounded in heterosexuality. As the letter exchange nears its end, the anonymous writer registers plainly his refusal to entertain Felipe's entreaties to resolve the enigma of Don Sandalio's death by seeking out his daughter. It is a significant refusal insofar as it protects his own image of the chess player by disavowing any sort of familial arrangement that would separate the two of them. In the penultimate letter, XXII, he dismisses the idea that a woman can provide the answer to the enigma:

> [Y]ou've missed, in the course of this long correspondence, the presence of a single woman. And now, you expect the novel you're looking for from me to take shape, to gel, with the appearance of a woman. The missing She! The old story of "her." As in: *Cherchez la femme.* But I don't intend to seek out Don Sandalio's daughter nor any other "she" or "her" who might have been involved with him. (220, trans. mod.)[27]

His vehement rejection of the heteronormative paradigm—the "old story" of a man and a woman—is impossible to overlook. Discarding the daughter's possible role in the imprisonment and death of Don Sandalio, he maintains that the only woman for Don Sandalio was the queen of the chessboard. Sinclair also sees Felipe's allusion to a woman at the end of text as a mistake and affirms that what is truly important is "the relationship of himself [the letter writer] to Don Sandalio" (193). The absence of a woman is by no means a sign of homosexuality, but it does further suggest that the bonds between them are not homosocial ties based on a rivalry for a female object of desire. Instead, the possibility that something other than rivalry for a woman may be the motivating force of their relationship leads the narrator to offer in letter XXII a brief exposition on the topic of identity, one that forecloses the possibility that sexuality is what links them.

Let us look more closely at letter XXII.[28] "I don't recall what writer obsessed with the sex 'problem' said that woman is a sphinx without a riddle. Perhaps. But the most profound problem of the novel or play of our life does not lie in the sexual 'question,' any more than it lies in our stomach" (221).[29] The phrase "a sphinx without a riddle" can be read as an oblique reference to Unamuno's play *La esfinge* (The Sphinx, 1898), but it is also, and more importantly, an allusion to Oscar Wilde's definition from "The Sphinx without a Secret." The story, which circulated in Spain in a version translated by Ramón Gómez de la Serna, narrates the conversation of two men who debated whether a deceased woman had an untold secret. The mention of Wilde's definition draws a parallel between the two tales, which ironically happen to share a common thread: a character has a secret, but the nature of that secret is left unrevealed by the narrative denouement. Nevertheless, the narrator's reference is not meant to establish this parallel but rather to distance himself from Wilde's definition. That he should mention the expression at all, or even attribute it to someone else, is curious; the absence of information begs the question of why it was suppressed in the first place. Wilde, symbol of the love that dare not speak its name, cannot be named in the narrative: he is identified only by circumlocution. Homosexuality too is rendered oblique, reduced to the more general category of "sex." The refusal to name Wilde is not, I would argue, meant to reflect an unfamiliarity with the author on the part of the letter writer. At the turn of the century the name of Oscar Wilde was already "sacred" among Spanish *modernistas,* and Wilde's public image was firmly established in Spain by 1910, due in large part to a theatrical production of *Salomé* in Madrid (Fernández Cifuentes 100–102).[30] Mira similarly claims that Wilde and the adjective "wildeano" were becoming increasingly associated with homosexuality in the late 1910s and early '20s ("After Wilde" 33). The definition of woman as a sphinx may also have had a certain resonance as an invocation of Wilde's homosexuality, as Juan Gil-Albert, a Spanish gay writer, suggests when he remarks, "A sphinx without a secret, as he tried to define women, with knowing that he was much more certainly defining himself" (14).

The veiled allusion to Wilde and the repression of the topic of sexuality is significant at this juncture in the correspondence. The letter writer seems to distance himself from his connection to Don Sandalio as if the letter exchanges with Felipe were becoming too intimate or revealing. Unamuno claimed in his brief essay "Cartas a mujeres" (Letters to Women) that a man should ideally confess to a woman: the proximity between two men would produce a lack of discretion that would allow for too much confidentiality between them (8: 903–4). *Don Sandalio,* in using the letter form for a confession between two men, seems to corroborate Unamuno's point. Drawing on Wilde's definition, the letter writer shifts the focus from sexuality to our general existence, to what he calls "personality" ("personalidad"): the profound problem of our lives, he asserts, is not our appetite—our desire—but rather our identity—"being or not being" ("de ser o no ser") (221; 91), a phrase that undoubtedly echoes Unamuno's own metaphysical meditations on *serse,* or achieving a coherent identity. In short, the letter writer asserts that the objects of our attraction and need—love and nourishment— are less significant than how we conceive our own subjectivity. In some sense, this is a psychoanalytic insight, insofar as Freud locates subjectivity not in the objects that we seek but in the fantasy structure that underlies our desire for certain objects. At the same time, however, his sudden refusal of desire as a category, of what his relations with others say about him, rings a bit hollow, for up to this point his entire correspondence has been concerned with his connection to Don Sandalio as a means of finding himself.

By way of explicating what he means by "personality," the narrator offers two categories, two types of "novels" or "life-stories": "There may be sphinxes without riddles—and those are the novels which most please members of the Casinos—but there are also riddles without sphinxes" (221).[31] On the surface he seems to say that there are those people for whom an uncomplicated world is preferable, while for others the enigma of life is more intriguing. The earlier definition of "woman" as a sphinx without an enigma would seem to have gone by the wayside, as the narrator has deliberately moved away from the categories of sexual difference. Nevertheless, he reiterates that definition when he returns to Don Sandalio's relation to both "woman" as sphinx and woman as "queen" of the chessboard to sever the link between the image of the chess queen and real women: the lack of "bust, breasts, and face" ("busto, senos y rostro") means that it is no sphinx but that the queen harbors an enigma. The enigma at the core of his and Don Sandalio's respective "personalities" is not resolved by finding a female object of desire. It bears asking, in some respect, if a sphinx without an enigma is a woman, is an enigma without a sphinx a man?

Between the sphinxes and enigmas that evoke the figure of Wilde, Unamuno's text is also a reworking of the myth of Oedipus and its Freudian reinterpretation. In rejecting the female object of desire as the teleological outcome of the narrative, the letter writer in effect rewrites the story of Oedipus. The myth of Oedipus is clearly alluded to through the invocation of the sphinx and the enigma, but no explicit mention of Oedipus is made. In the original myth, Oedipus answers the Sphinx's enigma and thus frees Thebes from her control. Nevertheless, the answer to the enigma is what allows Oedipus to enter Thebes as king, marry his mother, Jocasta, and fulfill the prophecy. In other words, the answer to the enigma condemns Oedipus to his predetermined fate. The letter writer, in choosing to contemplate the enigma over the sphinx, to ignore the sphinx altogether, refuses in a sense to adopt the position of Oedipus. Oedipus fulfills his fate by answering the enigma: he kills his father and marries his mother. Such is the telos of heterosexuality as reinterpreted by Freud. For Freud, the "normal" outcome of the dissolution of the Oedipal complex consisted in the strengthening of the relationship to the father and, by extension, the reestablishment and reconsolidation of heterosexuality.[32] If the identification with the mother is strengthened, and the object-cathexis for the father not given up, the "negative" Oedipal complex results in homosexuality for the male child. But the letter writer denies the normal Oedipal outcome as the answer to his and Don Sandalio's enigma: the answer, he suggests, lies elsewhere. The refusal of Oedipus is, implicitly, a refusal of the modern social order constructed around the heterosexual unit of the family with the clearly defined roles of mother, father, son, and daughter.

Unamuno's narrative works often address the struggle of individual desires within the social structure of the family. *La tía Tula* (*Aunt Tula*, 1921), for example, dramatizes one woman's struggle with maternity. In essence, the narrative seeks to answer the question: what drives a woman who cannot have and does not want to produce children of her own to establish a maternal relationship with someone else's children? *Don Sandalio* follows this pattern by asking, what other affective relationships are possible, outside the heterosexual family unit, between two men? The question remains unanswered, the epistolary introspection comes to a close. The letter writer is no longer a *robinsón* in the Ortegan sense of the word. The editing and repackaging by Unamuno, who insists that the letters are written by Don Sandalio himself, invariably begs the question of why he would need to recur to such a novelistic strategy to "hide and reveal his 'truth.'" From a psychoanalytic point of view, the subject's decentering and splintering between the ego and the unconscious compels him to engage in the creation of a coherent authorial identity. If psychoanalysis argues that sexuality is a stumbling block in the subject—a void or gap around which we construct a house of cards known as identity—self-knowledge of our own sexuality often eludes us. The anxiety produced by the relationship with Don Sandalio and the self-questioning that the letter writer pursues in his correspondence suggest that the relationship was of such a nature or intensity that it needed to be ventriloquized through a third person. The implication is that the letter writer's and Don Sandalio's "truth," as Unamuno calls it, remains something of an enigma for the writer himself even after the confessional exchange with Felipe has ended. On the other hand, the fact that he wishes to continue his conversation with Felipe in person hints at the possibility that he did not want the answer to circulate in his letters.

Unamuno's refusal to provide the solution to Don Sandalio's life leaves that truth for the reader to decipher, but the epilogue does in some ways ward off certain interpretive possibilities.[33] The editor of someone's private letters ostensibly maintains control over the correspondence by organizing and giving it meaning (Pagés-Rangel 14). It could be argued, for example, that Unamuno's insistence that the letters are the product of a single mind eliminates any further inquiry into the relationship between two men. Yet Unamuno ultimately undermines the interpretive authority he wishes to exert over the letters, for in the end the act of retransmitting the letters, rendering them public documents, wrests control from the editor and grants it to the reader. The transferential circuit alters their reception so that the original meaning of a letter is not necessarily conveyed or even available to the new addressee (Duyfhuizen 5; Pagés-Rangel 33–34). This view is, in fact, in accord with other statements in which Unamuno grants interpretive authority to the reader. In the preface to his drama *El otro* (*The Other,* 1932), he asserts: "The idea that an author forms of his own work influences very little the idea that the public has of it. And a tragic, dramatic or comical character belongs more to the public than to its author. Just as, in general, it matters less what a writer says than what he says without meaning to" (12: 801). By unmasking the letter writer's authorial ruse without supplying a final answer, Unamuno's epilogue initiates a hermeneutical path in which a queer reading of the homoerotic potential of their relationship is not foreclosed.

Don Sandalio offers, through its dramatization of the confessional and autobiographical function of letters, an example of the shifting conceptualization of the epistolary novel as a psychologizing instrument. The struggle with desire is presented here as the writer's own dilemma, a psychic burden that is the very motor of the epistolary enterprise. Rescued from the depths of the archive as a novelistic trick, the letters of *Don Sandalio* invite the reader to spirit back into existence a phantom desire by decoding the writer's sexual identity. Unamuno's story is, in this respect, a reflection of the psychoanalytic and postal epoch that sees the letter as a portal into the psychic life of a writing subject. Read alongside Lorca's correspondence or essays on epistolarity from the turn of the century, *Don Sandalio* offers us a glimpse into the evolving function of epistolarity as a form of letter closet. The discourse of friendship, the use of epistolarity, the types of secrets that letters could contain: all point to the potential of homosexual desire being found beneath the seal of the envelope. Unamuno may not have *intended* to

write a homoerotic love story but the discursive association of letters
with confession and sexuality generates an interpretive map that allows
us to see *Don Sandalio* as a representation of the vicissitudes of the emergence of same-sex desire in early-twentieth-century Spain.

But what we find in the archive of correspondence is not so much
the coherent product of a sexual identity but a disruption of the cir-
cuits that link identity and desire. There is no outing of the anonymous
correspondent in Unamuno's novel, even as his letters appear to offer a
glimpse into the veiled space of his sexuality. In the end the queer interpretation is significant not for what it says about the letter writer or
Don Sandalio but rather for what it tells us about the very call for interpretation initiated by Unamuno's framing of the text—a call to read
that, based on the letter writer's discussion of sexuality and personality,
draws the reader's attention to the topic of sexual identity. We seek out
keys to a person's identity in letters, and because sexuality, as Foucault
has argued, is the primary secret of subjective relations, we invariably
search for evidence of a letter writer's sexual identity. This is true for
both authentic and fictional correspondence; hence the contemporary
proliferation of collections of letters as a form of biographical insight
into the affective lives of gays and lesbians, or the debates that emerge
about a given individual's sexual identity when admissions of homoerotic desire are found in his or her correspondence.[34]

Yet Derrida's deconstruction of correspondence in *The Post Card*
amply demonstrates that the writing subject is never fixed, for like literature, letters are subject to the vagaries of language: the letter can be a
poor medium for the communication of a singular identity. Our knowledge of sexual identity will always fall short, due to the limits imposed
by the partial and incomplete framework provided by epistolary correspondence. Even if letters are subject to the rhetorical indeterminacy of
all writing and thus open to interpretation, we nevertheless hold onto
them as a potential portal to our innermost selves—and to the innermost selves of others—because they are considered among the most
private and personal of exchanges. Our attachment to the possibility
of a coherent subjectivity leads us to place our most intimate thoughts
in the supposed sanctuary of the envelope and to desire urgently to read
the intimate writings of others as an entry into their private lives. A

queer reading of Unamuno's novel, rather than simply recuperating a hidden queer subjectivity, unmasks the ideological function of the letter in the aegis of the postal system. *Don Sandalio*, read alongside the emerging discourses of homosexuality in the early decades of twentieth-century Spain, reminds us that the search for sexual secrets beneath the seal of the envelope is a reflection of a modern understanding of sexuality that attempts to transform the fragmented expressions of desire in epistolary correspondence into irrefutable evidence of a sexual identity.

CHAPTER 2

Specters of Lesbian Desire:
Love Letters and Queer Readers in
Carmen Martín Gaite

In Edgar Allan Poe's "The Purloined Letter," Inspector Dupin's ingenuity in resolving the mystery of the missing missive resides in his insight that the letter, had it been concealed, would have been found. Instead, he reveals that the minister, who anticipated the detective techniques of the Parisian police, did not attempt to conceal it at all. The basic plot of Poe's story is that the minister has stolen a letter addressed to the queen, the contents of which she would prefer to keep private. The minister exercises his newly gained power to exert pressure on the queen while the police search for the letter. Because the minister left it in the open, Dupin concludes, it remained undetectable. But the fact is, he did conceal the letter—in another envelope with another stamp. As Dupin narrates: "It had a large black seal, bearing the D—— cipher *very* conspicuously, and was addressed, in a diminutive female hand, to D——, the minister, himself" (21). Dupin, naturally, recognizes it immediately to be the object of his search, in spite of the radical difference in appearance from the description given to him by the prefect. The original seal had been small and red, with the ducal arms of the S—— family, while on the new envelope it was large and black in the D—— cipher. More important is the description of the writing of the address: "Here, the address, to the Minister, was diminutive and feminine; there the superscription, to a certain royal personage, was markedly bold and decided" (21). A seemingly insignificant detail, the point of the change in exterior appearance is to hide the letter while remaining in plain view.

In his "Seminar," Lacan also notes that the letter's envelope has been switched and is now addressed with a "delicate feminine script"; he proceeds to examine the relationship between a letter from a woman and its recipient, the minister. Although Lacan stresses the inability of the king and the police to read the letter because "that *place entailed blindness*" (50), such an insight leads to another blind spot in Lacan's formulation: so concerned is he with the minister and the female body that he overlooks the relationship between this letter and the search for the queen's letter. The minister concealed the letter from the police by altering not only the addressee on the envelope but also the author of the letter: by restamping the envelope and writing the script in "diminutive female hand," D—— effectively changed the gender of the original letter writer. With a large, black stamp designed to conceal, the travestied letter is rewritten by a man as a woman's letter. The masquerade is successful since at no moment did anyone consider that an epistle penned by a woman—an epistle which may be a love letter, although that is never stated—could be addressed to the queen. In plain sight but unnoticed, the purloined letter is haunted by a desire that remains wholly unintelligible within the gender and sexual expectations of the police: this desire is the possibility of an amorous correspondence between two women.[1] Lesbianism in Poe's text exists as an absence, an absence that marks a heteronormative blind spot.

Implicit in Poe's story is the association of women's writing with the genre of the letter, and specifically the love letter, which has been, in the words of Elizabeth Goldsmith, "perhaps the most tenacious of gender-genre connections in the history of literature" (viii). The long-standing link between letters and women's writing—a means of keeping women from the masculine-dominated domain of literature, some might argue—has been revalorized in contemporary feminist studies as a mode of rescuing and recuperating the suppressed voices of women. The notion that the letter functions as a space of knowledge and confession subtends the metaphorical view of the letter as a "window into the intimate, and usually feminine, self" (Favret 10). In recent studies of epistolary fiction, Anne Bower and Diane Cousineau have upheld the longstanding notion that the letter can function as a space for women writers, where writing can become a means of reconstituting oneself as

a subject (5; 26). In the Spanish context, a cursory examination of epistolary studies reveals the same gender-genre alignment. In his introduction to the *Epistolario español* (Spanish Letter Collection), Eugenio
de Ochoa writes that "it is a noteworthy observation that on this point
[the expression of emotion in letters] women have the advantage over
men" (vi). Pedro Salinas also avers women's superiority in letter writing due to their capacity for spontaneity and flirtation (69, 72). In turn,
critics of Spanish literature have emphasized the use of the letter by
Spanish women writers for the creation of a female writing subject.[2]

As invaluable as the study of feminine epistolary correspondence has
been for feminist studies and the revalorization of women's writing,
the association of women with letter writing can also unintentionally
reify a traditional, normative view of femininity and sexual difference.
Critics of epistolarity reiterate that the image of the female letter
writer, the lettered woman, oscillates between conformity and liberation, between the imprisonment of the gendered norms imposed on
letter writing and the escape from such confinements that writing
allows. Mary Favret and Barbara Zaczek have remarked on the cloistering effect of epistolarity, how women write under the shadow of a
male vision of femininity, in which women's access to a voice in letters
remains enclosed within prescribed roles such as the heartsick lover
(12; 12). In the *Heroides,* Ovid's deployment of Sappho's voice in a
ventriloquistic masquerade is a key example of the male creation of
the woman letter writer. By contrast, figures such as Heloise remind
us of the subversive potential for women that letter writing affords.
As both Peggy Kamuf and Linda Kauffman point out, Heloise's letters
to Abelard reveal that her apparent submissiveness to her tutor and
lover are crafty rhetorical maneuvers designed to undermine Abelard's
own authority and provide a space for her own desire (8; *Discourses* 67).
Women letter writers are thus seen as rehearsing a feminine performance dictated by men or, conversely, deploying the letter as an authentic outlet for their true selves. Nevertheless, in both cases, the link
between letter writing and femininity remains fundamentally dependent upon men. The erotic activity of writing letters is construed as
inherently heterosexual, where men must be the addressees of women's
love letters. From Ovid's ventriloquism to Guilleragues's masquerading

as a Portuguese nun (whose letters may have been penned by Mariana Alcoforado), from Heloise's letters to Abelard to Clarissa's letters about her seduction by Lovelace, women's epistolarity is circumscribed by male interlocutors and prescribed gender and sexual norms.

Shari Benstock's reading of Derrida's *The Post Card* stands out as an example of an attempt to read against the grain of the gender-genre alignment of epistolary fiction. She admirably teases out the ways in which Derrida's text exposes the radical suppression of female desire within epistolary fiction, subordinated to men: "Epistolary fiction only poses then as feminocentric writing; it only gives the illusion of woman writing. Underwritten by masculine assumptions about woman's writing, the epistolary genre only seems to compose itself under the auspices of the feminine" (266). Yet Benstock too turns a blind eye to the radical possibility in epistolarity for female desire. Poe's "The Purloined Letter" suggests yet another possibility for thinking of the letter as a signifier: the letter becomes the site of a foreclosed desire that continues to haunt the literary text as an unrealized possibility. For while authentic correspondence has been significant for the study of lesbianism (the letters between Virginia Woolf and Vita Sackville-West, for example), little attention has been granted to a subset of the epistolary genre that emphasizes same-sex desire between women, how the very "masculine" assumptions about women's desire are both duplicated and undermined by a feminocentric desire.[3] In Laclos's *Les liaisons dangereuses,* for example, Merteuil eroticizes her relationship with the young Cécile Volanges, who in turn writes to her friend of the passions that the elder woman has aroused in her. Honoré de Balzac's *La fille aux yeux d'or* (*The Girl with the Golden Eyes,* 1834–35), while not a *roman par lettres* (although Richardson's characters Clarissa and Lovelace and Laclos's *Les liaisons dangereuses* are explicitly mentioned), uses letter writing to convey the same-sex relationship between Paquita Valdés and the Marquise, Margarita-Euphémia Porrabéril. Henri de Marsay intercepts a letter, whose confessional dimension allows him to discover that the author of the letter is, in fact, a woman and not a man, as he had believed. In both cases, the epistolary love is never consummated, and the authors are men, reflecting the predominant masculinity that critics have noted in epistolary fiction.

Carmen Martín Gaite's *El cuarto de atrás* (*The Back Room,* 1978) shares close company with these works, in spite of the fact that it not usually associated with the epistolary genre.[4] During a stormy evening, a woman writer who closely resembles Martín Gaite is awakened by a mysterious man dressed in black who claims to have arranged for an interview. The protagonist, known only as "C.," does not remember having scheduled the interview but nonetheless allows him entrance to her apartment, at which point they spend the night in conversation. The novel is a series of often interrupted dialogues, confessions, and internal monologues in which the man in black serves as a catalyst for C.'s reflexive pursuit of past memories. The recollection of her past begins, however, just prior to the arrival of the man in black. In the first chapter, the protagonist rummages through a sewing basket in her bedroom and discovers a lost letter hidden at the bottom. The letter, composed on pale blue paper, glows mysteriously and begins to take over the space of the narrator's hallway as she continues to unfold it. In spite of its overwhelming size, however, the letter immediately begins to flee, propelled by a gust from an open window, and thus foregrounds the fleeting presence letters will have in the novel.

> It is a long letter, in cramped handwriting, addressed to me. It bears no date. My body is hiding the place where the signature must be. I change position, consumed with curiosity, thereby revealing a blurred, indecipherable initial. The ink appears to have run, as though a tear had fallen on it. (13–14)[5]

The image of the tear-stained amorous epistle is, of course, a conventional one. Martín Gaite employs it ambiguously, however, in that C. describes the blurry letter "as if" an anguished lover's tears had fallen onto the page. As she begins to describe the letter to the reader, a quick interjection clarifies the author's gender: "it's a man writing because the adjectives that refer to him are in the masculine gender" (14).[6] But as a reader of her own letter, C. is incapable of remembering who wrote to her or why, nor does she remember having read it before. The interlocutor is not identified, and thus the epistolary circuit is rendered incomplete; the meaning of the desire conveyed in the letter remains open to interpretation.

As in Poe's narrative, desire appears, at least initially, as heterosexual, residing comfortably within the traditional parameters of the love letter. C.'s declaration of her epistolary interlocutor's gender would seem to foreclose any further inquiry into her sexual desires. Furthermore, she has spent the evening recalling various love affairs with men from her youth, and the relationship between these two interlocutors has been tinged with eroticism from the outset. Yet C.'s need to clarify the sex of the addressee of the blue letter opens up the possibility that her epistolary interlocutors could have been women. Her comment foreshadows the subsequent discovery by the reader that her relationships with women—her childhood friend, the enigmatic Carola—are similarly mediated by the epistolary mode. In the protagonist's past, disordered under the influence of conversation and pills, there persists a desire between women that seductively suggests and simultaneously resists the label "lesbian." Brad Epps has argued insightfully that in Martín Gaite's text "lesbian love cannot even be imagined, let alone named" ("Virtual Sexuality" 330). Lesbianism indeed cannot be imagined, at least not by the protagonist, but it is named. After C. mentions her strong affection for a female friend from her childhood, the man in black asks rather unexpectedly: "Were you a lesbian?" (195).[7]

El cuarto de atrás vacillates between heterosexual friendship and female eroticism, memory and fantasy, lost and recovered letters. The novel is an exploration of the back room—both a literal space in the narrator's home and a figural expression of the narrator's own memories—"the attic of one's brain, a sort of secret place full of a vague jumble of all sorts of miscellaneous junk" (87).[8] Like the murky space of the unconscious from which the repressed returns, letters resurface in the back room and other secreted spaces, functioning as signposts of foreclosed desire, of libidinal activity that has been buried and ostensibly forgotten. Or, to anticipate my reading, the letter hidden in the back room will lead us to yet another figurative space: the closet. At the risk of oversimplifying, we might say that El cuarto de atrás is a lesbian novel without lesbians and an epistolary novel without letters. This is undoubtedly too succinct a formulation for the complexity of both aspects in the novel, but it nonetheless aptly captures the ways in which desire between women, most readily seen in the novel in the circulation of letters, is rendered illegible within the presumed heteronormativity of women's epistolary writing.

Remembering the past and recuperating the forgotten, *El cuarto de atrás* is a novel of memories but not a memoir, autobiographical in detail but not an autobiography, historically accurate but not an official history (Castillo 814). Like many other writers, Martín Gaite began to look back at the Franco regime in the early years of the transition to democracy, yet she chose a hybrid genre—the fantastic memoir—as a means of approaching that era without falling into the trap of solipsistically recalling one's own memories; in the novel, the protagonist notes that there has been a proliferation of memoirs, and that other people's memories are of little interest to her (142). *El cuarto de atrás* plays instead with the border between fiction and reality by framing the entire conversation between the man in black and C. within the genre of the fantastic; Tzvetan Todorov's *Introduction à la littérature fantastique* is an explicit intertext. The dialogue between the man in black and C. is, in many respects, exemplary of the considerable emphasis Martín Gaite places on the function of communication—both oral and written—in her narrative works. In "La búsqueda de interlocutor" (The Search for an Interlocutor), for example, she conceives of writing as the search for another to establish a form of idealized communication. Nevertheless, the reader never knows if the man in black is a figment of the protagonist's imagination or a real person who has mysteriously appeared in the middle of the night. Similarly, the main character resembles the author, lives in an apartment in Madrid (which resembles the one where Martín Gaite lived for years until her death in July 2000), has authored a number of works that bear the same titles as those published by Martín Gaite, but she is never named as Carmen.

The turn to the fantastic, to the border between reality and fantasy, is in part a measure of Martín Gaite's literary evolution from the social realism that characterized her early work toward postmodernism and a view of history as a narrative open to revision. Memory functions in the novel as a strategy not merely for recovering the past—both national and personal—but also for overturning and rewriting it from the point of view of a woman writer. Steeped in national history and politics, in romance novels and sentimental *boleros,* in childhood fantasies and postwar experiences, the novel has been a profoundly influential work for Hispanist critics' exploration of gender norms and women's subjectivity during the Franco regime because of its emphasis on the memories of a woman growing up during the dictatorship. This was not, to be sure, the first instance of Martín Gaite's engagement with the social pressures of gender norms. Her first full-length novel, *Entre visillos* (*Behind the Curtains,* 1958), takes up that issue with the main character Natalia's refusal to marry in spite of the pressure to do so. In *Ritmo lento* (Slow Rhythm, 1962), David engages in a series of recollections with a psychiatrist, and he notes that women remain complicitous with social oppression by failing to resist cultural norms.

But it is in *El cuarto de atrás* where gender, tied to the history of the Spanish state under the Franco dictatorship, is refracted most powerfully through the lens of memory. This point is made early in the novel when C. attempts to remember a specific type of cloth. *Género,* the Spanish word for gender and genre, also carries as one of its definitions "any type of cloth" (Real Academia Española 1033). "That cloth had a name, I don't remember what it was, all fabrics had one, and it was essential to know how to tell a shantung from a piqué, a moiré, or an organdy. Not to be able to recognize fabrics by their names was as scandalous as to call neighbors by the wrong names" (5).[9] C.'s comment on cloth underscores the ways in which cloth, like gender, is a form of normative categorization; women of her age and class are expected to make such distinctions or suffer the consequences of a social faux pas. Like gender and genre, C. learned the conceptual need for classification through the names of cloth. Gender and genre—*género*—are tied to the act of remembering, and in her attempt to recall the names of fabrics, C. points to the transgressive and ultimately scandalous act of forgetting, deliberately or not, the names of *géneros* and consequently crossing their borders.

After the man in black gives her a "memory" pill from a little gold box, C.'s memories become disordered, allowing her to narrate an alternative story to the official version of women's subjectivity under Franco. "The pill," as Debra Castillo notes, "stimulates memories of a past not necessarily faithful to fact or even to verisimilitude, while at the same time it provokes a studied disorder, a feigned forgetfulness" (824). And those memories are always subject to revision, change, erasure, and evolution as the time between the memory and the recollection grows.[10] The self recalls and rewrites itself in the form of a fragmented narrative composed of memories in which the gaps are perhaps more telling than the main story. As Adam Phillips argues, the paradox of autobiographical writing, from a psychoanalytic perspective, is that the most significant memories are the ones most likely to be forgotten (66). Much of the third and fourth chapters are devoted to the sudden return of childhood memories of the Spanish civil war (1936–39) and Franco regime (1939–75), which contrast greatly with the freedom of the Second Republic (1931–36): "I could tell him that happiness in the war years and the years just after the war was something inconceivable, that we lived surrounded by ignorance and repression [. . .] and add the bitterness of my present opinions to the other sensations that I am dredging up from my memory tonight" (65).[11] Her memories recall the ways in which the Franco dictatorship, through the Women's Section of the Falange, the nationalist party of the regime, constructed and controlled female subjectivity.[12] Pilar Primo de Rivera, sister of José Antonio, the founder of the Falange, headed the Women's Section, whose purpose was to roll back the advances women had made under the Second Republic and to inculcate in young women the desire to accept a life of submission and remain in the home.[13] The laws that were quickly passed after the Nationalist victory over the Republicans in the civil war eliminated coeducation (boys had to be separated from girls in schools), prohibited women from working at night, used subsidies to encourage married couples to procreate, illegalized divorce and abortion, and made domestic education obligatory for women. Through the idealization of traditional female roles (the self-sacrificing mother and dutiful wife), women were subjugated under Franco in rather rigid ways.

Counterposing the official narrative, C.'s newly recovered and disordered memories allow her to narrate a personal history in which a different view of gender emerges. She confesses the curiosity she had about the women who did not follow proper gender norms or occupy roles considered appropriate for women: "Madwomen, bold women, scatterbrained women were skirting the limits of transgression" (123).[14] These women inspired in her a furtive desire to imagine how they would live if they were not subject to the scrutinizing gaze of others who condemned them to the margins of society. Given the oppressive force of gender, this was a private desire for the narrator—"I would not have dared to confess this to anyone," she comments (124)—but that secrecy did not prevent her from admiring the audacity of these women who defied the normative constraints imposed on them.[15] These same women would also appear, figured romantically, in the *boleros* of the singer Conchita Piquer: "Stories of girls who were not at all like the ones we knew, who were never going to enjoy the tender affection of the peaceable home and fireside that set us respectable young ladies to dreaming—girls drifting on the fringes of society, unprotected by the law" (152–53).[16]

As C. recalls, her childhood reading of the romance novel, *la novela rosa,* provoked her awareness of the possibilities of breaking with gender expectations, instructing her to overturn those expectations, to see in them an alternative course in spite of the novels' conservative portrayal of women's lives. She remarks that romance novels played a crucial role in shaping the sensibilities of young girls during the forties (138–39). When discussing the romance novel, C. questions the paradigm of marriage as the typical outcome of a novel (87–88; 92).[17] Remembering the novel *El amor catedrático* (Love and the Professor, 1910), she recalls the deception she felt upon reading the typical ending of the wedding scene, in which the female protagonist has sacrificed her career in order to marry. As young girls, she and a female friend attempted to create their own romance novel around the characters of Alejandro and Esmeralda. Through their youthful romantic fantasies, C. and her friend created a private oasis known as Bergai. This childhood creation of a private space illustrates one of the most trenchant repudiations of the heterosexual romance plot.[18] In a departure from the ideal outcome of the marriage ceremony, C. and her friend created a feminine homosocial refuge to escape the pressures of social norms. This metaphoric and literary place rewrites the traditional romantic plot in that there is no husband to be found (Ortiz 48).

It is within this larger framework of her memory about women that the relationship of the novel to the epistolary genre accrues its significance. The only letter that C. still has, on torn blue paper, is signed with a single, illegible letter. It is, significantly, the only letter that actually appears in the text. The importance of the letter rests not solely in its content—in the appearance of a man on the beach who agonizes over their lost relationship—but in the fact that the letter sends C. wandering through her past. She recalls her childhood practice of sending letters to herself through the mail, making herself her own interlocutor in a solipsistic loop. Attempting to fall asleep near the end of the first chapter, C. focuses on her heart, on the lost love that the unnamed letter writer has resuscitated, on the youthful acceleration of her pulse when watching Leslie Howard kiss Norma Shearer on screen. At the root of these reflections is the metonymic movement between letters, both alphabetical and epistolary—the "c" of her name; the "c" of *casa* (house), *cama* (bed), and *cuarto* (room); but most importantly, the "c" of *corazón* (heart). It is here that the letter, which in Spanish also begins with the letter "c" (*carta*), carries its force, for if the back room is symbolic of C.'s unconscious, the letter returns as a sign not just of lost love but the loss of the memory of that love altogether. It is, in a sense, a repression of love, one that leaves the man on the beach behind altogether ("the barefoot man has now disappeared from sight," she comments [16]) in order to return to her childhood self and her failed pursuit of love.[19] She ends the chapter drifting off to sleep, "'I want to see you, I want to see you,' with my eyes closed. But I have no idea who it is I'm saying that to" (18).[20]

This single letter, once forgotten and only partially remembered, becomes a map to the protagonist's past loves. "'The most terrifying thing about old letters is when one has forgotten where one has put them for safekeeping or when one doesn't even know if one has kept them, and then suddenly they reappear,' the man says thoughtfully. 'It's as though someone from another planet were giving us back a slice of life'" (39).[21] Yet the other letters that surface time and again throughout conversation with the man in black similarly reflect the failure of epistolary relations. In the second chapter, C. recalls the time she spent in Portugal, when two Portuguese men would send her and her roommate letters signed with a single initial. If those letters would seem to clarify the origin of the blue letter, no such connection is made. Instead, she recounts her failed attempt to deliver a letter of her own to one of them. At the last moment, however, he notices her presence, and she can no longer surreptitiously slip the letter into his pocket (48; 53–54). The delivery is never realized as the epistolary connection is short-circuited. But she admits that the inability to slip the letter into his pocket was the least important aspect of the exchange. Before running from the scene of failed delivery, she had gone to the park to reread her letter: "I went out into the park and read it all over. It was altogether literary. The person to whom it was addressed mattered not at all. I was in a transport of narcissism" (48).[22] Afterward, she runs upstairs to her hotel room and destroys the letter. In the end, the interlocutor is a pretext for the writing of letters, as she becomes her own interlocutor. As is the case with the writing of some of Martín Gaite's literary predecessors, such as the letters of the seventeenth-century Portuguese nun Mariana Alcoforado to a French chevalier, letter writing is transformed into a mode of desire that is close-circuited, rerouted, and turned back upon itself. In *Lettres portugaises* Alcoforado initially conveys the sorrow she suffers due to the chevalier's absence and indifference only to recognize that the act of writing sustains the passion she feels, that the chevalier is a mere pretext.

In *Usos amorosos de la postguerra* (*Courtship Customs in Postwar Spain,* 1987) Martín Gaite recalls the remarkable power of epistolary writing for young women in postwar Spain. She notes that girls were envious of friends who displayed a rhetorical talent for writing letters, since the ability to carry on a letter correspondence with a man was one of the possible ways of starting a romance (175). In *Desde la ventana* (Through the Window, 1987), a volume of essays on the topic of women's writing, Martín Gaite expands her line of thinking and asserts that women have turned to letters and diaries in order to find the proper interlocutor for their intimate thoughts (59). For Martín Gaite the epistolary form was an ideal means for women to express their literary talents, allowing them to create ideal interlocutors that did not exist in real life: "if that 'you,' the ideal receiver of the message, disappears or has never existed, the need for dialogue, for confiding, leads to its invention. Or, in other words, the passionate quest for that 'you' is the driving force of feminine discourse, the primordial motive for breaking through the feeling of enclosure" (59).[23] In *El cuarto de atrás,* the search for the ideal "you" in epistolary relations comes to signify a failure of communication, or, to be more precise, a failure of amorous connection, as that interlocutor is only imagined, never reached in person.

As a result, C. emphasizes the loss of letters: she used to keep them in a tin chest only to burn them later, as if in a ritual of purification. Pressed by the man in black to explain her motive, she claims that letters lose their content; they are no longer what they were when originally sent (38–39; 45). For C. love letters come to signify a disruption, a breakdown in the chain of human relations. Their loss is a reflection of her inability to reach an epistolary interlocutor, to establish a desiring connection with someone other than herself. Yet that failure is also, paradoxically, a success, for the primary *destinataire* is, in fact, herself: her own self and the amorous relation imagined in the letter are more significant than the letter's addressee. Her former relationships are thus rendered unreadable through their incendiary destruction, the traces of her desire in the form of amorous epistolary discourse erased. As if following Todorov's precepts for the fantastic genre, unknowability and unreadability become the trademark signatures of epistolarity in *El cuarto de atrás*. "Fantastic literature has a great deal to do with letters that reappear [. . .] With those that disappear as well" (39), C. comments.[24] Epistolarity thus becomes a destabilized and destabilizing concept that emphasizes the indeterminacy of the addressee and the circuit of transmission, in spite of the ontological status that traditional epistolary discourse attempts to achieve through recourse to these formal aspects.

Traditional epistolary fiction duplicates the reading process by publishing the letters within the narrative (thereby rendering the letters of internal readers available to the external reader), but in Martín Gaite's novel access to these letters is summarily impeded since they are illegible fragments. The epistolary mode also often depends upon a mimetic reflection of the real-life process of exchanging letters between two or more interlocutors. In Martín Gaite's work, that mimetic reflection is shattered as the transmission and reception of letters is frequently an unstable process in the text: it is often not readily apparent to whom they are written or who in fact wrote them, even if they reach their destination; as readers we are cut off from their content. In spite of the presence of letters in the novel, nearly all the features that would define

epistolary discourse as a genre are elided. But if Martín Gaite undermines the formal conventions associated with the epistolary genre, she
also interrogates the gender-specific norms of letter writing. For example, C.'s nostalgic retelling of the attempt to deliver the letter to the
young Portuguese man shows how she broke with gender conventions,
"since no decent and decorous young lady of that day would have had
the audacity to write a letter like that" (48).[25] Her words evoke the gendered parameters of epistolary correspondence that dictated the ways
in which women could have recourse to letter writing. The loss of this
and other letters also marks the continual (albeit incomplete) erasure of
compulsory heterosexual desire in the novel; the unrecovered messages
symbolize the ways in which the heteronormativity of the epistolary
genre is itself "purloined."

Like the letters themselves, the genre of epistolary fiction also occupies a sort of spectral space in the novel: "This would be a good time to
change the subject and talk about the epistolary genre, just to see what
would come of it. He appears to be inviting me to do so" (193).[26] Just
as the protagonist cannot recall the author of the blue letter, neither can
she bring herself to discuss the genre of epistolary fiction. As much as
men are connected to letter writing, they are also seemingly secondary
to it, at a distance, forgotten, and at times even irrelevant. With the husband written out of the romance plot and the sentimental letters no
longer destined for their male addressees, letters instead become vehicles
for connections between women. Indeed, it is by no means coincidence
that after C. offers a lengthy discussion of the influence of the Franco
period on gender, the conversation is interrupted by another woman:
Carola. She calls C.'s apartment in search of "Alejandro." Although the
identity of Alejandro is never clarified, C. presumes that it must be the
man in black, only later to doubt the connection between the two male
figures. (No clear answer is given to resolve the dilemma of Alejandro's
identity. Nevertheless, the one piece of information that suggests the two
male characters might be the same is the fact that the man in black alerts
her that someone might be calling for him and to say that he is not present.) During the course of their telephone conversation, Carola reveals
that Alejandro jealously guards a large stack of letters whose authorial
identity remains unknown to her. Although they are signed with a C.,

the narrator does not remember writing them and, as a result, suggests that perhaps Carola herself wrote them: "What if she wrote them herself and doesn't remember that she did? She has the impression that she's never liked writing letters, much less love letters, but she may be mistaken. What does anybody ever know about himself or herself?" (173).[27]

Displacing Alejandro as the link between the two women, these letters form an alternative homosocial epistolary circuit in which the roles of reader and author become ambiguously convoluted. Here the importance of the letters resides not so much in their content—although they are love letters—but in the very act of reading. As Darian Leader has argued, in the exchange of love letters the content often matters less than who reads them and where (124). C. comments to herself after asking Carola to read them aloud, "How much I wanted to ask her to do that!" (169).[28] Yet once again the letters fail to arrive. Carola attempts to read them over the telephone so that C. can verify if she is the author, but the communication is never completed as Rafael, another male character, interrupts the process. Both women as readers and possible writers of these letters are linked in this epistolary circuit that never completes its course. The letters never reach C. in spite of her request to have them read over the phone.[29] The burnt letters of past loves never return complete. These letters, like the original letter in blue from her sewing basket, disappear and reappear in the text, but their meaning ultimately escapes C. At the same time, however, the issue of their authorship is rendered a moot point, for in the end they have traced a new postal circuit between the two women. At the end of the conversation, Carola says, "I'd like it if you were the one in the letters." C. responds, "I'd like to be her too . . . Let's hope I was" (176).[30]

The lack of clear authorship, of explicit addressees, and of recuperable content erodes the textual evidence that would serve to clarify the amorous and sexual relationship between two epistolary interlocutors. Paradoxically, the failure to communicate this information is not a failure to communicate. Rather, given the topos of the lover's letter as a synecdoche for the lover's body, the lack of access to this synecdoche opens up a critical space in which sex, gender, and sexuality are not fully disclosed or established. In narratological terms, paralepsis becomes paralipsis: the lack of information is suggestive of more information than

we are provided with by the narrator.[31] As the novel continually undermines heterosexuality in the discourse of letter writing, the epistolary
genre also functions as a feminine homosocial form of communication
for C., albeit one that is disturbed by the presence of male interlocutors.
In her recollections of the pieces of writing she stored in her tin box,
C. mentions letters from her first close female companion. This particular epistolary interlocutor is the only one whom she remembers with
any clarity. Only later in the novel, after the telephone conversation
with Carola, when C. and the man in black begin their final dialogue,
does it become clear that this initial correspondent was also the girl-
friend with whom she created the imaginary island of Bergai.

The effect of the protagonist's drug-influenced trip down memory
lane is certainly not without its liberatory release: as Robert Spires
suggests, the intertextual network of personal memories and historical
data allows the former to free itself from the latter (147). In particular,
the heteronormativity imposed on women, as expressed through the
romance novel and the love letter, is undermined as the demand for
marriage is nullified. Yet for all the novel's liberatory movement from
past to present, some elements refuse to return from rejection, remaining ever so hidden, packed away in the back room's dusty contents.
Linda Gould Levine has perceptively drawn attention to the absence
of any mention in the novel of the author's marriage to Rafael Sánchez
Ferlosio, from whom she was estranged, and the absence of any mention of her sexual life in general (169). Martín Gaite's novel focuses on
gender at the expense of sexuality—pushing the envelope, so to speak,
of the gender and genre expectations of the letter novel and of women's
subjectivity during the Franco years, but refusing to entertain the effects
that the transformations of gender roles may have had on the discourses
of sexuality during this period. Not that sexuality is wholly absent, for
it infiltrates the relationship between the man in black and C., it appears
in her retelling of various love interests in the past, and, as the man in
black will suggest, it appears in her relationships with women. But the
desire that passes between C. and her interlocutors rarely moves beyond
a hint of eroticism: objects of explicit sexual desire they are not.

C.'s friend reappears in the novel literally as a ghost. "I fall silent, how
difficult it is to tell all that without talking about the principal miracle,

the fact that even though she's dead now, she still keeps flying hand in hand with me. It's rather spooky" (186).[32] In the description of her childhood friend and the secret island of Bergai, C. recalls that "she was crazy about her" (195).[33] This final comment leads the man in black to ask about C.'s sexuality. It is, to a certain extent, a mise en scène of a psychoanalytic exchange, in which the man in black engages in the critical interpretive act of calling attention to the possibility of lesbian desire. Nevertheless—and this is an important point—he does not offer an affirmative statement but rather poses a question with the expecta-tion of a rejoinder. In so doing, the man in black's exchange with C. invites a comparison with one of the most famous cases in psycho-analytic literature on sexuality: Ida Bauer, better known as Dora.[34] Dora complained that her father was trying to give her to his friend Herr K. in exchange for Herr K.'s wife, Frau K. Freud considered her case a fail-ure since the analysis only lasted a few months. Lacan's return to Freud's case history in "Intervention on Transference" (1951) argued that underlying Dora's so-called hysteria was her interest in Frau K. If Dora transferred her anger toward Herr K. and her father onto Freud, Freud himself engaged in a countertransference that rested on his implicit identification with Herr K. Lacan claims, in short, that Freud's counter-transference blinded him to the lesbian subtext—to the possibility that Dora desired Frau K. from the position of a man and that a relation-ship with Frau K. offered Dora an answer to the question of her desire (69–70). Freud would have preferred that Dora simply accept Herr K. and live a happy heterosexual romance. But Lacan, unlike Freud, does not assume that Dora is heterosexual or lesbian. Instead, as Heather Findlay points out, he questions Dora's identification with Herr K. as a means of answering the question of her own identity as a woman (334–35). Lacan's move is not to close down desire by categorizing it but to keep it open by questioning Dora's attempts to solve the mystery of her identity through identifications either with men or with women.

It is in this sense that the man in black engages in a queer reading (which by no means is meant to imply that he himself is queer), for his use of the word "lesbian" here is meant to challenge the supposed stability of C.'s sexuality. The distinction between "lesbian" and "queer" is not a simple one, to be sure, and the relative value of these terms has been a point of debate within critical circles. On the one hand, "queer" challenges the notion of a stable identity and underscores the contingent nature of identity politics surrounding sexual desires. On the other, as a single signifier it potentially erases significant differences between gays and lesbians. Judith Halberstam points directly to the problem of terminology in discussions of sexuality: "'Queer' . . . performs the work of destabilizing the assumed identity in 'identity politics.' However, by continuing to use and rely upon the term 'lesbian,' we acknowledge that identity is a useful strategy for political and cultural organizing. 'Lesbian' is a term that modifies and qualifies 'queer,' and 'queer' is capable of challenging the stability of identities subsumed by the label 'lesbian'" (259). In this respect, "queer" denotes something less tangible, more opaque: it remarks less on the firm foundation of identity than on the fissures and exclusions against which one grounds an identity. Rather than having a clear content, queer denotes a position in opposition to a norm.[35] Like Lacan, the man in black also questions the meaning of C.'s identifications. What he exposes is the tenuous, often fragile border between desire and identification: he interprets her admiration for her friend as a sign of lesbian desire (196; 193). He suggests, with a wry smile, that the object of desire may have been her friend's curly hair and thus remits the reader to an earlier moment in the text when C. mentions the dictator's daughter Carmencita Franco's hairstyle. Identification and desire, which Freudian psychoanalysis generally posits as mutually exclusive psychic activities, give way in the man in black's interpretation to a slippery temporality in which neither identification nor desire supersedes the other as a psychic state but instead coexist simultaneously in the same subject and for the same object.[36]

Just as Freud's analysis of Dora was tinged with a countertransferential desire, so too an erotic charge passes between the man in black and C. Not blinded to the lesbian subtext, however, he avoids the pitfalls of analysis that Freud, according to Lacan, could not. By opening up the question of her desire, the man in black asks not only about C.'s identity but about the definition of the word "lesbian," since he does not specify what he means by the term. "'Lesbian' is a word written in invisible ink," asserts Elizabeth Meese, "readable when held up to a flame and self-consuming, a disappearing trick before my eyes where the letters appear and fade into the paper on which they are written" (18). Meese elaborates a theory of lesbian desire as a form of Derridean *différance* in a series of letters addressed to L., the very form of her work exemplifying the construction of lesbianism as something that struggles to be written and read. Judith Butler too has argued that it is unclear in what contexts and under what circumstances the lesbian signifier, unstable and continually shifting, will in fact signify at all ("Imitation" 2). A similar situation obtains in *El cuarto de atrás,* for the man in black's interpretation of the strong bonds of affection between C. and her childhood friend could be seen as a reflection of Adrienne Rich's "lesbian continuum," which posits a wide spectrum of identification and desire among all women, or, on the contrary, her rejection of the normative dictates of gender is suggestive of Monique Wittig's trenchant repudiation of any connection between the categories "woman" and "lesbian" (13).

Left unspecified by the man in black, the term "lesbian" erupts into Martín Gaite's text as a question, not only of desire but of definition itself. C.'s response thus begins not with the memory of lesbianism as a desire but with the memory of lesbianism as a concept. There was no space for the idea, no expectation that such a concept could exist, she claims. There was no memory of lesbianism as a discourse, much less a desire that she experienced personally: "But I did not encounter the word *homosexual* and *lesbian* until years later, in Madrid, and it was very hard for me to understand their meaning, I had no place ready in my mind to receive such concepts" (196).[37] The Francoist construction of female identity in Spain negated lesbianism as a possibility. Women's sexuality was reduced to maternity, censorship of sexuality in the public sphere eliminated references to brassieres and retouched photographs, and religious authorities established firm limits on the acceptable lengths of women's skirts and shirt sleeves (Eslava Galán 263–65).[38] It is not only that the dominant discourses around sexuality drew their moral basis from Catholicism, and thus reaffirmed homosexuality as a sin; it is also that same-sex desire between women simply did not figure conceptually in juridical prohibitions, even if the laws themselves were so broadly worded as to apply to them. Lesbianism was rarely, if ever, named as such. Lesbianism would not gain a discursive foothold until feminist groups beginning in the second half of the 1970s and in the early '80s began to engage with women's sexuality.

If official history is heterosexual, then personal memory serves up a different version of events. The man in black, it is important to recall, asks, "*Were* you a lesbian?" Same-sex desire is cast in the past tense, although its effects may still register in the present. His interrogation of her desires adopts, in some respects, a rather Freudian position insofar as Freud's Oedipal narrative of sexual development, at least the so-called positive outcome, likewise locates homosexuality in the past, repressed within the deepest recesses of the mind, a libidinal cathexis whose sexual aim has been diverted and transformed into identification.[39] If memory rewrites the conditions of gender under which women struggled during the nearly forty years of dictatorship, sexuality in general, and homosexuality in particular, is continually forgotten, pushed aside, by the protagonist. What C.'s resistance to this question suggests is that lesbianism in Martín Gaite's novel is a loss that never was, a loss for which there is no memory. Desire for the woman, disavowed from the outset in the form of a forgotten letter, refused as a signifier of affection between C. and her friend, cannot be named "lesbian," for "lesbian," for C. at least, did not exist as a signifier. The foreclosure of the possibility of explicit desire between women in the context of Francoist Spain emerges in *El cuarto de atrás* as a loss that never occurred, as a possibility proscribed from the very beginning.

Lesbianism represents the limits of Martín Gaite's transgression of gender: C. may reject the normative parameters imposed by the Women's Section of the Falange, but she unequivocally states, when she finally responds to the man in black, that she was not a lesbian since she could not conceptualize her own desire in those terms: "'No,' I say, 'a thing like that never occurred to me. One can be a lesbian only when one can conceive what is meant by the term, and I'd never even heard that term" (196).[40] Remaining on the literal level of the signifier "lesbian," C. interprets the question to be one of naming, of self-identification: did she in fact ever use the word "lesbian" to describe herself? Clearly not. C.'s rejection of the category of "lesbian" is not necessarily a rejection of the desire that persisted between her and her childhood friend. Rather, she opposes conceptualizing this desire as "lesbianism." The man in black's queer reading, we might say, does not claim that C. is a lesbian but rather that she cannot be one, even if eroticism permeates her relations with women. "Lesbian" cannot signify desire between two women for C. because at the basis of the man in black's question is the crystallization of that desire within a normative category—giving it a name—which is especially important to recall for a character who resists being named at all, except for the use of a single letter. Although it is clear that C. shares the same name with the author and with Carmencita Franco, at no point in the novel is she referred to as "Carmen." The distinction between C. and Carmen—the inability to be fully named—is crucial here.

The act of naming effectively interpellates a subject into existence. This naming produces the subject by making the individual comprehensible—readable, as it were—according to a matrix of culturally constructed cognitive schema: naming is a mode of *address*. The use of the term "lesbian" in C.'s case is problematic in that the act of interpellation cannot be completely negated by denying that very identity. The man in black's naming forces C. to negotiate her own identity in relation to that term. In so doing, she duplicates similar rejections of being identified with a label (escapist, madwoman) that occur earlier in the novel. At one point, the man in black calls her an "escapist" ("fugada"), to which she responds hastily, "Me an escapist? That's really funny, nobody's ever told me a thing like that before."[41] The man in black asserts definitively, "Nobody may have told you so, but it's obvious" (122).[42] During their phone conversation, C. comments to herself after Carola refers to her as a "madwoman": "I have the dizzying suspicion that I may perhaps have deserved that description. I can feel on my skin, like a stigma, that unsuspected identity, 'runaway, madwoman,' that has been conferred upon me" (146).[43] In a similar manner, C.'s first thought in response to the man in black's question is that no one had ever asked her that, which alludes to the previous episode of being called an "escapist" or "runaway." Furthermore, C. endorses the belief that our knowledge of ourselves is incomplete when she remarks during her conversation with Carola that people are not a single self but many selves, and thus the subject is an amalgamation of puzzle pieces that can never be put together to create a coherent, single image (170;

167). This is not to suggest that C. is, in fact, a lesbian. Rather, her remark underscores the lack of control over identity and the ways in which self-knowledge and identification by others do not always coincide. C.'s explorations of her identity are a testimony to the volatile and unstable dynamic of recognition and misrecognition involved in identification. In spite of the fact that C. does not identify herself as a lesbian, the man in black's query demonstrates the possibility of being identified by another as such.

Amid these letters, hidden and rediscovered, where the question of desire was posed as a question, Martín Gaite made it clear to me that, for her, there never was a question. In a letter sent to me in reaction to an earlier published version of this interpretation, Martín Gaite maintained that the man in black had made a mistake. The scene, she corrected me, was meant to be ironic, to show the man in black seeing something that was not there.[44] Martín Gaite is right, as we have seen, that the man in black misreads C.'s desire as "lesbian." Her desires cannot be reduced to that signifier. Yet throughout the novel he has shown himself to be a most perceptive reader. If at the beginning of the novel C. bristles at his insistent questioning, likening it to a form of police interrogation, she soon acquiesces and accepts that "he always hits the nail on the head" (53, trans. mod.).[45] As the man in black comments just after this scene concludes: "The thing is that I understand literature and know how to read between the lines" (200).[46] If lesbianism runs the risk of being "unread," its spectral presence alludes to something that, because of its ineffable quality, cannot merely be dismissed.[47] The man in black draws attention to the traces of lesbianism that have been ostensibly foreclosed from the text, the maneuver of dismissing that desire unwittingly producing the very conditions for reading its ghostly traces. Moreover, he explicitly stakes a claim upon his capacity to read her correctly as he adds: "Tonight I think that my readings have not been off track: you've spent your life without ever leaving your refuge, dreaming all by yourself" (200, trans. mod.).[48] Nor is it clear why this particular question would seem to be the most appropriate one for irony, for an error in judgment. His attitude toward same-sex desire is never expressed; his own subjectivity is suppressed for the sake of exploring C.'s memories of the past. It is not readily apparent if his question is motivated by homophobia or a disinterested curiosity. Neither can the reader assume that his masculinity indicates a particular disposition toward lesbianism. The man in black's own intervention does not appear to be a self-gratifying fantasy, one that allows him to participate in C.'s relationships with her childhood friend. He remains outside that circuit of same-sex eroticism even as he draws our attention to it.

It cannot be mere coincidence, in light of the history of sexuality in Spain under the Franco regime, that it is precisely when the topic turns to *sexuality* that the man in black's interpretive skills ostensibly have led him astray. From the point of view of Freudian psychoanalysis, resistance—in this case, resistance to interpretation—is always related to sexuality. Resistance to psychoanalysis is part and parcel of psychoanalysis itself, whereby the resistance to analysis is, in fact, the starting point of analysis. Martín Gaite would no doubt disagree, as her resistance to psychoanalysis has been well documented. Her resistance is not to the theory but to the couch: she refutes the practice of psychoanalysis between a doctor and patient while advocating the curative dimension of sharing one's thoughts. In another novel, *Retahílas* (Yarns, 1974), the protagonist Eulalia rejects therapy as a talking cure: "if you go to a psychiatrist to tell him the ills of your soul and you are capable of telling them half correctly, what purpose does the psychiatrist serve?" (185). Marcia Welles has argued that the resistance to psychoanalysis in Martín Gaite's work is paradoxical: she endorses dialogue as a form of "talking cure" at the same time that she rejects the disciplines of psychoanalysis and psychiatry.[49] But there is a difference between confession and psychoanalysis: if confession is good for the soul, psychoanalysis causes a confrontation with unanticipated readings. In "The Question of Lay Analysis," Freud distinguished between confession and psychoanalysis, arguing that the patient in analysis knows more than the confessant tells the priest (189). The purpose of therapy is precisely to allow the analysand to come to terms with the knowledge he or she has. For Freud, the patient must put aside all reservations that prevent his or her reporting certain thoughts or memories. There are, he asserts, "things that one likes to conceal from oneself" (188).[50] It may well be the confrontation with the unknown, the unexpected, in a psychoanalytic exchange, which is most disturbing. At one point in the novel, C. describes the man in black as a mirror, but in this scene the man in black, playing the role of an analyst, would appear to know something more than C., reflecting more in the mirror than she herself can see.

In the course of their conversation the man in black sees something that C. cannot: he perceives in the spatial and psychic topography of the back room the way in which love letters provide C. with an alternative means of obtaining love. This metaphorical notion of space is transformed throughout the text from a back room to a mental attic, a false-bottomed suitcase, a tin box, and a fictitious island named Bergai. These spaces are also the places of letters. The tin box, the sewing basket, and the false-bottomed suitcase are the repositories of C.'s epistolary correspondence. As spatial metaphors, they function like a closet—or, to be more precise, a closet whose door can never be opened. Indeed, shortly after asking about her desires, the man in black turns to the topic of letters, which she is surprised to hear him bring up, and he declares that the interlocutor is a pretext: what is at play is a different form of desire, one that, in the form of a written letter, substitutes for the erotic pleasures of the flesh and allows for fantasy to take over. Writing, he suggests, functions as a form of libidinal pleasure. In Freudian terms, we might say the sexual aim is inhibited and the energies redirected in another fashion so that the affective dimension of the exchange remains untainted by the erotic cathexis that has motivated it, or, at least, remains *consciously* untainted. The letters that circulate phantasmatically in *El cuarto de atrás* are not lesbian love letters, but, unmoored from their (male) addressees, the desire contained within is unfettered from the normative constraints of heterosexuality.

Purloining lesbian sexuality even as it insinuates its presence, *El cuarto de atrás* exposes the ways in which homoeroticism between women during the Franco years is erased and rendered unintelligible except to the subtle eyes of a reader of lost love letters. It does so through its deft manipulation of generic parameters, in particular, in the way the novel diverges from the formal and gender conventions of the epistolary genre. Martín Gaite's handling of epistolarity continues the tradition of viewing the letter as a repository of one's desires but her text shows that the letter reveals more about the subject than the confessional contents alone suggest: her transgressions of genre and gender uncover the ideological component of women's letter writing that seeks to inscribe it solely within a heteronormative framework, where female desire is directed only toward a male correspondent. The history of women's letter correspondence, as Poe's story reminds us, is marked by the presumption of heterosexuality. Martín Gaite's dismantling of the telos of romantic union between man and woman associated with amorous and sentimental letter fiction opens up the possibility that the love letter, once destined for a man, might be written for and read by another woman.

PART II

※

CLOSET CONFESSIONS

CHAPTER 3

The Ethics of Outing in Luis Antonio de Villena

> We read, ethically and politically, when something demands a
> response we cannot give, at least not only the basis of anything
> we know or have under our control, but that we cannot
> avoid giving.
>
> —THOMAS KEENAN, *Fables of Responsibility*

"In reality this story is nothing more than a confession," writes the protagonist of *Amor pasión* (Love Passion) (50).[1] First published in 1983 and revised in 1986, Luis Antonio de Villena's novel begins as a letter of confession from Arturo to his friend César, after the latter makes an oblique reference to the rumors that at one time Arturo had a sexual affair with another man. Although the temporal frame of the letter's events is not clearly stated, the reader can easily discern from references to Franco, university student riots, and musical appearances by Lou Reed and the Rolling Stones that the events of his letter span approximately from 1973 to 1981, with Arturo composing his letter some time later. As a university professor, his first contact with homosexuality takes place when he dines with Diego, a senior colleague, and meets Diego's male lover, thus confirming rumors of his colleague's homosexuality that had circulated among the faculty. Later, sitting with Diego on an outdoor terrace, Arturo sees a young prostitute named Sixto. Arturo is awestruck by the beauty and slightly ambiguous body of the youth; his curiosity piqued, he arranges for a sexual encounter. In the course of his letter to

César, Arturo details his relationship with Sixto, off and on for nearly a decade; the conflict it created for his marriage, which later ended in divorce; and the eventual realization that he had not only been sexually attracted to another man but also in love with him.

The nostalgic retelling from one heterosexual male friend to another of a series of transient and ephemeral homosexual encounters is a recurring structure in Luis Antonio de Villena's fiction. A member of the *Novísimos,* a generation of writers born after the Spanish civil war who begin to publish out of a sense of political alienation during the transition to democracy, Villena self-consciously embraced transgression as an aesthetic impulse in both his poetry and narrative writing. In his study of Villena's literary oeuvre, Chris Perriam corroborates the view that Villena's aesthetic approach to literature emerges from a self-conscious embrace of marginal and exotic cultural scenes (9). This aesthetic embrace of marginality extends also to his authorial figure, for Villena is an openly gay writer who self-consciously cultivates an unconventional image as a contemporary dandy. Sexuality is thus intimately linked to his vision of transgression; but, as a rejection of a dominant cultural order, homosexuality forms part of his transgressive literary aesthetic only insofar as it refuses to cohere in the form of a gay identity. Perriam asserts that many of Villena's stories reflect a strong ambivalence toward a coherent gay subjectivity in which, on the one hand, women are not objects of sexual desire and, on the other, women are objects of sexual desire who disrupt an all-male, homosocial world; marriage, for example, is often portrayed as a fall into bourgeois conformity (97–98, 106–7).

In Villena's fiction, homosocial and homosexual relations tend to be precarious and fragile, the idealized world of countercultural and transgressive desires difficult if not impossible to sustain: his narratives often end with a retreat from homosexuality and a (reluctant) return to bourgeois banality. In "La bendita pureza" (Blessed Purity), one of the two stories that compose *El mal mundo* (The Evil World, 1999), a middle-aged father of two daughters waxes nostalgically about a high school friend with whom he had an intense sexual relationship one summer. In "El amor celeste" (Celestial Love) Rainer and Max spend their time reading books about ancient Greece and the works of Karl Heinrich

Ulrichs. Upon exploring the "uranism" that Max extols in Ulrichs's works, Rainer becomes disillusioned with the German author and sees modern homosexuality as a degenerated version of the same-sex practices of ancient Greece. Their friendship disintegrates, and Rainer eventually marries. *Fuera del mundo* (Outside the World, 1992) narrates Álvaro Alba's rejection of bourgeois life and his initial embrace of the counter-culture, with numerous homoerotic encounters, even as he maintains sexual relationships with women, until his cocaine habit leads to a violent death by stabbing. At one point the narrator states: "It's useless to want to apply a homosexual paradigm, since the story didn't allow for that name, even if it was that" (101).

Amor pasión remains highly ambivalent about homosexuality and sexual identity, following the general pattern of Villena's writings. But unlike his other works, the narrative depiction of homosexuality owes its ambivalence in part to the use of a confessional discourse that invariably locates the representation of desire within a narrative of sin and redemption.[2] The traditional script for confessional narratives is that the subject, burdened with a secret, reveals his transgressions in exchange for penance and a peaceful integration into the subject's community. In his *Confessions,* for example, Augustine recounts the various sins of his life—impure sexual desires, stealing pears for pleasure—as an integral part of the process of receiving God's grace. His confession of sexual misconduct is the beginning of a conversion: his sexual sins are the mark of a fall, a will that loses control, and only through the grace of God does he recuperate his path. Whereas Augustine may have preached about sexual sins, Arturo's concern, although it suffers the same weight of Christian morality around sexual acts, is the burden of coming to terms with a *sexuality,* with a discursive organization of subjectivity in which sexual desires are the central axis around which a sense of identity is formed.[3]

Eve Sedgwick wrote in her pioneering study of the closet that modern definitions of sexuality were not constructed by the supersession of older models by newer ones, but, rather, that different models overlapped and persisted in an "unrationalized coexistence" (*Epistemology* 47). The closet then is an accretion of distinct and even competing historical modes of conceptualizing homosexual and heterosexual difference that gives rise to a definitional incoherence. Not only is that incoherence epistemological, as Sedgwick forcefully argues in teasing out the dense network of binary operations that compose the closet (e.g., secrecy vs. disclosure, public vs. private), it is also ethical. In the second volume of *The History of Sexuality,* Foucault shifts his focus from the juridical and religious discourses that codified sexuality as the subject's truth to the ostensibly more difficult question of analyzing how individuals recognize themselves as sexual subjects. The fundamental question for Foucault becomes: "how, why, and in what forms was sexuality constituted as a moral domain?" (10). For Foucault, morality refers to, on the one hand, a set of values and rules that govern behavior and which are communicated and reinforced through various institutions (family, school, church), and, on the other, the actual behavior of individuals in relation to those rules, whether they comply with or disregard them (25). In contrast, the ways in which a given subject makes sense of or rationalizes the imperative to adhere to moral rules and values is the domain of ethics. There are, he argues, numerous ways of adhering to a moral code and thus constituting oneself as an ethical subject. An ethical subject is one who adopts a specific position vis-à-vis a moral code or law, delimits the aspects of his or her life that come under the purview of that code, and elects a specific course of action to constitute oneself as such a subject.

Arturo's quest to explain his past to César involves not only a recognition that he desired another man sexually—that much becomes apparent rather quickly in the narrative—but also how he relates such activities to dominant moral codes. Interrogating his own ambivalence regarding homosexuality, Arturo admits to César that he writes so that he might better understand what his homosexual experience means for his own sense of self (8). The irruption of homosexual desire in Arturo's life and the need to explain it to someone else initiates a form of ethical self-analysis. But in the movement from secrecy to disclosure, what emerges is the *undecidability* of Arturo's sexuality. The evocation of multiple and often competing modes of conceptualizing sexuality in Arturo's letter produces a radical lack of resolution regarding his identity. My interest here, then, is not solely the emergence of homosexual desire in Arturo's life but also the rhetorical strategies he uses to justify his actions. For at the end of his confession, it is not clear that Arturo has in fact come out of the closet. The incoherent resolution of Arturo's confession obfuscates the function of his narrative: Is César to understand that Arturo is trying to tell him that he's a gay man or, on the contrary, that he is a straight friend who had a one-time gay experience? The struggle of a subject, Arturo, to come to terms with his own sexual identity in light of his lengthy affair with another man becomes the struggle of a male confidant to respond adequately to his friend's confession.

As a confessional letter, Arturo's disclosure of secrets to a friend is not entirely faithful to the structure of a traditional confession in which the speaker demands absolution from a figure of moral authority.[4] Although it shares with religious confession the introspective interpretation of one's thoughts and actions in order to arrive at some notion of truth about the self, Arturo's letter entails a secular relationship of confidentiality: César is not a figure of moral or legal authority—a priest or officer of the law—but rather a friend and confidant. Arturo justifies his confession out of a sense of obligation, a duty rooted in his friendship with César. While they share an evening of drinks in a hotel terrace—"one of those splendid moments of communion, of profound communication, that only come with a good, deep friendship" (7)—César touches on the "dark points" ("puntos oscuros") of Arturo's life.[5] It is precisely this gap in their friendship that induces Arturo to confess: "if I were such a good friend of yours as I felt (and I feel) it was my obligation to undo those *dark points*" (8).[6] The verb *deshacer* in Spanish is rather ambiguous, however, since in this context it could mean to clarify or to correct the rumors, so it is not apparent to the reader whether Arturo intends to divulge secrets from his past or dispel the rumors altogether.

As a testament to the confidential bond they share, Arturo declares that he will tell César everything. César's role as addressee, both as friend and heterosexual male, thus conditions the scope and language of Arturo's confession. Arturo's desire to bridge the gap between himself and César initiates a series of rhetorical strategies that will govern his representation of homoerotic desire. Arturo anticipates César's objections and withholds information. He draws out the narrative, adds extraneous material, and digresses. Expecting a question regarding the boy's youth, for example, Arturo offers a proleptic commentary: "And you'll ask, was he an effeminate boy? Are you talking about a little kid with girlish airs? No, naturally not. He was ambiguous because he was an adolescent, but not feminine. That boy did not remind me at all of a woman" (21).[7] The description of Sixto's body as masculine, though ambiguously adolescent, underscores that the desire in this case was indeed homosexual. At the same time, Arturo refrains from telling the *whole* truth, respecting a certain heteronormative assumption that César would not want to be exposed to the details of homosexuality. "I promised to touch very little upon the physical aspects of our love. I will uphold that promise" (30).[8] Arturo's discretion about the sexual relationship thus undercuts the transparency of his confession. Yet this discretion does not prevent Arturo from commenting on his own sexual desire for the young male, which he discloses openly, claiming that what he experienced was true sexual desire (31). Arturo's admission is key, for he confesses quite plainly his erotic desire and declares that he wishes he could give César a full account: "It's obvious that I'm not telling you everything. But I would like to" (23).[9]

Perhaps recognizing César's discomfort at the details of the homosexual desire he recounts, Arturo qualifies his desire by stating that it was not so much the masculine body of Sixto as his beauty that attracted him; throughout the text he refers to Sixto as an angel, thus downplaying the physicality of their encounters (43, 65, 71). In seeking to communicate with César as a friend and to avoid sexual details, Arturo conceptualizes his homosexual affair as a form of *friendship*. The effect is not simply to brush over Arturo's sexual relations with Sixto but also to render homosexuality intelligible to his interlocutor. In *Amor pasión* friendship and eroticism are conflated throughout the text, as the meanings of "friend" and "friendship" ("amigo" and "amistad") apply to both heterosexual and homosexual relations, a mode of conceptualizing same-sex desire among men that appears frequently in Villena's works. (My use of the term "homosexual" here is not meant to suppress the pederastic dimension of the relationship but rather to emphasize, as Arturo does, the centrality of same-sex desire in their relationship;

he meets Sixto when Sixto is about to turn sixteen, and their relationship ends when he is nearly twenty-three.)

The instability between friendship and eroticism surfaces quickly in the novel. In some instances, homoeroticism stands in opposition to friendship. Referring to the secrets circulating on campus, for example, Arturo remarks on how the rumors left a shadow on his relationship with César, marking a territory "forbidden to friendship" (48). When he calls Sixto's house and speaks with his mother, Arturo describes himself as only a friend; obviously in such a case, "friendship" works to mask the intimate dimension of their relationship. At other times, homoeroticism is portrayed as a form of friendship, such as when Arturo's colleague Diego reveals his own homosexuality by referring to his lover as "a very close friend" (11). Arturo's account of his relationship with Sixto deploys a similar rhetoric, for in a later encounter he describes their *erotic* connection as a "true friendship" (59). What Arturo means by "true friendship" is slippery, for the concept of friendship continually shifts throughout the text even as he continues to evoke it as if it were a stable term. Friendship is a relationship of equals, as when he speaks of the desire "to be his friend (not his elder brother, nor his tutor), his friend, his companion" (60).[10] Yet the meaning of this concept of friendship is also not certain, for he qualifies the relationship of equals as a friendship of adolescence, of youth: "it was as if his presence rejuvenated me or more precisely returned me to adolescence" (62).[11] Friendship in this instance conjures up an image of boyhood sexual freedom divorced from identity, a period of experimentation in which sexuality is not indicative of any future predilection.

This shared sense of pleasure in a homoerotic relationship with a beautiful adolescent, a pleasure that does not displace his desire for women, initiates Arturo's later attempts to render his desire intelligible by recourse to a (mythic) Greek model. The model of heroic comradeship would seem to allow him to incorporate homoerotic desire within the preexisting framework of his heterosexual life. Recognizing that he and Sixto are not equals in age, Arturo begins to conceive of his "friendship" in terms of a Greek concept of homosexual relations between an older and a younger man: "a companion, friend, comrade, young warrior who receives guidance from an elder" (71).[12] In *El libro de las perversiones*

(The Book of Perversions), a book of essays on sexuality, Villena situates the origins of Greek homosexuality in the Doric period, in which the adult male and a younger partner formed in a pedagogical relationship within a military context. "The purpose was to transmit to the youth—having left childhood behind—the virtue of war, the concepts of honor, responsibility, loyalty and valor—basic concepts in a military society—through a pedagogical relationship of companionship and friendship" (83): a summary, as it were, of Arturo's concept of his relationship with Sixto.

In his study, Villena distinguishes between an earlier model of heroic comradeship, or friendship between warriors, and the later model of classical Athenian pederasty. He argues that with time the relationship shifted as Athens evolved into a civil society and pederasty became much more of an educational practice (86). In his important study of Greek homosexuality, David Halperin similarly distinguishes the paradigm of the older warrior and younger male charge who share a strong emotional bond from the pederastic model that is most often associated with the term "Greek love." In constrast with Villena, however, Halperin views the paradigm of heroic comradeship not as the origin of "Greek love," not as a precursor to pederasty, but as the final playing out of an earlier narrative tradition, in part because it is not entirely clear in the comradeship model who played what role, who was "active" or "passive."

Although Halperin's conceptualization of heroic comradeship differs from Villena's, both concur that there is a significant difference between a Greek model of sexual relations as a reflection of political status and a modern concept of sexuality that depends almost exclusively upon the sex of the object of desire. Halperin remarks that contemporary understandings of homosexuality often fail to understand the intimate relationship between the sexual practices of two men and the social and political framework that governed classical Athens. The Greeks did not distinguish between homosexual and heterosexual relations in terms of object-choice: what did distinguish sexual practices was active versus passive roles, organized around a phallic principle that men were active, women and adolescent boys passive. As Halperin summarizes, "What is fundamental to their experience of sex is not anything we would regard as essentially sexual; it is something essentially outward, public, and social. Instead of viewing public and political life as a dramatization of individual sexual psychology, as we often tend to do, they see sexual behavior as an expression of political and social relations" (*One Hundred* 37). Erotic relations in classical Athens were in strict alliance with the social practices that organized the political domain. The social meanings of sex were thus utterly bound up in the political and social roles that free adult men would exercise as citizens. Halperin remarks in a footnote that homosexual relations as such would be "heterosexual" in the sense of "different" or "other" insofar as the adolescent or female partner was "other" to the Athenian male citizen (34).

By appealing to a Greek model, Arturo uncritically imports concepts that are opposed to contemporary models of sexuality. Put another way, Arturo's gesture points to the ways in which older structures that once governed sexual relations continue to inform and inflect contemporary modes of conceptualizing sexuality. The structure of the letter-confession calls attention to the conceptual misunderstandings at play in evoking a Greek model of sexuality—be it pederasty or heroic comradeship. The incompatibility can be seen most saliently in Arturo's recourse to such a model within the framework of a confessional letter. The concept of sexuality that Arturo articulates makes little sense as the topic of a confession of sin: it is his need to confess that betrays his subjection to a concept of sexuality rooted in morality, one that is alien to the Greek concept (at least as he voices it). In "Christianity and Confession," Foucault distinguishes between a Greek model of confession in which self-examination follows from a series of moral precepts of conduct as a source of self-development and a Christian model in which the search for truth is a self-examination that deciphers a hidden element within the self—the site of sin that must be expelled.

Arturo's recourse to a Greek model would therefore seem to suggest that he is struggling to articulate a model of sexuality that will allow him to incorporate his homosexual experience into his own life narrative. Arturo grapples with a desire that interrupts the normative arrangement of his life, forcing him to contemplate a profound transformation in his domestic arrangements and affective relationships. The function of

Arturo's letter, then, is not simply to voice his homosexual desire for Sixto but rather to attempt to determine whether his desires are indicative of a shift in identity. Arturo thus oscillates anxiously between heterosexuality and homosexuality. His confession to his wife Carmen of his "amor-pasión" (her words) ends their relationship, and Arturo attempts to reestablish a similar domestic relationship with Sixto, which ultimately fails. Some years later, Arturo marries a woman named Lucía, with whom he eventually has a son, also named Arturo. Yet the marriage to Lucía is predicated on his need to overcome the absence of Sixto in his life (53). The family unit produced as a result of the birth of his son strikes Arturo as an impediment to his relationship with Sixto. The concepts of paternity and fraternity impede one another: he cannot be both companion and mentor to Sixto and father to his own son. As a form of compromise, Arturo maintains a relationship with both Lucía and Sixto, with each of them aware of the existence of the other. His relationship with Lucía is presented as a form of agape, a warm domestic love also linked with reproduction, while the passion that Sixto inspires in him is seen as eros and pleasure. His heterosexual relationships are thus equally shot through with contradiction and ambiguity. In fact, at one point he admits that he while he desires Lucía sexually, he is not in love with her (53).

It is because of this conflict between competing visions of sexuality and subjectivity that *Amor pasión* cannot easily be categorized as a "coming out" story. According to Perriam, the scene in which Arturo and Sixto dress in formal tie and jacket for a dinner engagement and then kiss just prior to leaving the house is what provokes the writing of the letter: "[the scene] compels the reconstruction of identity which is Arturo's decision to write his long letter to César and, along a tortuous route, to come out as gay" (77). For some scholars, to speak of the closet in Spain is an imposition of Anglo-American constructions of identity politics. Pointing to the decreased emphasis on the self-disclosure of sexual identity in the Spanish context, Paul Julian Smith has argued that "the idea of the 'closet,' even when framed in Sedgwick's deconstructive terms, has less resonance in Spain than in the English-speaking world; indeed, there is no single equivalent for the term in the Spanish language" (*Laws of Desire* 10). Smith's argument is that the concept of identity rooted in one's sexuality is less central in Spain, that Spanish writers and artists are skeptical of claims of gay subjectivity—a claim that must be seen as historically contingent; in the 1990s the phrase *salir del armario* was introduced and integrated into the Spanish lexicon.[13] My aim is not to disprove Smith's thesis about the applicability of the term "closet." Rather, I want to underscore that in Villena's novel the ambivalence around homosexuality is not a radical skepticism of the putatively oppressive constraints of gay identity. After the birth of his son—an event to which he was opposed—Arturo comments that he longed for Sixto, but not sexually, only in terms of a nostalgic friendship. Once again Arturo's discourse of friendship not only reveals the fleeting quality of homosexuality, its shadowy presence as a mere episode in his life, but also the inadequacy of friendship for conceptualizing homosexuality. The emphasis on friendship appears to annul the sexual dimension of their relationship, redirecting the sexual energy provoked by Sixto's beauty into a more "normal" affective relationship. At this point in the narrative, he even qualifies his desire as "a rare (for me) and bygone passion" ("una pasión rara [en mí] y pasada"), thereby effectively undermining his previous accounts (83).

Arturo's letter wavers between two forms of confession, between the admission of a secret in confidence, on the one hand, and on the other, a psychic process of coming to terms with his homosexual desires. He admits to subjecting himself to constant self-analysis, and throughout the letter he reflects on the shifting terrain of his emotions toward the young man. At an early point in the narrative he searches for a name for what he experiences, and he deliberately opts for the word "desire" rather than "love" (41). It is not until the final pages of his confessional letter that he finally issues forth what could be read as the crux of his endeavor: the realization that his desire—an aesthetic response to beauty, a sublimated friendship, a singular passion—was, in fact, love. What provokes this realization is not Sixto's absence but his reappearance, at the age of twenty-three, with only hints of his former beauty. "All of a sudden, upon seeing him changed, I realized that I loved Sixto, that I loved him, that I had loved him ever since that first time long ago" (89).[14] The final experience of seeing Sixto catalyzes a shift in Arturo's perception, and he recognizes that his shifting conceptualizations of desire between beauty and friendship, between passion and domesticity—these were all forms of love for Sixto.

Arturo's confession of love for another male strips homosexuality of stigma, freeing it from the coercive veil of impropriety that covers it—or at least strives to do so. The construction of sexual identity based on confession that Foucault masterfully traced in volume one of *The History of Sexuality* is rooted in shame, guilt, and morality. In light of Foucault's arguments, one might object that Arturo's introspective search for meaning plays into the confessional matrix of power that coerces a subject into narrating a personal truth.[15] Yet Arturo's confession overturns the immorality of homosexuality by presenting his self-disclosure as an ethical act. Admittedly, Arturo's comments scattered throughout the text about love and its meaning—whether true love is more profound, whether it depends fundamentally on beauty, whether eros is more valuable than agape—border on the banal when taken at face value.[16] Much more could be said about the ideological force of love, about its conventional and repetitive nature, about the inability to define love with any precision. Love may be, as Lacan puts it, the gift of nothing, a gift of what one does not have ("The Meaning of the Phallus" 80; *Séminaire* 8: 46). Love may be, in short, an imaginary relationship (*Seminar* 11: 268). For Lacan, love is impossible because our relationships are asymmetrical: what we want from someone else is not what they want from us, which Lacan condensed in the expression "there is no sexual relationship" ("il n'y a pas de rapport sexuel") (*Séminaire* 20: 17). On a *psychic* level, love may be deceptive, narcissistic, and an imaginary fantasy, but on a *social* level heterosexual love is affirmed while homosexual love is discredited. The social value accorded to love exerts a powerful ideological force that continually separates homosexuality from the domains of affection and attachment.[17] One of the powerful and damaging messages of heterosexism is that homosexual love is something of a contradiction in terms, asserting that love is, by definition, an emotion shared between a man and a woman.[18]

Arturo asks rhetorically near the end, "But if it were all love (a passionate, strong love that excluded almost everything else), why hadn't I known it before, and why did I realize it only as it was ending? That was the unquestionable enigma" (91).[19] The remaining enigma, which in part motivates this written confession, is why Arturo took so long to reach this conclusion. For as much as Arturo stresses his desire to tell everything, there is always something else—a remainder, if you will—at play in confession. All confessional discourse, by its very nature of having kept a secret, fails to dispel the suspicion that some secrets are still being kept, leaving the impression that there is still more to tell. Recalling Freud's distinction between the confessant and the analysand, we might ask what is it that Arturo refuses to tell? What does he know but resists acknowledging? There is a resistance to analysis here, a resistance to an alternative to the heterosexual world in which Arturo operates, a resistance in the final analysis, to a homosexual *identity*. Arturo valorizes his homosexual experience as a form of love only then to isolate it as a singular experience: a discrete moment, located in the past, whose transcendence is limited to the text that we now read. It is for this reason that Perriam reads Arturo's story as one of a failure to take up "a truly dissident position" as he returns to a heterosexual marriage at the end (82).

One could argue, *pace* Perriam, that the truly dissident position here is the recognition of a desire that cannot be taken up under the banner of identity but rather persists and insists on recognition in spite of the subject's avowed identity. Arturo's reflections on the incompatibility of eros with human relations may sound hollow and hackneyed, but in fact they reflect a psychoanalytic perspective that sees desire as inherently conflictive to any notion of identity and the self. Undoubtedly the initial references to both Barthes and Lacan at the outset of the novel—César spoke continuously of them after studying in France (8)—are reflected in the vision of love that Villena's character presents near the end of his letter. As Judith Butler describes the importance of the Lacanian notion of the instability of identity, "it may be that the affirmation of that slippage, that failure of identification is itself the point of departure for a more democratizing affirmation of internal difference" (*Psychic Life* 86). Butler gives voice to the fundamental basis of the queer critique of gay and lesbian politics in which the revindication of "gay" and "lesbian" as terms of identity remains indelibly marked by the matrix of confession that gave rise to sexual identity as we currently understand it. The political gesture of "coming out" cannot be divorced from the larger framework of confessional practices that instill a "will to truth" or the discursive construction of the self as an intelligible, coherent subject. The sense of pride associated with redeeming a stigmatized sexual identity is, following Foucault, the end result of a confessional practice in which the community at large exonerates the subject of his guilt. Foucault's argument is seductive and powerful, as is Butler's affirmation of the failure of identification as the signpost of internal difference, and the conceptual rigor of both arguments for critiquing identity politics is not to be dismissed. Nevertheless, the failure to affirm homosexuality as an identity does little to displace the normative power of heterosexuality as the only acceptable form of sexual identity.

The argument for a "queer" vision of sexual identity in *Amor pasión* would be more convincing if it were not for the fact that Arturo's ambivalence toward homosexuality tends to bracket this affair, for him, as an *exception* within a seemingly coherent heterosexual identity. I have already suggested that the resistance to identity is, in Villena's work, part of a transgressive ethics. In this case, however, Arturo's refusal is neither a self-consciously marginalized position vis-à-vis society nor an embrace of the fluidity of sexuality. Arturo's initial description of Diego, for example, belies his own lack of comfort with the topic of homosexuality. His feelings toward Diego's lover, Jesús, reveal his own homophobia, which trickles to the surface of the text when he writes: "I wasn't like him, and although I presumed not to have any prejudice neither did I like being mixed with him" (57).[20] Arturo attempts to distance himself from Jesús, who is portrayed as a stereotypical, dandyesque figure, at precisely the moment in the narrative when Jesús is engaged in a relationship with Sixto, during one of the periods between the "episodes" with Arturo. Metonymically linked by their shared object of desire, a parallel is drawn between the two men that Arturo is loath to accept. Arturo's ambivalence about homosexuality also manifests itself in his inability to experience erotic desire with men other than Sixto. During a trip to Almuñecar, Arturo begins to watch a youth at the hotel's pool; he dubs the youth "Lolito" in an explicit reference to Nabokov's *Lolita*. While he fantasizes about engaging the youth in masturbation, he establishes a clear distinction between the affair with Sixto and the fantasy construction of "Lolito" as nothing more than a wish for an adolescent experience between two boys—an event between equals in which neither participant views the act of desire as an expression of a sexual identity: "It was merely a sexual fantasy that had very little to do with my own true feeling" (50).[21]

Much of this vacillation occurs admittedly before his restructuring of his desire as love, but as much as Arturo valorizes the affair as love, his newly found perspective does little to alter his life. The struggle he faces between choosing his family and wife over his homoerotic desire might be understood as a clash between two visions of ethics— between a Kantian ethics of duty and a Lacanian ethics of desire. If Kantian ethics emphasizes the obligation or duty of the subject against any notion of desire, Lacan argues that desire itself is the original source of ethical obligation. A rather traditional approach to morality would say that to do what is good or right we need to restrain or control our desire. In his seventh seminar, *The Ethics of Psychoanalysis,* Lacan argues instead that the primary ethical question is: "have you acted in conformity with the desire that is in you?" (314). It is our singular structure of desire, Lacan argues, that makes each one of us a subject. Our responsibility, then, is to our own desire, or to be more precise, to the structure of our desire. It is for this reason that Lacan suggests that the only thing of which one can be guilty, from an analytical point of view, is of having given ground relative to one's desire. If, for Lacan, desire is central to our sense of identity, to our notion of being, then to deny the place that desire holds in our psychic lives is, in a sense, to deny oneself as a subject. Lacan is not simply saying that we should enjoy our desire and not feel guilty—he is not offering an unmitigated endorsement to pursue our desires without reflection or cause for concern. Nor does he argue that we should somehow try to make our desires conform to normative prescriptions, since generally those moral rules have led to a subject's psychic troubles. For Lacan, psychoanalysis is ethical since it should not offer a prescriptive approach to how one should be: it is not a morality, a set of rules that judge one's behavior. Instead, psychoanalysis charts a narrow course between shoring up the ideals society establishes as morally good and the equally duplicitous choice of forsaking responsibility for pleasure. The two opposing poles are, for

Lacan, Kant and Sade: Kant's version of morality is the adherence to a categorical imperative of moral duty at the expense of pleasure, while Sade represents the adherence to all pleasure regardless of moral duty. Both maintain the same relationship to the law; both, in short, are imperatives that command the subject.[22] The ethical dimension obtains when examining one's position between them.

In the novel Arturo's attempt to come to terms with his desire and his subsequent valorization of it as a form of love conflict with his perceived duties as a father and a husband. In this respect, to a certain degree, a Kantian ethics wins out over a Lacanian one. The portrayal of homosexuality as an impossibility is a sign of Arturo's resistance to his own desire, for as much as he has come to accept it as love, he cannot face up to his own lingering heteronormativity (if not homophobia) and accept that homosexual love would be possible if it were not for his inability to act upon his desire. Arturo succeeds in vindicating his homosexual affair, yet his own confession simultaneously underscores his inability to disregard the social constraints that would allow him to acknowledge his desire as something other than impossible. In the end, we might say, Arturo is guilty not of homosexuality but of giving up his desire.

Arturo assures César that he has not seen Sixto again, that his sense of nostalgia is on the wane, that his attachment belongs to a former, now surpassed self (94). But more importantly, he adopts a moral stance in which he rehearses precisely the social opprobrium that condemned his relationship with Sixto: gay love is impossible, it has no future. "I don't want to seem like a harsh and sententious moralist. But no other path occurs to me" (94).[23] The only path, he suggests, is the one that he has taken. An alternative social and affective relationship is simply not possible, and thus Arturo justifies his actions by designating homosexuality as an impossible love, one that is so intense that it runs counter to domesticity. He refers in his final paragraph to the "moderately happy" state of his present marriage, and assuages his own sense of guilt by reiterating, for himself, the notion that "the immense happiness doesn't exist" (94).[24] The ethical quest of his self-examination and confession to César ends on this nostalgic note of ambiguity, somewhere between the desire to recapture his lost love and the desire to bring that chapter of his life to a close, expelled in the form of confidential letter.

François Jost has distinguished between two types of letters in epistolary fiction: the *lettre-confidence,* which narrates events the receiver did not take part in, and the *lettre-drame,* which constitutes a specific action to prompt a reaction from the receiver (e.g., a request for sexual favors) (124). The 1986 version of *Amor pasión* blurs the line between the two types of letters identified by Jost, since Arturo's letter prompts a reaction from César, enfolding him into those events as a respondent: that is, confidentiality leads to a response, to an action that affects the events narrated in the first letter.[25] The dialogic nature of correspondence, as critics often reiterate, brings into relief the role of the addressee, perhaps more so than any other genre (Altman 148; Violi 88). For while other genres such as autobiography may implicitly establish a connection with the reader, the letter's structure requires an addressee, even if that addressee remains unspecified.[26] Not only does César's role as addressee influence the narrative Arturo provides but the very act of writing is predicated on the implicit demand of a response even though Arturo explicitly tells César that there is no need for one: the structure of letter writing anticipates a call to another that mirrors the request inherent in a formal confession.

Nevertheless, the epistolary call to another is rather fragile, for the expectation of a response may not be fulfilled. The response may be offered but never arrive, or the response that does arrive may not be the expected outcome. The distance that protects the writer depends on the letter as a material vehicle for the confession, and thus the retention of the tangible document of the letter gives discursive control to the confidant, who may choose to betray the writer's confidentiality and disseminate the letter. Letter writing, we might say, establishes a sense of responsibility for an interlocutor, a responsibility based on the obligation of a response (both "response" and "responsibility" derive etymologically from the Latin *spondere,* "to say yes"). The confidant bears responsibility for the confessed material, and his or her response— directly to the letter writer or to a third party, the safekeeping of the epistle or the public revelation of its contents—determines whether the confidentiality of the letter has been maintained or broken (53).

César informs the reader that he fulfilled his obligation by calling Arturo directly upon reading the letter and speaking at length. He reveals that the university faculty members did in fact gossip about Arturo's alleged affair with a young man, and he expresses his own gratitude to Arturo for his disclosure. At an earlier point in his letter, Arturo relates to César how Diego came out of the closet to him, and it occupies a significant place in the narrative for the way in which it stages what Arturo perceives as the proper response to coming out of the closet. Arturo recalls that his own response was to thank Diego for his honesty, and he describes himself as a "sympathizer" ("simpatizante") (12). The episode is important, for it establishes a paradigm for the disclosure of homosexuality: as with the exchange between Diego and Arturo, César has been in the position of listening to a confession of homosexuality predicated on a bond of friendship. Arturo reiterates the same paradigm when he relates his experience with Sixto to his former mentor's lover, Jesús, who responds in kind: "And naturally he reciprocated my confidentiality (which, in the end, was what I was hoping for)" (57).[27] César, in turn, states that Arturo's letter "offers intimate and courageous details (that I appreciated and respected in my friend)" and that by the end he shared Arturo's own sense of sadness at the loss of the relationship (97).[28] He does not explicitly judge Arturo's actions, either by applauding the failure of a gay relationship or questioning his decision to remain married.

Just as Arturo's letter was shaped and conditioned by the identity of his addressee, so too César's response is conditioned by the audience to whom he directs his comments. Describing Arturo's letter, César writes: "The letter from Arturo that *I just transcribed* certainly did not surprise me as he feared" (97, my emphasis).[29] César does not direct his response to Arturo. Instead, he refers to his friend in the third person, and in so doing redirects both the letter and his rejoinder to a third party, implicitly the external reader. César's transcription of the letter also raises the question of its authenticity, since the mediation of his story by the transcriptor's hand severely limits our ability to know that he has not dramatically transformed Arturo's version of the story. More importantly, César's rejoinder alters considerably the reception of the story by undermining the tenuous boundary between public and private spaces so germane to epistolary discourses. Had César simply responded to Arturo's letter with one of his own, addressed to Arturo directly, the reader would have access to letters that were destined for someone else. This is, of course, the nature of epistolary fiction, in which all letters are purloined. But César has already responded to Arturo in person, and yet he feels compelled to give another response, one in which he transcribes the letter for another party, breaking the bond of privacy and confidentiality that engendered the letter's composition, at least for Arturo, in the first place.

César's need to reply again may reflect a sense of inadequacy about his prior response. Arturo's letter demands a response, but that demand is unclear because of his oscillation between various concepts of sexuality. Moving between pederasty and friendship, Arturo has not declared a homosexual identity even as he asserts that what he experienced was love. César must negotiate Arturo's appeal to multiple and competing systems of sexuality in order to deduce the conscious and unconscious demands of his confession. As Adam Phillips asks about the relationship between autobiography and psychoanalysis: "The psychoanalytic question, at any given moment in the story, is: what is the unconscious nature of this demand and who is it addressed to?" (72). César attempts to give Arturo what he thinks Arturo asks for, but since Arturo's petition is never articulated, César cannot be certain that his own response is adequate, that he has in fact given Arturo what he wanted. His rejoinder reflects that insecurity, offering a response to Arturo whose performative effect remains subject to multiple interpretations. Is the public response a strategy to distance himself from Arturo? Or, on the contrary, is it a mode of remembrance, in order to hold onto that past, one that reaffirms the bond between César and Arturo? Does Arturo's ethical struggle, made public, offer evidence of an alternative to heteronormative familial arrangements? Or, on the contrary, does it fulfill a traditional confessional speech act, making Arturo a public spectacle of expiation that will then allow for redemption?

Pedro Salinas calls private letters made public "betrayed letters" ("cartas traicionadas") (39). Has César betrayed Arturo's confidence? In

Arturo's letter there is no evidence that leads the reader to doubt César's friendship with Arturo. Still, his transcription of the letter raises questions about his motive for doing so, especially since breaches of confidentiality in correspondence were especially sensitive and significant during the Franco regime.[30] In a 1946 review of the juridical norms governing epistolary correspondence, Félix de Llanos y Torriglia stated that the legal debates about intellectual property and letter writing were fundamentally connected with anxieties about the right to secrecy and the history of violations of correspondence in Spain.[31] Letters are protected by the right to privacy ("el derecho a la intimidad") and the secrecy of correspondence ("el secreto de la correspondencia").[32] For his part, Juan Pemán Gavín notes that while inviolability of correspondence is guaranteed, the history of correspondence in Spain suffers from extensive violation (reported in "Un joven profesor" 16). In an illuminating analysis of correspondence in Spain, Jesús García Sánchez claims that during the civil war, censors opened letters from individuals in search of military information, while military officials attempted to have their own correspondence excluded from the practice.[33] (Ironically, Franco was among those whose correspondence was most inspected, to the point that most of his letters arrived opened and read by others; orders were eventually given to the censors to not interfere with his correspondence.) In 1940 there were fifty-four censorship offices (with one in the capital city of each province), which continued to inspect and censor the mail on a daily basis, until they were closed after World War II. Nevertheless, the postal system continued to exercise the right to "inspect" (as opposed to "violate") mail to guarantee that dangerous items were not being mailed ("Cartas violadas" 21).[34] The passage of the Fuero de los Españoles in 1945 reinstated the inviolability of correspondence, but García Sánchez cautions not to take such legal changes at face value; in fact violations of correspondence continued to occur without judicial support throughout Spain until the promulgation of the 1978 constitution.

As sensitive as the discourses around correspondence may be to the issues of privacy and secrecy, the putative violation of secrecy of a private correspondence nevertheless depends upon the performative effect of the information that is rendered public. In simpler terms, determining whether César's transcription is a violation depends upon how homosexuality will be received and interpreted by the public audience to whom César directs his response. On the one hand, the public disclosure is construed in some respects as an act of solidarity in which César maintains fidelity to his friend. As an act of solidarity, the transcription continues the circuit of communication by replicating the letter, giving it a second life. Arturo's letter took several days to complete, and the prolongation of and meditation on the composition provided him with the space and time in which to relive his affair through the nostalgic lens of memory. The continual deferral of the end and the solipsistic introspection of his writing likewise suggest, as is often the case in epistolary writing, that the letter was just as much for the writer as for the addressee. This potential is intrinsic to confessional practices in which speaking about one's desires becomes a way of reexperiencing them. The confessional practice is designed to eliminate the very desires that are being disclosed to the confessor, yet the confession itself comes to substitute for the homoerotic relationship. As César writes: "And Arturo wanted to preserve his failure, to be able to recall—beautifully—its glory" (103).[35] In effect, César's transcription of Arturo's letter, in its archival function, allows him to hold on to lost time and to preserve that loss as a fleeting moment of passion. César's transcription of Arturo's confession in this case articulates an ethics of outing in which he outs Arturo—to say that his friend's admission of homosexuality is not immoral—and declares his solidarity as a friend.

On the other hand, the desire to ensure narrative closure implies a need to contain this desire to a single moment, foreclosing the possibility of future episodes: César states clearly that the goal of his response is to "put an end to this story" (98).[36] Arturo claims throughout that he felt this passion for no one other than Sixto. César's efforts to provide an ending to the story seem to suggest that he too has believed Arturo's version, that there is no other possibility of homoerotic desire for Arturo. In fact, by the end homoeroticism has been erased as a possibility, rendered a memory with no hope of a future realization. The "finality" of desire, from this perspective, would constitute an attempt to reestablish the homosocial bonds between them. For Perriam, this is precisely the function of the narrative: "Their linked roles in the telling and enacting of this tale and their common capitulation to the demands and discourses of conventional behaviour and expression make it, in part, a story of male bonding" (86). Indeed, there is evidence to support this reading as César engages in his own private reflection on the relationship between transgression and conformity, and in so doing realizes that they are all conformists to heteronormativity, himself included (102). The possibility of homoerotic love is contained at the end by having the object of desire, Sixto, become "Arturo" to yet another unavailable youth. As a result, César both confirms and denies Arturo's homosexuality by testifying to the relationship with Sixto and by emphasizing its finality. The public declaration both exposes Arturo's past homosexual activities and yet exonerates him of any guilt or suspicion by reiterating the singular, episodic nature of that relationship. In this case, homoerotic desire does not necessarily undermine or displace heterosexuality: the confession of homoeroticism potentially functions as a means to strengthen the heterosexual bonds of friendship.

In these interpretive scenarios, their friendship is reaffirmed as an act of solidarity that either confirms and valorizes Arturo's homosexual experience or reasserts their shared heterosexuality. The difference in valence is significant, for it bears on how the reader is meant to understand, in the final analysis, the place that homosexual desire occupies in Arturo's psychic life as well as César's attitude toward it. At no point does César offer his opinion in an unequivocal manner. The two interpretations advanced thus far suggest either a recognition of Arturo's homosexual experience as a form of love or a consolidation of heterosexuality through the disavowal of homosexuality as a singular experience. In both instances, however, homosexuality is cast as a form of desire but not an identity. Arturo remains, for César, a heterosexual male. Another potentially less affirmative interpretation of César's action is that in transcribing this letter for the public he effectively outs Arturo as a gay man, suggesting that Arturo's love for Sixto is what defines his subjectivity. "Outing" did not enter the Spanish lexicon nor emerge as a political practice and intellectual debate until the 1990s, hence to speak of "outing" in *Amor pasión* is, admittedly, to run the risk of anachronism. Nevertheless, Villena's text does engage with the ethical issues concerning the dissemination of personal information about one's sexuality in a public forum.

Sedgwick has observed that modern definitions of homosexuality are splintered between a "minoritizing" view that holds that some people really are gay and a "universalizing" view in which same-sex desire could be shared among those who identify as heterosexual (*Epistemology* 85). Read from this perspective, César's betrayal of confidentiality is an attempt to distance himself from Arturo and redefine his heterosexuality by appealing to a minoritizing view that denies the possibility that he too could experience homosexual desire as a form of "friendship." It follows from his emphasis on the past that César's rejoinder is a public disclosure of information about himself, given that the rumors about Arturo's homosexual experiences were already entering the public sphere of the university. By transcribing the letter and thus establishing his own friendship with Arturo for the reading public, César effectively makes himself an accomplice in the homoerotic circuit between Arturo and Sixto. The blurring of boundaries between friendship and homoeroticism, by virtue of the connotations of "friendship," implies that César's own response *as a friend* is haunted by the specter of homosexuality. Although César may not confess to having had any homoerotic experiences of his own, Arturo's rhetorical use of friendship recharges the meaning of the term "friend," and as a consequence, César's own use of the word cannot entirely negate the connotations that it now possesses.[37] Just as Arturo, a married man, suddenly discovered homosexual love, so too César might find himself repeating the same steps. Friends—true friends—are not lovers, César seems to say, and through his transcription of the letter and his commentary he may also be attempting to regain his authority as confidant by shoring up the boundary between friendship and love upon which homosocial male bonding depends, to reinterpret the word "friend" in a less erotic way than Arturo would have it. The public display, the spectacle of Arturo's letter, could be seen in this manner as a kind of spectacle of exposure, whereby César distances himself and publicly displays *himself* as a straight male.

The "outing" that César performs, assuming the appropriateness of the term, is complicated by the fact that Arturo has not, in fact, come out of the closet. Given the emphasis on the right to privacy in Spain, the ethical value of outing has been the subject of much debate among

Spanish gay and lesbian activists and scholars. Outing is a form of coerced or ventriloquized confession, but the ethical value accorded to outing often depends—so the argument goes—on who performs it. At least two points of contention emerge around outing, whether defined as the political pressure to come out of the closet and affirm a gay identity or the involuntary disclosure of one's sexuality by being outed. Advocates see outing as a viable political tool, while critics argue that it potentially operates as a coercive force that violates one's right to privacy. In a roundtable discussion on homosexuality among various activists and writers published in 1997, Ricardo Llamas adopted the first position, arguing that the right to privacy was actually the force that kept gays and lesbians in the closet. In contrast, Oscar Guasch asserted that the imperative to come out may not apply to everyone, even those who engage in homosexual sex, since they may not necessarily identify as gay (Aliaga and Cortés, *Identidad* 229–30).[38]

Arturo's multiple and, at times, incompatible concepts of desire—as friendship, as mentoring, as agape, as eros—troubles César's, as well as the reader's, capacity to assign a homosexual identity to him. César's publication of the letter would, in this instance, not only out Arturo as a gay man, imposing a sexual identity that he has not adopted: whether intentional or not. César's response also brings Arturo's activities within a legal purview. The legal discourses during the early years of the transition to democracy still criminalized homosexuality, a point to which Arturo alludes, albeit ironically, when he describes one of his sexual encounters with Sixto in a lawyer's office in the midst of bound volumes of laws (24). At this time, the Law of Social Dangers was still in effect, but it was not the only legal prohibition on homosexuality: Article 431 of the criminal code, which outlawed any act that offended "decency" ("pudor") and caused a "public scandal," was in effect until 1988. The fundamental difference between the two laws is significant, for while the former permits the courts to label men who engaged in habitual homosexual acts a "social danger" and incarcerate them, the latter prohibition could potentially punish any homosexual act that came to light.[39] In his 1963 *Contemplación jurídico-penal de la homosexualidad* (Juridical-Criminal Contemplation of Homosexuality), Luis Vivas Marzal argued that the crux of the legal issue resided with the terms "scandal" and "transcendence" (16). The supreme court, in various cases, had set the precedent that only those acts that were accompanied by public knowledge—either at the time or afterward—were punishable by law.[40] When "indecent" acts, even though immoral, take place in private quarters and remain a secret with no possibility of public knowledge, they cannot be prosecuted under Article 431.[41] The burden of "transcendence" was lifted for cases involving minors, as is the case in *Amor pasión,* since it was held that the notion of "scandal" was always transcendent due to the gravity of the offense.

The very definition of "transcendence" would seem to imply that if somehow a homosexual act were brought to the court's attention, it would necessarily satisfy the requirement of this term and thus could be prosecuted. Victoriano Domingo Lorén underscores this apparent legal paradox in which any public knowledge of homosexuality already constitutes a scandal (37).[42] Domingo Lorén cites a case from 1977, after Franco's death, in which the court affirmed that such acts had to be absolutely clandestine "because the acts of pederasty, of homosexuality, acts against nature and sodomy are by nature facts of grave scandal and transcendence, offensive to decorum and to good customs" (37–38). The only case he mentions that involved men of adult age who were convicted without any public knowledge involved the subsequent discovery of two photographs of men engaged in oral sex; even though the sexual relationship was held in secrecy at the time, the supreme court deemed the recording of the act to constitute "transcendence" (22–23). Domingo Lorén mentions that various supreme court decisions confirmed the notion that any act "realized consensually in secrecy and privacy by persons of age that later came to be known to a third individual, under any circumstances, even by confession of the involved parties" was subject to criminal prosecution under Article 431 (55). (Domingo Lorén notes, in numerous interviews with various judges, that merely speaking about homosexuality to someone less than twenty-three years old constitutes, according to Spanish jurisprudence, an act of moral corruption.) The right to secrecy in epistolarity thus runs counter to the possibility of public scandal and homosexuality. Given that expressions of homosexuality via letter were enclosed and therefore not "transcendent," the confession of homosexual desire in letter writing escapes detection by the law. But as the letter always hovers on the border of public knowledge, it contains information that could divulge one's secrets and thus fall, potentially, under Article 431. In other words, given the structure of the story and its historical moment, César exposes Arturo's homosexual activities at a time when crimes of public scandal were still being adjudicated. Furthermore, Arturo's sexual activities implicate him in the crime of moral corruption for engaging with a male prostitute who was, at the time of their relationship, also a minor.

My argument is something of a legal fiction: this is, after all, a literary exchange of letters. Nevertheless, Villena's use of the confessional letter allows for a series of interpretive possibilities that emerge from the ambiguity surrounding Arturo's desire and César's response. These interpretive possibilities are derived from the formal structure of letter writing, the ambivalence regarding the demand (conscious and unconscious) of a confessional mode, and the legal constraints on homosexuality at this historical juncture. These interpretive possibilities coexist, paradoxically and uneasily, at one and the same time. Didacticism and moral instruction are of course part and parcel of the epistolary genre. Rousseau's *Julie* and Richardson's *Clarissa* are prime examples of epistolary novels in which the letters are either designed to educate and mold the addressee (Julie) or articulate a series of moral precepts (Clarissa). Yet César's decision to share Arturo's letter offers no simple moral lesson. Does the confidant's response return his friend's petition for friendship or is it meant to annul the homoerotic desire and reaffirm his heterosexuality through a violation of privacy? The reader cannot endorse either interpretation of César's outing with certainty. Occupying a no-man's-land between acceptance, sympathy, and renewed friendship, on the one hand, and on the other, betrayal, condemnation, and self-righteous distance from the events, César's response, entitled "the final serenity," is anything but serene. The narrative's lack of resolution, in contrast with moralistic epistolary predecessors such as Muñoz y Pabón's *Amor postal,* subverts the confessional expectation of absolution and moral rectification, and it removes the ground on which the reader stands to interpret the motive for the transcription and publication of the confessional letter. The ambivalence that the reader faces at the end troubles the interpretation of *Amor pasión* as a familiar narrative of the closet.

In his analysis of ethics and reading, Thomas Keenan argues that reading is an "experience of responsibility" in which we face a text whose complexities cannot be solved like a simple riddle by following preestablished rules, and as such, responsibility is not "a moment of security or cognitive certainty" (1). There is nonetheless something promising about insecurity, about the refusal of closure. In spite of the dynamics of power that confession exerts on its participants—the compulsion to share in order to achieve moral satisfaction, the affirmation of moral authority in the confessor's gesture of absolution—the ambivalent depiction of confidentiality and friendship in *Amor pasión* allows, in the end, for homosexuality to persist as a ghostly trace of desire. The passion Arturo shared with Sixto is neither whisked away as a sin by the strong arm of moral law nor is it sublimated as a single episodic moment of passion that can be nullified through male bonding. Articulated in the space between these two opposing poles, queer desire appears as a disruptive love that foregrounds the tenuous line between eros and agape, amor and amistad. In this interstitial space of uncertainty, César delivers a final message as he reflects on Arturo's melancholic demeanor upon seeing Sixto for the last time: "Perhaps because *love*—perhaps—does not belong to us either" (104).[43] The comment is strikingly Lacanian in its formulation, echoing the psychoanalyst's own view of love as a fantasy about an object that the subject tries to give to someone who does not exist. Another interpretation is possible, though, in which César recognizes that his and Arturo's words no longer belong to them, their correspondence cast adrift to the reading public. César's line implies that neither he nor Arturo has the final word on the meaning of love in the novel, that another ending may be possible. The novel does not offer a countercultural transgression, a queer politics that refuses the cloistering space of gay identity. But even as it courts the conformity of the closet, a reluctant return to heteronormativity, perhaps we can discern in their exchange a touch of queer sentimentality, the lingering trace of homosexuality as a request for love worthy of a confidential and affirmative response.

CHAPTER 4

A Witness to Mourning:
Memory and Testimony in Carme Riera

There may be a cure for symptoms but there is, from a
psychoanalytic point of view, no cure for memory. The past, ghost-
written as desire, is driving us into the future.

—ADAM PHILLIPS, *On Flirtation*

Testimony is the disjunction between two impossibilities of bearing
witness; it means that language, in order to bear witness, must give
way to a non-language in order to show the impossibility of bearing
witness.

—GIORGIO AGAMBEN, *Remnants of Auschwitz*

"Jo pos per testimoni les gavines" ("I Call upon the Seagulls as Witness," 1977) begins with a letter addressed to Alfons Carles Comín, who
was the director of Editorial Laia in Barcelona at the time Carme
Riera's first literary works were published. The letter is not signed by
Riera but destined for her. Comín is simply meant to deliver the letter
to Riera, who is identified as the author of "Te deix, amor, la mar com
a penyora" ("I Leave You, My Love, the Sea as a Token," 1975). The brief
missive is signed "illegible signature." In a second letter, immediately
following the first and explicitly addressed to Riera, the unnamed
author apologizes for her epistolary intrusion. Her purpose is ostensibly straightforward: to share with Riera's readers her own version of the
events narrated in "Te deix, amor, la mar com a penyora," a short story

in which a woman writes a letter to an unidentified interlocutor reminiscing about their former love affair from ten years earlier. In "Te deix," the writer recalls their burgeoning romance, their furtive yet passionate lovemaking, and the fear of discovery that overshadowed the relationship. She composes the letter on the eve of childbirth. Believing that she will not survive the delivery, she offers to name her child after her interlocutor, Maria. Only in that moment of naming at the end of "Te deix" does the reader learn that the addressee was another woman, and hence the letter one of lesbian love. In "Jo pos," the letter writer states that Riera's story has strangely replicated her own life, with the exception of some modifications that Riera made: "I believe that this story of mine, corrected by you, even rewritten, if you will, might interest those who read your first book, as a testimony of real-life events" (10).[1]

Published in 1977, "Jo pos" portrays lesbianism in a radically public light. The unnamed letter writer expresses her sense of indebtedness to Riera for the first story: seeing her life transposed into fiction has emboldened her to take an unprecedented step and voice her sexuality in the public sphere by publishing a letter of her own. Where "Te deix" plays with the reader's expectations, hinting at a lesbian relationship but deferring the answer until the end, the later story is explicitly about lesbian desire: the reader familiar with the first story knows from the beginning that the writer is in love with another woman. Her story is, as she describes it, a *testimony* about the lived experience of a lesbian in Spain during the Franco regime. As expert or eyewitness information given in a legal setting or as a narrative relayed by a survivor of traumatic historical events (e.g., the Holocaust, slavery, genocide), testimony is a speech act that is grounded in the privileged experience of a subject who can bear witness to that reality by translating the experience into language; it is a first-person narrative in which the speaker denounces social and political abuses on behalf of a larger community. To speak of lesbianism in the first person, in public, would indeed be unprecedented in 1977 in Spain. The text defies the standards of epistolarity by taking a private, intimate form long associated with women writers and granting it a public status. But more importantly, in the context of the early years of the post-Franco era, to give voice to lesbian desire, still illegal under the Law of Social Dangers, is a speech act that necessarily engages with religious and juridical interdiction, a form of testimony that implicates oneself legally and morally.[2]

The writer thus confronts the historical legacy of lesbianism as a desire cloaked in invisibility and shame. From the outset the writer's letter skirts cautiously, even precariously, the border between testimony and confession, appealing to the reader to listen to her story because of its factual value but all the while revealing the difficulty of not slipping into a confessional mode when speaking of her sexuality. At the end of her cover letter, she requests not to have her name revealed, and the editor of the letters obeys her wish (130). With an illegible signature, the lesbian writer is rewritten not only into anonymity but into illegibility—as a form of writing that cannot be read, or read only as illegible; her anonymity likewise redoubles the sense that this is not a singular testimony but a collective experience. The gesture of outing oneself may be something of a public confession, but the text does not truly "out" the letter writer, since her identity is protected. As much as the writer testifies to her lesbian desires, she nonetheless remains hidden from the public eye, acquiescing to the social pressure of "discretion."[3] So powerful is the force of decency and discretion that, even as she recalls her fear that her younger lover would pronounce words of love and desire, she still cannot utter them (13). Her memory, years after the relationship, remains overwhelmed with guilt: "my most beautiful memory, the one that would have been enough to fulfill my life, is an incomplete memory, mutilated by my guilt" (16).[4] Oscillating between testimony and confession, between bearing witness and seeking absolution, the letter writer struggles to speak of lesbianism free from stigma, sin, and guilt.

For Riera, narrative itself is a confessional act. Her narrative works frequently make recourse to confessional and epistolary modes of writing as autobiographical genres that privilege self-reflection and introspection.[5] Offering something of a confession of her own, Riera locates the beginnings of her own literary endeavor in her childhood practice of confession:

My confessor was absolutely obsessed with sexuality, and the questions he asked me were dreadful. They had a great effect upon me. At any rate, I continue to believe that literature begins, at least in part, as self-examination. The act of confessing—and Saint Augustine is the antecedent here—of delving into one's own wretchedness, one's faults, is an antecedent of literature. (Glenn, "Conversation" 39)

The religious roots of Riera's interest in confession and storytelling confirm the critical role that her education under the nuns of Sacred Heart played in her literary formation: she attributes her facility with the epistolary form to them (Glenn, "Conversation" 40). As Mary Vásquez points out in her discussion of "La seducción del genio" ("The Seduction of Genius"), a short story from *Contra el amor en compañía y otros relatos* (Against Love with a Partner and Other Stories, 1991), epistolarity and confession often go hand in hand in Riera's fiction, as both forms invite the narratee into a privileged space of intimacy and confidentiality (188). Riera has remarked that successful literature seduces its reader, and the letter form provides a writer with the confidential and intimate tone necessary for that seduction to take place (Aguado 35).[6]

If the explicit confession of lesbian desire and the use of letter writing in "Jo pos" are any indication, Riera's fiction excels in manipulating and overturning the reader's expectations for literary genres, especially as they concern gender and sexuality.[7] "Te deix" is exemplary in this respect, for it uses the illegibility of lesbian desire in order to seduce the reader into making certain assumptions about the relationship. The reader who assumes that the addressee of the letter is a man rather than a woman is seduced by the text's suppression of explicit gender markers. Gender, sexuality, and seduction also figure prominently in her 1987 novella, *Qüestió d'amor propi* (*A Matter of Pride*). The text is a long letter of confession from Àngela to her friend Íngrid about her failed love affair with Miquel. Àngela is a writer well versed in rhetorical strategy, who asks for forgiveness from Íngrid for not having written in the past (for which she blames Miquel) and attempts to convince her to seduce Miquel. Her plan is to have Íngrid feed him false information about Scandinavia, which he will use in his own writing, in order to discredit him. As critics have noted, Riera's use of letter writing complicates what may seem at first glance to be a deceptively simple love story. Akiko Tsuchiya argues that the woman writer is so transparent in her strategies to convince her interlocutor that she undermines her own narrative authority. For Noël Valis, the narrative's emphasis on Àngela's struggle to achieve success as a novelist reflects the precarious status of women writers in Spain. Brad Epps too sounds out the ways in which gender, sexuality, and epistolarity press upon each other in the text, analyzing how the conflicting desires for love, friendship, and revenge are themselves figured as conflicts of correspondence (written and emotional): Àngela's demand for love from another, he argues, conflicts with her own need to love herself ("A Writing of One's Own" 139).

Published a decade earlier, "Jo pos" is similarly shot through with issues of narrative authority and conflicts of love and desire. The epistolary themes staged in *Qüestió*—the play of absence and deferral between interlocutors, the construction of an authorial voice, the historical association with women writers and sentimental expression—all bear powerfully on the representation of lesbian desire in "Jo pos." But the importance of letter writing is not limited to formal qualities alone, for those epistolary qualities are rendered all the more salient by the writer's language: Catalan. To enter the public sphere with a letter on lesbian desire in Catalan is to issue a challenge to lesbian invisibility in a form and in a language that have often been designated as "minor." Even more so when the language in question is, to be precise, the Mallorcan strand of Catalan, which, viewed from a Castilian-centered perspective, is "minor" indeed.[8] Although she is the first winner of the National Award for Literature for her novel *Dins el darrer blau* (In the Furthest Blue, 1994) and has published several volumes of literary criticism in addition to her narrative fiction, Carme Riera remains at the margins of national literary discourses in Spain. As Riera herself states: "Bear in mind that I am a marginal person, because I am a woman, because in Spain I form part of a minority literature (Catalan rather than Castilian), and furthermore within this minority literature, I'm not from the center (Barcelona) but from an island (Majorca)" (Glenn "Conversation" 53).

Riera's relationship to language is complex since her parents' language at home was Castilian and thus her primary education was in Spanish; as a result, she grew up entirely bilingual (Servodidio, "Introduction" 8).[9] A professor of Spanish literature at the Universitat Autònoma de

Barcelona, Riera writes books of literary criticism in Castilian on Castilian writers. In her work there is no clear opposition of Catalan to
Castilian, even as her fiction often reflects the vexed histories of power
and oppression that surround Castilian and Catalan.[10] In an interview
with Cristina Dupláa she states unequivocally:

> As you can see, I love both of these languages. I can write in Catalan and
> teach Spanish literature written in Castilian at the same time. I consider
> myself a bilingual person, and I've paid a price for it, because I've never been
> one hundred percent behind either side. I've never considered myself a Span-
> ish nationalist or a Catalan nationalist. (60)

Riera regularly translates her work into Castilian, and thus her choice
of language is not so easily read as a capitulation to the market demands
for Castilian nor as an imposition of the dominance of Castilian by a
reading public unwilling or unable to read Catalan texts.[11] Instead,
Riera's own labor as translator reflects a continual revision of her own
fiction in a dynamic process of translation and transformation. This is
not to suggest that the decision to read Riera's fiction in Castilian over
Catalan is ideologically innocent and should not take into consideration the respective histories of the two languages.[12] But neither can one
overlook the fact that Riera often dramatically alters the translations,
in some cases to such a degree that the Castilian versions are nearly
autonomous, distinct texts from the Catalan originals. "Te deix" and "Jo
pos," for example, were initially published separately as the title stories of
two collections, *Te deix, amor, la mar com a penyora* and *Jo pos per testimoni
les gavines*. In 1980 Riera translated a selection of those stories into Castilian and joined them sequentially in a single anthology, *Palabra de mujer*
(Woman's Word). The Castilian version of the second story differs from
its Catalan counterpart in that the framing letters have been removed and
the story placed immediately after "Te deix"; the distance, both temporal and textual, is eliminated. The combined effect is to strengthen the
sense of correspondence between the two stories, making them almost
seamless: "Y pongo por testigo a las gaviotas," stripped of the interven-
ing letters and coming immediately after "Te dejo," functions as a form
of response. As a result, the two narratives mirror each other in order

to offer a different perspective on the relationship—the first from the younger lover who dies, the second from the older lover who survives.[13]

The differences are not limited to language and form: the content and tone are also radically altered. Kathleen Glenn notes that in the Castilian version the atmosphere is more oppressive, and that the narrator is now permanently confined in a sanatorium in which the doctors attempt to control her ("Reading and Writing" 59). For her part, Mirella Servodidio reads the alterations to the stories and their order as a sign of Riera's own ambiguous relationship to issues of lesbianism ("Doing Good" 66). Whether or not we can deduce the motive for Riera's changes from the stories' content, it is nonetheless clear that the formal, thematic, and linguistic changes significantly alter the reception of the stories and how lesbianism is portrayed. Riera's revisions and translations, moving ambiguously between Catalan and Castilian, between public and private spaces, reflect not only the duality of her own linguistic and national history but also the negative space to which lesbianism has traditionally been consigned in Spain.[14] If a written testimony already influences the representation of lesbian desire, the removal of the framing letters further eliminates the need to consider the thorny matter of the publication of private correspondence and its relationship to public confessions of sexuality.

It is the movement between reality and fiction, between the privacy of letters and the public nature of literature, between the speech acts of confession and testimony as they influence the legibility of lesbian desire of the Catalan original that interests me here, even as I attend closely to the differences of the Castilian version. Unlike the Castilian translation (or, for that matter, "Te deix" and *Qüestió d'amor propi*), "Jo pos" is not addressed to a single third party: although initially addressed to Riera, the public is, as the writer states clearly, the readership she has in mind. The question that emerges, and the focus of this chapter, is the nature of the demand her letter places on the reader. This demand begins, of course, with Riera herself, and it turns on the issue of narrative authority. The unidentified letter writer, when expressing her thanks to Riera for the initial rendition of her life in a literary form, mentions the last letter she received from her lover and offers to show it to Riera. She nevertheless qualifies that offer by stating that *Riera already knows the letter.* The "real life" letter, she implies, was the principal source that Riera used to write the first story. The use of quotation marks here is deliberate since Riera's text, as a fictional narrative, never claims to be an "authentic" testimony. The publication of these letters from an outside reader is a foil, of course, for these letters are clearly the work of Riera's own pen. In this sense, the text might be called a *testimonial fiction,* even if the term appears to court a contradiction.[15] Playing with the relationship between authentic informant and literary author, Riera ostensibly cedes her authorial voice to the letter writer, an accomplice who passes the testimony to her readers.

"Would you mind if I start my story by borrowing some words from you?" (11).[16] The fact that the narrator begins with a request, a gentle, even respectful, petition of permission to use Riera's own words may seem contradictory when her goal is to tell her own story, to offer a testimony that is, in fact, hers and hers alone. Yet her citation of Riera is, in a sense, a way of closing the book, almost literally, on *Te deix, amor la mar com a penyora,* as she takes the quotation that appears at the close of the volume: "To close my eyes with enough sleepiness so as to dream of you one more time and to deliver you afterwards like an offering— no debt, no sea—to the necessary oblivion where I have so often awaited you" (11).[17] The original volume ended with "to be continued," and by invoking such words as her own, using them as her point of departure, the writer usurps Riera's own voice in order to supplement her citation with the following addendum: "To pronounce with these sad lips, which still burn with passion when spelling a certain name, a final word, so that no else will ever write another commentary, nor say that they knew me or knew her. Nor change the ending to make it a happy one so that it ends well, as one would have liked it to end because one identified a little too much with the story" (11).[18]

In his subtle analysis of "Te deix," Brad Epps focuses on the ways in which lesbianism appears unreadable, and at the same time, readable as absence, in Riera's text. That absence appears in the narrative in the form of letters written but never sent, in lovemaking remembered but not reexperienced, and in the intruding presence of men: lesbian sexuality is consigned to a state of virtuality, a space of ontological lack, where the lesbian is not quite real. Lesbianism is a phantom, a ghostly desire, on the border of visibility, so much so that when the addressee is finally named, she remains subject to misreading: readers assumed that "Maria" was missing an accent, as "Marià" in Catalan is a masculine name (Nichols 210).[19] The act of naming Maria, the older lover, is both undone and replicated in the second story. Marina, not Maria, is the name of the younger lover in "Jo pos," which similarly evokes the maritime imagery so prevalent in "Te deix." But there can be no mistake: Marina is a woman's name. Repeating Riera's own words, the writer of "Jo pos" announces in effect that she will submit "Te deix" to a number of significant revisions. For example, her version does not situate lesbianism within the realm of the heterosexual couple: there is no husband, no pregnancy, no death from childbirth, and the lesbian relationship is reconfigured outside the paradigm of the heterosexual family. This is not to suggest that "Jo pos" portrays lesbianism any less ambiguously than "Te deix," only that the ambiguity of lesbian desire takes on an entirely different valence.

In the case of the first story, the sea is seen as the eyewitness of their love, the only space allowed for lesbian desire. The young lover misses the sea, and she invokes it at the very beginning of her letter. The writer recalls the sublime experience of lesbian lovemaking, the experience that the writer of "Jo pos" was never able to fulfill: "Without salvation, for that was the only way for us to be saved, because down there, in the realm of the absolute, the inexpressible, beauty was waiting for us, beauty dissolving in your-my image when I looked at myself in the mirror of your flesh" (36).[20] Lesbian sex is cast as a fall from grace, and yet, the fall is the only salvation, paradoxically, as a salvation from the religious proscription of their desires. For in breaking with the compulsory heterosexuality of official Catholic Spain in the 1960s, in assuming the sin attached to lesbianism, they have saved themselves from repression.[21] The tone of "Jo pos" is decidedly more pessimistic than "Te deix." The narrator's depiction of their lovemaking is brief and saturated with guilt since she never fully abandoned herself to the passion of the experience. As Epps suggests, "lesbian love is here only retrospectively acknowledged as a desire that is at once overlaid with guilt and impossible of being

realized in the flesh: as if Riera had to amend the sexual act, the lesbian fact, of the earlier text: correct, unwrite and undo it, volatilize and
virtualize it" ("Virtual Sexuality" 331). Unable to overcome the moral
prohibition of lesbianism, she acquiesces to the dominant standards of
sexual behavior and abandons her younger lover. In "Jo pos" the amorous space of the sea is turned into a watery cemetery for Marina. The
narrator asserts that she sees roses growing out of the sea, indicating the
place where Marina's body has come to rest.

As the rewriting of an earlier text, "Jo pos" distinguishes itself from
its predecessor, ironically, in its use of writing. Referring to the numerous letters the narrator of "Te deix" wrote and kept in a locked drawer,
Epps observes that they are rendered illegible for the reader, their contents unavailable for reading (324). The protagonist of "Te deix" remembers her letters, recalls how that scriptural activity substituted for her
absent lover: "I definitely spent the whole night with you. Sometimes
the pen would move so slowly and delicately across the paper that it
felt as if I were silently caressing you" (42).[22] The use of the letter as a
form of substitute object, as a material representation, is a topos of epistolary literature, one that nevertheless does not appear in "Jo pos." There
are no remnants of writing to be recalled, no love letters. Marina's letter to the unnamed author in "Jo pos"—the one that Riera supposedly
uses as the basis for "Te deix"—turns out to have been a suicide note,
a last will and testament.[23] Her goal, in the end, is to stop writing, to
devote herself to remembering her dead lover. The sense that writing
is itself tinged with fatality, with an awareness of the futility of writing,
is exacerbated in the Castilian version, which opens, "I know that these
notes will never get published, and in spite of that, I keep writing" (33).[24]

Although she offers no fond remembrances of love letters, memory
remains central to the narrator of "Jo pos": "Memory is everything for
me. Thanks to it I live still awaiting the prettiest smile in the world,
when I'm capable of remembering her profile" (13).[25] Her retelling of
the story is an effort to write against time, bemoaning the loss of a lover
whom she cannot revive: "I would exchange all of the hours that remain
of my life to relive that one, but in order to repeat it, enjoying each second with great relish, in spite of knowing their lethal fleetingness"
(15).[26] Marina persists as a spectral figure revisited in her mind, immune

to the passage of time: "And the memory of her returns her to me, palpable and real: she appears in front of me, an adolescent, beautiful" (18).[27] Her memory, described as a doll that she can caress, substitutes for the lover much as letters became substitutes in "Te deix." Yet while "Te deix" can be read as a single love letter from one woman to another, "Jo pos" is a narrative of depression, darkness, and utter lack of hope. The narrator describes her memory as filled with "phantoms that besiege me to that point that I can't go on, and I start screaming like a crazy woman" (15).[28]

In *Black Sun*, Julia Kristeva writes, "For those who are racked by melancholia, writing about it would have meaning only if writing sprang out of that very melancholia" (3). The writer's emphasis on memory and guilt, on holding onto the past, suggests that the composition of her letter is an expression of a failure to mourn, a means of testifying to a loss that has never been fully voiced and thus has remained within the domain of melancholy. Hers is a loss that she cannot accept, that cannot be accepted as loss. To speak of melancholy is, by necessity, to invoke Freud, if only at least as a point of departure. In his 1917 essay "Mourning and Melancholia," Freud attempted to distinguish between the two modes of responding to the loss of a love object. For Freud, the loss of an object leads to the task of mourning, whereby the attachment or cathexis is severed and given up. What one gives up in mourning is not only the object but the love for it, allowing the subject to reinvest, as it were, that love in another object. Melancholy results from the impossibility of mourning, in which the loss is disavowed. The subject unconsciously refuses to give up the object and thus incorporates it by allowing for part of the ego to identify with that object.

Mourning, it is important to recall, is a *conscious* process, whereas no declaration of melancholia can be made: it refuses to be rendered into language. In their work on mourning and melancholia, which they develop in terms of introjection and incorporation, Nicolas Abraham and Maria Torok claim that "incorporation results from those losses that for some reason cannot be acknowledged as such. In these special cases the impossibility of introjection is so profound that even our refusal to mourn is prohibited from being given a language" (130). If the melancholic subject cannot recall, cannot remember what was lost, and thus cannot grieve, the mourning subject is precisely the one who does remember. It is only through remembering that the lost object is no longer incorporated into the ego as a loss that cannot be voiced. As paradoxical as it may seem, memory allows the unconscious element that was masked and encrypted to enter consciousness and hence to be forgotten. Remembering, from a Freudian psychoanalytic perspective, allows one to give up the past. The distinction is key for our discussion of "Jo pos." While the narrator's desire dresses itself in the trappings of melancholia, she is not necessarily a melancholic. She does remember: memory is, in fact, all she has. She is, however, refusing to mourn. As Abraham and Torok note, there are "resistant cases of mourning" that do not produce melancholia, for the subject is aware of the loss (129). Trapped somewhere between mourning and melancholia, the narrator refuses to let go of the past by recalling it ceaselessly, agonizingly, as her "inalienable right to continue suffering an overly depressive neurosis" (12).[29]

But mourning and melancholia are not only approaches to loss. They are also treated, in various theoretical writings, as a matter of gender. Juliana Schiesari has argued persuasively that there is a "gendering" of melancholia, a cultural association of melancholia that privileges loss for men as a source of artistic energy and devalues female experiences of melancholia as mere depression. She notes that numerous feminist critics—Luce Irigaray, Kaja Silverman, and Kristeva—have interrogated the ways in which the female subject is addressed in Freud's writings on mourning and melancholia. For example, Schiesari interprets Irigaray's argument in *Speculum of the Other Woman* that women cannot experience melancholia to mean that women, sexually and socially devalued, are barred from the "privilege" of melancholia, cannot express their loss in culturally meaningful ways (65). In contrast, in *The Acoustic Mirror* Silverman refutes Irigaray and argues for female melancholia not as a pathology but as a psychic condition that emerges from the female version of the positive Oedipus complex. The female subject both desires and identifies with the mother, and upon facing symbolic castration in the Oedipal complex, must devalue the mother, give her up, and invest her desire in the figure of the father. The lost maternal object is then incorporated within the ego as an identification, one that produces the conditions for depression, since the woman must identify with a devalued object (158). In her aforementioned study of melancholia and depression, Kristeva adopts a more negative approach that emphasizes the difficulty of desire and identification for women. She analyzes the pathological dimension of grief in terms of an incomplete or unsuccessful detachment from the mother, for the female subject must engage in a form of "matricide" in order to establish her own identity: melancholy and depression are symptomatic of the impossible mourning for the maternal object (9).

If feminist critics have confronted the limits of Freudian psychoanalysis for women, rethinking the place of loss and lack in women's subjectivity, so too have queer theorists attempted to rework psychoanalytic theory for understanding lesbian desire. Psychoanalysis has, to be sure, struggled with lesbianism, especially as it continually defines lesbianism in relation to masculinity. In "The Psychogenesis of a Case of Homosexuality in a Woman" (1920), Freud interprets the female patient's love for an older woman as a substitute for her mother and revenge on her father for having given a child to his wife rather than to her, thus rendering lesbianism a triangulated affair of two women with an invisible man as witness. In his "Intervention on Transference," Lacan reinterprets Freud's argument, arguing that the young woman offers a challenge to her father by showing him how he should really give a gift of love to a woman. Turning away from the phallus and male identifications, queer theorists have theorized loss of femininity, rather than identification with masculinity, as the basis for lesbian desire. Teresa de Lauretis's theory of lesbianism as a form of fetishism, in which lesbian desire arises not out of castration but rather because of the loss of the woman's female body (and a subsequent disavowal of that loss), attempts to rework psychoanalytic principles in order to theorize lesbianism in terms other than the phallus.[30] De Lauretis's goal is to move beyond the limitations of psychoanalytic theory to see how lesbian desire is different from female heterosexual desire (226). She argues that the woman does not disavow the loss of the phallus: the castration complex results in "the lack of a libidinally invested body-image, a feminine body that can be narcissistically loved" (262). As a result, the lesbian disavows the lack of female body she can desire, converting it into a fetish that in turn structures the desire to recuperate the "absent (lost, denied) and wished-for female body" (263).[31]

Judith Butler's subsequent work on melancholia and gender theorizes, in ways similar to yet distinct from de Lauretis, lesbianism as a form of originary loss or foreclosure of the woman as a love object. Butler's argument dovetails with Irigaray's and Silverman's work insofar as it privileges melancholic lack in the constitution of the female subject. In *The Ego and the Id* Freud recalls his earlier work on melancholia and notes that the process of identifying with the lost object is much more common than previously assumed and plays a significant role in the formation of the ego itself: "when it happens that a person has to give up a sexual object, there quite often ensues an alteration of his ego which can only be described as a setting up of the object inside the ego, as it occurs in melancholia" (23–24). For Butler, following Freud, the process of losing a homosexual attachment—the lost possibility of lesbian desire, for example—becomes the foundation for the melancholic identification with a woman. In short, a woman identifies with the woman she could never love (*Psychic Life* 136–37). Butler makes such a claim—one that she recognizes cannot account for all forms of gender identification—in order to seek a plausible explanation for the way guilt adheres to homosexual desire and why the mourning of the loss of homosexual attachments is often difficult (both of which are present in Riera's story). If lesbian desire is renounced through a prohibition, as Butler argues, then the melancholic identification of the ego with the lost object invariably produces ambivalence and anger within the subject's psyche, for that identification with a lost lesbian desire preserves it as *loss:*

> The prohibition on homosexuality preempts the process of grief and prompts a melancholic identification which effectively turns homosexual desire back on itself. This turning back upon itself is precisely the action of self-beratement and guilt. Significantly, homosexuality is not abolished but preserved, though preserved precisely in the prohibition on homosexuality (*Psychic Life* 142).

This preservation paradoxically does not eliminate homosexual desire but strengthens it as a prohibition, as something to be renounced or lost.

The successful lesbian, it would seem from these works, is the lesbian who does not successfully mourn the loss, cannot give it up, for to do so would eliminate the very loss that produces desire. As Butler puts it, "The 'truest' lesbian melancholic is the strictly straight woman" (146–47). To experience lesbian desire in these terms would be akin to being trapped, not unlike the narrator of "Jo pos," somewhere between mourning and melancholia, to be perpetually mourning the loss of another woman (the maternal figure, one's own female body, an idealized female love object), and thus trying to recuperate it through sexual desire.

My purpose here is neither to champion nor to criticize the theoretical contributions of feminist and queer critics such as Irigaray and Silverman, de Lauretis and Butler, but rather to sound out the ways in which Riera's text enters into dialogue with a body of theoretical work that, in the case of Irigaray and Silverman, attempts to redeem women's melancholia as culturally significant, and in the case of Butler and de Lauretis, views the loss of a woman's body—conceptualized as fetishism or melancholia—as irremediably linked to female desire for another woman.[32] The utility of their work in this context is that it supports the view that the writer's grief-ridden disposition is, in a sense, a reflection of her own psychic means of preserving her lesbian lover in the face of a social prohibition and her only means of rendering that loss intelligible to others. The turn to the past is not meant to mourn that loss successfully, for it is precisely her inability to let go of her (lost) object of desire that allows her to retain that melancholic loss as a substitute for the lost lover. *Melancholic guilt becomes the space of lesbian desire.* This is much more apparent in the 1980 version of Riera's story, in which the narrator is not voluntarily resting in a seaside home that belongs to her friends but rather is confined in a mental ward and refuses to "rehabilitate," refuses, that is, to overcome her depression. As Servodidio suggests, her long-term struggle with therapy—she has been institutionalized for some time—suggests that her letter is not a talking cure to work through her depression ("Doing Good" 76). (The word "rehabilitate" is used deliberately here for its resonance with the 1971 Law of Social Dangers, which stipulated measures for "rehabilitating" gays and lesbians.)

The writer's refusal to rehabilitate, her claim to the right to her depression, is symptomatic of her deliberate attempt to undermine the letter's confessional tone. As Servodidio aptly puts it, "she courts guilt not expiation" (76). The publication of her letter as a form of self-disclosure of lesbian desire might imply that it functions as a therapeutic mode of exorcising one's own psychic demons in order to achieve some form of atonement or absolution. Ann Cvetkovich, in her analysis of lesbian sexuality and trauma, addresses the distinction between confession and therapy; she views testimony as performing, under certain contexts, a therapeutic function in which the witness to the testimony would not be a voyeur or a moral authority, as in confession (93). The paradox of the writer in "Jo pos" is that she adopts a testimonial mode that attempts to refuse both confession and therapy. Of course, the motives behind personal confessions are rarely about absolution alone. As Paul de Man argued in his analysis of Jean-Jacques Rousseau's *Confessions,* the motives behind confessions are always difficult to ascertain and corroborate since a confession is always splintered between the referential and cognitive dimensions of the speech act—that is, between testimony and penitence, between what actually happened and how the confessant feels about it (280). On the one hand, there is the event itself which took place and is recounted by the confessant (testimony), and on the other, there is the motive for the confession such as guilt, shame, a desire for absolution (penitence).

As readers of Rousseau know all too well, his confessions continually overturn the petition for absolution that supposedly motivates his writing. For example, Rousseau justifies his refusal to admit to stealing a ribbon and subsequent blaming of Marion in book II in his *Confessions* by claiming that he was too ashamed to confess his guilt at the time: "It was my shame that made me impudent, and the more wickedly I behaved the bolder my fear of confession made me" (88). For de Man, however, Rousseau does not confess but instead offers an excuse. "I have been absolutely frank in the account I have just given . . . But I should not fulfil the aim of this book if I did not at the same time reveal my inner feelings and hesitated to put up such excuses for myself as I honestly could," Rousseau asserts (88). The "inner feeling" of guilt he finally confesses cannot be verified in the same manner as the actual event of the stolen ribbon, since we only have Rousseau's word. De Man writes: "No such possibility of verification exists for the excuse, which is verbal in its utterance, in its effect and in its authority: its purpose is not to state but to convince, itself an 'inner' process to which only words can bear witness" (281).

In "Jo pos," a deferential tone characteristic of confessional writing admittedly seeps into the letter at times, such as when the writer states: "It really hurts me to justify myself in front of you, now that it is no longer possible to correct, amend so many mistakes" (17).[33] Nevertheless, justification, although it expresses a certain deference to Riera (already present in her "indebtedness" for the first story), is not a demand for absolution. Her mistakes, she confirms, are irremediable. She does not, indeed cannot, seek absolution or forgiveness from Riera. María Pilar Rodríguez rightly notes with regard to "Te deix" that the narrator's memory of lesbian love is and is not confession: it is introspective, yet it distances itself from moral law (110). So too in "Jo pos," where the writer does not seek redemption for her lesbianism but rather for her failure to act upon it. She writes not out of guilt for being a lesbian but for *not* being one, that is, for abjuring the love that the younger woman offered her. The letter thus takes on the guise of a confession of guilt for not making love: she blames herself for her lover's suicide. By writing about her guilt, rather than assuaging it, she resists in her own anguished way the overwhelming force of a psychic prohibition that prevented her from reciprocating the love that Marina offered her.

Yet if the writer's confession about the guilt stemming from her lover's suicide is not an attempt to overcome it, what is the compulsion to narrate her story? Is it simply to tell the truth, as she claims? How do we, as readers, even know if what she says is true? Confessions and testimony are traditionally conceived in terms of transparency and sincerity, in which the reader believes the author to be telling the truth. Glenn has pointed up the conflict between invention and factual testimony in "Jo pos," rightly asserting that we have no real reason to believe the narrator, that she may be lying ("Reading and Writing" 57–58); Rodríguez similarly questions the veracity and authority of her story (133). Testimony is a speech act, one that depends upon the performative act of the speaker and a community of listeners, in which the individual gives a first-person account of something he or she experienced individually, solely: the testimony is the property of that individual alone, translated into language from the vantage point of memory. But memory is hardly infallible, and the narrator's memory, filled with phantoms, may not be the most reliable source of information. This is exacerbated by the use of letter writing, for Riera has commented that by nature the letter form may be duplicitous, that the reality forged in letters may differ completely from the world outside them ("Grandeza y miseria" 156). Such is the dilemma of testimonial discourse. Derrida argues that since testimony always claims to testify in truth, it "always goes hand in hand with at least the possibility of fiction, perjury, and lie" (*Demeure* 27). For Derrida, testimony and literature, truth and fiction, remain irrevocably linked. A similar predicament arises in critical discussions of the Latin American *testimonio,* which, as a denunciation of political abuse, also claims to testify or bear witness to a reality outside the speech act. In the case of testimonial novels, the authority and authenticity of the testimony remains a sticking point, for critics invariably wonder how much the author has manipulated the informant's story. For example, Doris Sommer asks: "Is it really 'authentic' history? How much does the intellectual interlocutor interfere with the informant's narrative transmission?" (914).[34]

The writer's testimony thus remains susceptible to charges of inaccuracy and even mendacity: such is the paradox that Rousseau deploys to great effect, claiming that he wants no veil to separate him from his readers, all the while exploiting language's capacity to conceal and manipulate. The evidence for her story rests in the supposed existence of roses that grow in the very spot where Marina committed suicide, a sign that Marina's body remains at the bottom of the sea. The letter writer adopts, in the final line, a juridical discourse, already announced in the title and in the use of the word "testimony": "I have seen them [the roses], I swear, and I call upon the seagulls as witnesses" (19).[35] To bear witness is not the same act as being a witness: for although the seagulls were witnesses to their love and to Marina's suicide, they cannot speak, cannot testify on her behalf, cannot *bear witness.* Whatever knowledge they have, it remains incommunicable to others, and without speech, there can be no witness who testifies. The appeal to a witness who cannot testify runs the risk of capitulating to the very conditions of illegibility that have prompted the letter writer's testimony in the first place. As a narrative that cannot be verified, her final appeal to a witness who cannot corroborate her version of events forms a most fragile defense.

"Fragility" is not a haphazardly chosen word. In "La fragilitat de l'escriptura," Epps argues that Riera's writing reflects an awareness of its possible disappearance, that in spite of its permanence as printed matter, such permanence is never guaranteed. This sense of the fragility of writing is exacerbated in the case of the Catalan (or more precisely Mallorcan) language, given its history of erasure, censorship, and prohibition (73). Like Basque and Galician, Catalan was banned from television, radio, newspapers, and schools during the first decades of the Francoist dictatorship in a concerted attempt at unifying the nation through Castilian. The effect on literature was devastating. Books could not be published in Catalan until 1946, and while in 1933 Catalan literature represented over 23 percent of the entire literary production in Spain, in 1975 it was only 4.5 percent; at the end of 1977, there were fewer books published in Catalan than in 1936 (Ruiz et al. 197). One of the results of Franco's linguistic politics, Epps argues, is that Castilian inhabits a public and permanent space, while Catalan is relegated to a private, more intimate realm (78, 80), a discursive alignment that also leaves its mark on Riera's use of letter writing in her fiction, since privacy and intimacy are, of course, fundamental to the epistolary genre (83–84). The history of correspondence reiterates this division between Castilian and Catalan: telegraphic communications in Catalan were prohibited first in 1941 and again in 1961 (Ruiz et al. 199).

Similarly, the right to privacy in correspondence did not safeguard the language of composition when the "obligatory" language of the nation was Castilian, for a letter, as private as it may be, had to be addressed, publicly, in Castilian to reach its destination. In a brief article entitled "El problema de los Idiomas en Correos" (The Problem of Languages in the Post Office), published in a post office periodical in 1976, the unnamed author responds to an article published in a Galician daily newspaper in which a young woman contested the corrections that a postal official made on several packages addressed to "Xulia," in Galician, as opposed to "Julia" in Castilian. The anecdote serves to remind readers that "the national language is Castilian, and all Spaniards are obligated to write the addresses on envelopes and on the front of packages in Castilian" (5). Postal officials, the article continues, are not required to know other languages, and the frequent use of other languages leads to the contamination of the Spanish language; the article makes reference to a similar case in Alicante. There is of course a contradiction in affirming the purity of "our idiom" (Castilian) in the face of "the different idioms of our country" (Catalan, Galician, Basque). They are all in fact languages of Spain. Yet the article's conclusion is that the "other" languages are obstacles to the smooth functioning of the postal system.

The narrator's testimony thus risks going unread or, at the very least, remaining illegible for readers unfamiliar with Catalan. As fragile as her writing may be, however, we ought to pause to consider that its form and language may be, paradoxically, its greatest strength. In her analysis of *Qüestió d'amor propi*, Tsuchiya argues that Àngela's use of a seductive epistolary tool, of a "duplicitous discourse," leads to a loss of her narrative authority because "duplicity, by definition, is self-betraying: the overdetermined nature of duplicitous discourse inevitably leads to the loss of authority, because it calls attention to its condition as language" (282). That may be true for *Qüestió,* but in the case of "Jo pos," a discourse that calls attention to its status as language may have the opposite effect, increasing the letter writer's narrative authority. It bears repeating that from the outset the writer declares her discursive authority over the events, that this is meant to be the final commentary.[36] For while the writer's testimony may be duplicitous, it may also be completely sincere. The reader has, of course, no way of knowing. In this respect, the writer offers a form of testimony that, while fragile, is also paradoxically completely irrefutable: fragile, for the seagulls cannot testify on her behalf (whatever they witnessed cannot be communicated), but irrefutable for the same reason: they remain beyond examination and cannot be queried. She states that Marina had left a letter, a last will and testament in which she left her the sea as a token. The writer vaguely insinuates that Riera somehow saw that letter, had access to it, and thus based her story on it, altering details and the denouement. The writer not only complements and corrects Riera's first story but she replaces that letter—Marina's original one—with her own. But her substitution also forecloses any empirical access to the events outside

her narration: to their relationship, to Marina's suicide, and to the original letter that the writer obscures. Marina's own letter, her voice in-
scribed in the final missive, is what is never heard.

In the final analysis, the truth value of her testimony—its verifiabil-
ity or accuracy with regard to "what really happened"—may be the
least important aspect of her letter. In a remarkable analysis of the role
of confession in law and literature, Peter Brooks remarks that "certain
narratives—narratives of victimhood, of the irreparable, of what cannot
be undone—are not susceptible of rebuttal" (136). Wracked with guilt,
beleaguered by the painful space of memory, the letter writer produces
testimony that is irrefutable. No grounds exist for disputing her claims:
not only does the validity of her version of events rest entirely in the
speech act of her letter but we are also not in a position to deny the
validity of her pain. The truth of her testimony lies less in the exact
details of what took place with Marina than in the truth of the grief
and pain that she suffers. That truth—the truth of her depression, of
her interminable retracing of the past—is, in the words of Brooks, "the
truth of desire, of affect, of that which makes sense of things in an emotional register" (54). The emotional grief, the need to speak as a means
of recalling and reliving her loss, compels her writing. It is here that the
witnessing function of the seagulls accrues additional significance. By
deferring the witnessing function onto the seagulls, the writer ultimately
undermines any capacity for the reader to somehow occupy a position
of witness to the events that she narrates. Witnessing is not transferable.
The witness is burdened with the responsibility of solitude, of being
the one who is "privileged" to bear witness (Felman 14–15). By underscoring our own lack of access to the events, of access to the original
letter on which both stories are based, to the supposed real-life figures
of Maria ("Te deix") and Marina ("Jo pos")—whose names may not
be those at all, but chosen instead as metonyms to the sea—the writer
underscores how our own position, as readers, remains utterly incom-
mensurable with that of the seagulls. In "Jo pos" no one but the writer
can claim an intimate knowledge of her or Marina.

No rebuttal may be possible, but testimony is nevertheless dependent on a recipient, an addressee to whom and for whom that testimony
is given: without it, the testimony cannot be acknowledged, and thus

validated, as a speech act. Bearing witness requires a listener or a reader, in the case of written testimony. In her analysis of trauma and literature in relation to the Holocaust, Shoshana Felman asks how the act of writing is related to the act of bearing witness and raises the question of the reader's position: "Is the act of reading literary texts itself inherently related to the act of facing horror? If literature is the alignment between witnesses, what would this alignment mean? And by virtue of what sort of agency is one appointed to bear witness?" (2). In a juridical context, the recipient of testimony becomes judge and jury. The listener, as in a confession, determines guilt or innocence depending on the value of the testimony offered. Instead, Felman conceives the reader of testimony as a "listener" who neither judges nor witnesses but, later, can bear witness to the act of having been present for the testimony. The relationship between text and reader is therefore not a wholly collaborative one in the way that reader-response criticism has often posited a reader who completes the work by giving it meaning. While the reader is necessary for the testimony to be validated as testimony, to recognize the speech act as such, the reader's recognition of the text as testimony necessarily grants a narrative authority to the witness: only the witness can speak with authority about the events he or she experienced.

Wavering between mourning and melancholia, the narrator's writing renders lesbianism present and public, but it achieves a public, permanent status only as a form of loss, as a desire that must lose its object to be accepted. No justice, she seems to say, is possible. Her inability to reciprocate Marina's love is reconfigured as the reader's inability to know her experience. Just as she cannot work through Marina's suicide, we cannot respond adequately to her loss. The writer annuls, in effect, the capacity of the reader to adjudicate and cast judgment upon her past actions and present decision to write. She, in turn, undermines the construction of homosexuality as a secret or melancholic loss that needs to be confessed to someone who stands in the position of moral authority. For while the reader cannot occupy the position of the seagulls to bear witness to their relationship and to Marina's suicide, the letter burdens the reader with the knowledge of their failure. The reader becomes witness to the effects of the discursive construction of lesbianism as a desire rooted in prohibition and loss.

In *Homografías* (Homographs), a study devoted to contemporary gay and lesbian subjectivities in Spain, Ricardo Llamas and Francisco Javier Vidarte stage a hypothetical conversation to describe how heterosexuals react to the public confession of homosexuality: "It's as if due to the mere fact of having witnessed someone coming out of the closet the witness suddenly felt like a member of the oppressing community, recalled within seconds the times that they may have joked disparagingly about homosexuals, were invaded by a peculiar sense of guilt and needed a good cleansing of their conscience" (84–85). Llamas and Vidarte's choice of chapter title, "Del otro lado del confesionario" (From the Other Side of the Confessional), reiterates the link between the voicing of homosexuality and confession. But more importantly, their use of the word *testigo* (witness) raises the question of what it means to witness the speech act of coming out. The witness here is one who hears directly—has first-hand knowledge of—the other's confession. At the root of their argument is that the speech act burdens the listener with the dynamics of shame and guilt that have conditioned the very act of confession in the first place, and as a result it removes the confessor from a position of moral authority: shame and guilt are repositioned such that the homosexual's shame becomes the witness's shame.

In a similar fashion, in "Jo pos" the writer refuses the cloistering space of a lesbian identity that can only confer guilt and shame (even as she mourns interminably her lost lover as a substitute desire) and that refuses to conform to the norms of letter writing as a confessional practice. But, as we saw in the last chapter, a confession via letter writing is not simply a case of an oral exchange transferred to paper, in the way that classic epistolary treatises viewed letter correspondence as an *absentium mutuus sermo* or a substitute conversation. The medium of letter writing erects a linguistic barrier—the deferral and distance intrinsic to epistolarity—between the reader and the writer, confounding our pretenses to having some sort of direct access to the letter writer. It is not a "deferred dialogue," for no dialogue is possible. Kept at a distance, we have no choice but to listen and not respond, at least not to her. The dynamics of a public confession are overturned by a refusal of total self-disclosure. The letter affords her a mask, one that allows the confessional space to be twisted and transformed for a different purpose.

The letter, by virtue of the distance that it places between writer and reader, turns the closet into something other than the cloistered space of stigma and secrecy. In so doing, Riera's story twists the confessional dynamic in such a way that the text is calculated not to exonerate the writer of guilt but rather to shift the burden of her guilt on to the reader.

This is, as it were, the upshot of the writer's version of events. In authoring her own story, she garners an authority over her own history. But neither can we forget that the testimonial dimension of the story is a fiction, that Riera is, in the end, the author of the narrative. Riera's separation from the events—transforming herself into a reader rather than the writer of the original lesbian love letter—may seem to be a technique to distance herself from lesbianism. Luisa Cotoner, in her introduction to *Te dejo el mar*, for example, remarks on Riera's distance from her characters, allowing them to speak in their own voices in the first person (29). That may be, in the end, one of the unanticipated effects of the story. Riera distances herself from the narrative events of her story, but in so doing she paradoxically reinforces the movement between fiction and reality. It may be that Riera distances herself from lesbianism not out of a fear of lesbianism itself but rather to undermine the virtual state to which lesbianism in Spain has been consigned. If lesbian desire appears all the more phantasmic because it is so steeped in loss, Riera's use of the epistolary form serves to render that virtuality ever so real: drawing herself, as a reader of her own text, into the reality of lesbian existence in Spain.

As a "real life" testimony, the writer's careful use of the letter does indeed raise a number of questions about the closet and sexual identity in the Spanish context. In light of Foucault's writings on sexuality, a confession of one's sexuality would appear to be an acquiescence to power, a consequence of subjection to a modern episteme that locates the subject's truth in sexuality and compels the subject to articulate that sexuality openly in the form of an identity. If Riera's story is any indication, however, the refusal of identity, of coming out publicly as a lesbian, is not necessarily a guarantee of freedom from power, from the compulsion to locate one's sense of identity in sexuality. As we saw in the last chapter, there was, at this historical juncture, a decreased emphasis on the self-disclosure of sexual identity in the Spanish context. If the closet—as the hidden expression of an identity—is less indicative of how sexuality operates in Spain at the time of the story's publication, Riera's story shows that the discourse of confession nevertheless maintains a prominent role in the structuring of sexuality. The lack of a Spanish equivalent for the "closet" at this historical juncture, I would argue, reflects instead the social stigma and moral prohibition associated with homoerotic desire.

In an interview with Ana Maria Moix published in 1989, Geraldine Nichols drew a distinction between novels in Spain that represented "episodes of lesbianism," in which lesbianism was an option, and U.S. literary works that emphasized "coming out," in which lesbianism appeared as an exclusive identity (115). Moix concurs that lesbianism appears much more ambiguously in Spanish literature and that, at the time, few if any lesbian "coming out" novels had appeared. The message from Moix and Nichols's exchange is that the shift in focus from the presumably stable space of identity to the transient and fluctuating "episodes" of desire does little to strip lesbian desire of its stigma. Riera's story seems to communicate a similar message: it is not easier to confess to an episode of lesbian desire—to a single, failed relationship in the case of "Jo pos"—than it is to lay claim to an identity. The adoption of the closet as a discourse in contemporary Spain does not mean, however, that lesbians have emerged publicly in the same way as gay men. This is owed, in part at least, to the historical legacy of invisibility around lesbianism; even lesbian political emancipation groups, distancing themselves from gay liberation in the early 1980s, would continue to suffer from invisibility within the feminist movement (Llamas and Vila 202). In a recent article aptly entitled "Las últimas del armario" ("The Last Ones [Out] of the Closet"), Luz Sánchez-Mellado discusses how lesbians in Spain, having assumed their desire without stigma, nevertheless remain reluctant to come out of the closet. "Yes, they are lesbians, they desire and love other women and are proud of it. But, no thanks. They don't want to proclaim it in front of three million readers" (36). While lesbians are appearing more frequently as television characters, "actual lesbians, with first and last names, don't show their faces" (44). Although Sánchez-Mellado offers no hypothesis, it can be discerned from her reporting that the resistance to coming out has deep roots in the history of lesbianism in Spain. The closet may no longer designate a space of shame and stigma for lesbians, but it nevertheless maintains a cloak of secrecy, keeping sexual intimacy out of the public sphere.

Refusing surveillance and the voyeuristic gaze of others, lesbians in Spain remain more in the closet than out of it. "Jo pos" articulates the difficulties of coming to terms with lesbian desire, of carving out a space for one's sexuality that entails recognition and privacy at the same time. Such is the demand that Riera's letter places on its reader. Commenting on the fate of the narrator's letter in "Te deix," Epps writes that it returns to the living through reading and the assumption of responsibility, a delivery that "may be the truest of all" ("Virtual Sexuality" 338). Riera's rewriting of that earlier story in "Jo pos" reiterates the need for reading as a form of responsibility. In her interview with Aguado, Riera asserts that the reader of epistolary fiction is always the true addressee (36). By virtue of appearing as a textual figure, the initial recipient of the letter, Riera grants the text the very respect and acknowledgment it demands, as a testimony, from its reader. In contrast with César, whose response to Arturo in Villena's *Amor pasión* constituted an act of involuntary outing, she respects the wishes of the writer not to reveal her name. There is, nevertheless, another version of this story, one possible rebuttal: the act of reading—a letter, a literary text—always presumes a distance from the textual events, and we may just as well turn our back on the writer's testimony as easily as we turn the page, our reading complacent and indifferent. In short, the reader may elude the text's call, rejecting its demand as nothing more than a fiction, or dismissing the narrative as one of a "minor" genre (a letter) in a "minor" language (Catalan) about a sexuality that does not deserve recognition. This is, of course, the risk the letter writer takes in making the public the final *destinataire*. The success of her endeavor, of her testimony, hinges on the precariousness of (letter) writing as a mode of connecting and communicating with another. For while the use of the letter form would seemingly provide a space to voice one's identity, to communicate both love and desire, by the very nature of being written, the expression of one's sexuality is cast adrift from the writer's hand, and thus can be manipulated and appropriated for other ends, or simply ignored. It is perhaps in recognizing this predicament that the reader truly bears witness to the oppressive conditions that have left an indelible stamp on the construction of lesbian sexuality in Spain.

PART III

EPISTOLARY POLITICS

Pleasurable Insurrections:
Sexual Liberation and Epistolary Anarchy

> Tyrants are never born out of anarchy. One only ever sees them rise
> up in the shadow of laws; they derive their authority from laws.
>
> —MARQUIS DE SADE, *Juliette*

Lluís Fernàndez's *L'anarquista nu* (*The Naked Anarchist*, 1979) declares its
two main themes in its title: sexuality and politics.[1] The text consists of
fifty-six letters written between 1975 and 1976 by friends and a former
lover to Aureli Santonja, a gay Valencian anarchist exiled in Amsterdam.
On August 30, 1976, Aureli committed suicide with five packs of barbi-
turate suppositories. Writing from Valencia, Aureli's friends openly share
with him saucy anecdotes and failed love affairs. No longer constrained
by the guilt-ridden confines of the confessional, Lulú Bon, Carles Besada,
and Pipi Iaguer, to name a few, aim to astonish and scandalize Aureli
with tantalizingly explicit descriptions of homosexual acts, their various
erotic escapades infiltrating the institution of the Church and crossing
the boundaries between public and private spaces. Whether sex takes
place at the opera, in train station bathrooms, or as an erotic fantasy,
their sexual lives are expressions of a sudden burst from repression in
the final months of the Franco regime. Yet this decadent eroticism
is divorced from any political consciousness of their actions: two figures, Lita Vermelló and La Washingtona, for example, go to a political
rally only in search of a boyfriend. Frivolous and campy to an extreme,
the colorful characters of *L'anarquista nu* favor the transitory pleasures

of the flesh over organized political emancipation. Sex is subversive, politics is passé.

Winner of the prestigious Prudenci Bertrana prize in 1978 and published in 1979, *L'anarquista nu* emerges from the literary milieu of experimentalism that dominated the production of literature written in Catalan during the late 1970s by Valencian authors. Between 1939 and 1972, only two novels were published by Valencian authors in Catalan, and many critics concur that Valencian authors, during the 1970s, lacked a narrative tradition on which to model themselves (Salvador and Piquer 10; Iborra 115; Oleza 84). Joan Fuster famously claimed that Valencia suffered from a "singular lack" ("carència singular") of narrative works in Catalan (Iborra 47), and the new generation of writers had to struggle with, in the words of Fuster, "the desolating and extremely evident fact of not having a Valencian reading public" (Cucó and Cortés 168). This is not to suggest that the Valencian writers in the 1970s began ex nihilo. Instead, they rejected the scarce amount of narrative work of previous writers in a realist vein and embraced experimental and avantgarde techniques. In 1973, as the Franco regime was weakening, Eliseu Climent, editor of the Valencia-based press Edicions Tres i Quatre, inaugurated the literary prize Premi Andròmina dels Octubre and published Amadeu Fabregat's *Assaig d'aproximació a 'Falles folles fetes foc'* (A Critical Approach to "Wild Floats on Fire," a reference to the Fallas festival in Valencia) in 1974. Fabregat's novel, together with Joan Francesc Mira's *El bou de foc* (The Bull of Fire, a reference to a Valencian festival) of the same year, engendered an experimental wave characterized by urban settings and cosmopolitanism, existential angst, and verbal and formal innovation (Salvador and Piquer 12). Fernàndez's work emerges in the context of this new generation of writers, with *L'anarquista nu* standing out as representative of the embrace of a linguistic and formal "baroque and antirealist" experimentalism that focuses on political transgression and sexual freedom (Oleza 73).

The lack of a narrative tradition and a reading public in Valencia is intimately related to the history of the Catalan language—its prohibition under Franco and the particular relationship of Valencia with linguistic and national politics. In his study of Fernàndez's novel, Josep-Anton Fernàndez argues that Catalan authors faced the task of redefining

Catalan literature in light of the political project of establishing a national identity shared by all of the Catalan-speaking countries, or the *Països Catalans,* which include the País Valencià and the Balearic Islands (132). Valencia nevertheless has a complex history with that national project and with the Catalan language, as many Valencians refer to their language as Valencian (*valencià*) rather than Catalan, in some instances to avoid the confusion between "Catalan" as a geographic term ("of Catalonia") and as a linguistic term ("in Catalan language"), and in other instances to claim that Valencian is a language of its own and to uphold a regional Valencian identity. Among linguists there is considerable consensus that Valencian is a variant of Catalan, with some lexical and grammatical differences.[2] Historically Valencians have resisted only the name "Catalan," not the linguistic unity among Catalonia, Valencia, and Mallorca. In a letter to Vicenç Riera Llorca from 1953, Fuster wrote that "it still repulses Valencians to call themselves Catalans and to say that their language is Catalan" (Cucó and Cortés 243).[3] In *Nosaltres, els valencians* (We Valencians) Fuster reiterates both the specificity of Valencia's history and language at the same time that he exhorts his readers to embrace the nationalist project of the Catalan countries. The word "Valencian," he argues, is their way of calling themselves Catalan (39).

Yet the term *valencià* has also been deployed historically by the more Castilianized members of Valencia to distinguish themselves from Catalonia: the right-wing "secessionists" in Valencia are those who speak little to no Valencian and have no real interest in Valencian as a language (Sanchis Guarner 41–42). The "Valencianization" of the language is thus an attempt to root out any influence from Barcelona, the increasing distance from Catalan leading in turn to the increasing dominance of Castilian (Cuenca 80). Valencian nationalism, in the aftermath of the death of Franco, would emerge as a struggle between a leftist project aligned with the *Països Catalans* and a right-wing version that advocated a regional identity for Valencia, distinct from Catalonia and Mallorca and aligned with the Spanish state (Cuenca 61). The battle over the name of the language has led to the publication of separate grammar and spelling norms for the Valencian language. Valencian authors publishing in Catalan in the 1970s and '80s thus faced a considerably complex political panorama in which their literary endeavors, and more importantly, their use of language (Catalan vs. Valencian forms), were invariably imbricated in national and regional political struggles (Carbó and Simbor Ruig 18–19).

But in spite of the fact that Fernàndez shares company with other Valencian writers such as Fabregat, Mira, Isa Tròlec, Rafael Ferrando, Ferran Cremades i Arlandis, and Josep-Lluís Seguí, who sought to create a literary tradition of their own, Fernàndez occupies a somewhat ambiguous place in Catalan literature. At the time of its publication, *L'anarquista nu* was generally valued less for its literary contribution than for its representation of a gay subculture (Josep-Anton Fernàndez, *Another Country* 133). Josep Iborra, for example, described Fernàndez's work as a "chronicle of a gay ghetto" ("crònica d'un *ghetto gay*") that focuses on two types of gay men: the unsophisticated, ignorant, happy queen who is frivolous, and the intellectual, angst-ridden homosexual who is neurotic and obsessed with sex (57). With the exception of articles by Josep-Anton Fernàndez and Leora Lev, criticism of the novel is limited to reviews and interviews published at the time of its release.[4] But Fernàndez's ambiguous place in Catalan literary history is not linked solely to the particular history of Valencian authors at this time nor to the novel's tepid reception among critics but is also a reflection of his subsequent decision to write in Castilian. *L'anarquista nu* is his first and only work in Catalan: in the 1980s he began to publish in Castilian and moved into the Spanish literary world. Works such as *Desiderata* (1984) and *Espejo de amor y lujo* (Mirror of Love and Luxury, 1992), written in Castilian, receive little to no mention in Catalan literary histories, even though they share a thematic unity around sexuality and camp.[5]

The back cover of the Castilian translation of *L'anarquista nu* describes the novel in terms of "the Almodovarian aesthetic," an anachronistic association as the text was published before Almódovar achieved fame for his musical performances with Fanny McNamara and the 1980 release of *Pepi, Luci, Bom y otras chicas del montón* (Pepi, Luci, Bom and Other Girls on the Heap). Although Fernàndez's first novel is indelibly tied to the political and aesthetic project of Catalan literature, his movement toward Spanish literature is already foreshadowed in the novel's representation of gay society, reflecting the widespread changes in social relations and sexual attitudes across Spain that erupted in the wake of Franco's death.

The novel's commercial success and rapid translation into Castilian (and later into French and English) attest to the fact that *L'anarquista nu,* while intimately linked with the sexual politics of gays in Valencia, was similarly engaged with the political and sexual changes occuring at the level of the Spanish state. In this respect, the association of the novel with an Almodovarian aesthetic is not inaccurate, insofar as it suggests that the novel participates in the cultural effervescence of what would later be dubbed *la movida* and the sexual explosion of *el destape,* although those terms undoubtedly maintain a strong link to Madrid.[6] As Teresa Vilarós observes, Ocaña's transvestite performances in Barcelona, immortalized in Ventura Pons's documentary *Ocaña, retrat intermitent* (Ocaña, Intermittent Portrait, 1978), were central to the countercultural "underground" of Barcelona that gave way after 1978 to *la movida* in Madrid (188).

But unlike Almodóvar's wild escapades of the self-proclaimed pornstar tranvestite protagonist of *Patty Diphusa* and the lesbian sadomasochist adventures in *Pepi, Luci, Bom, L'anarquista nu* tells a slightly different tale. As a story of post-Franco gay liberation, *L'anarquista nu* exposes the absence of a truly liberating sexual revolution. Its portrayal of cancer as a lethal disease before the identification of AIDS, its critique of the failure of identity politics, and its concern for the place of love within gay relationships anticipate many of the problems that gay liberation movements would face in Spain in the late 1970s and 1980s. The demise of the Spanish dictator did not catalyze a full-scale political movement for gay and lesbian emancipation, as some might have hoped. No doubt the open expression of formerly repressed sexualities and the rise of gay pride parades beginning in 1977 have contributed to an exaggerated view of the freedom enjoyed by gays and lesbians. The drag queens who marched in the streets during the first gay and lesbian liberation march in 1977 were attempting to undermine the powerful stigma that has dominated the construction of homosexuality, a result of the collusion of the Franco regime's juridical repression and the conservative religious values that permeated the moral landscape of Spanish society. At the same time, the lesbian movement was in its initial stages of development from within the feminist movement, a point of origin that unfortunately stymied its organization due to still uncontested homophobia within feminist groups.[7]

Most significant of all is that the earliest gay political groups questioned the value of identity categories, and while seeking equal rights
under the law they also sought to move beyond labels such as "homosexual" and "heterosexual." Furthermore, these movements were in general subordinated to the larger opposition parties for democratic change,
such as the Partido Socialista de Obrero Español (The Spanish Socialist Workers Party, or PSOE) and had to combat internal resistance due
to homophobia within such groups.[8] Unlike North American coalitions
that emphasized difference and identity within a context where democracy already existed, Spanish gay and lesbian liberation movements,
operating under the need to establish and consolidate democracy in the
early 1980s, formed part of a larger movement of democratization in
which equality was emphasized over identity and difference. In the 1977
Manifesto of the Front d'Alliberament Gai de Catalunya (Gay Liberation Front of Catalonia, or FAGC), it became clear that gay and lesbian
liberation was not limited to the specific emancipation of homosexuals,
as it also called for juridical change regarding the equality of men and
women, the minimum legal age for marriage, and the decriminalization
of abortion (Likosky 207–8).[9] Juan Vicente Aliaga has argued that the
lack of a strong self-reflexive movement stems in part from the *indifference* that results from affirming equality over difference and identity
("Como hemos cambiado" 41). If early identity politics were marginalized with respect to a larger framework of democratization, homoerotic
desire ran the risk of disappearing or being recuperated within heterosexuality at the same time that it nevertheless persisted as a spectral
presence within a largely heterosexual movement of democratic emancipation. Due in large part to this political posture of equality, however,
identity politics and visibility for gays and lesbians have only recently
been foregrounded in discussions of gay and lesbian sexuality in Spain.

Still, the lack of a strong political movement for gay liberation in
Spain is often interpreted in a positive light as a self-conscious refusal
of identity politics by Spanish gays and lesbians. Several critics have
asserted that the Spanish concept of homosexuality and identity anticipated the notion of "queer" sexuality within Anglo-American academic
circles. For example, in his recent study of gay autobiography, Robert
Richmond Ellis asserts that the 1977 FAGC Manifesto "anticipate[s]

the postmodern conception 'queer'" (17). In a similar vein, Emilie L. Bergmann and Paul Julian Smith claim that the use of the term *entender* ("to understand")—as an epistemological marker of desire rather than an ontological one of identity—has foreshadowed the "queer" thrust of Anglo-American theory (12). The early years of the *destape,* a period of explicit sexual expression, and the explosion of *la movida madrileña* would appear to be initial signs of an increasing cultural acceptance of the Spanish modality of camp and effeminacy known as *la pluma.* For Vilarós, the apolitical approach of *la movida madrileña* and the pre-*movida* in Barcelona during the early years of the Transition marked the casting off of identity categories, avoiding any form of institutionalized political organization (185). Indeed, in the early post-Franco years— particularly in the aftermath of Colonel Antonio Tejero's aborted coup on February 23, 1981, a watershed moment for the consolidation of democracy—identity categories were cast off with little thought, in a period of frivolity and frenzied nightlife that appeared to usher in a new era of sexual freedom.

The celebratory vision of gay liberation that circulates even today tends to suppress the fact that the 1970 Law of Social Dangers was not repealed until 1979, four years after the fall of the dictatorship. Even after its repeal, the statute continued to exert its influence through the category of "public scandal."[10] This broad category allowed for the policing of Spanish homosexuals, since, as Aliaga notes, judges were still able to persecute gay sex under the label "lubricious acts" ("actos lúbricos") ("Como hemos cambiado" 31); sexual orientation was not included in the criminal code until 1996 (in Articles 510, 511, and 512), making homophobia a crime. On October 23, 1986, for example, two women, Arantxa and Esther, were arrested under the provision of "public scandal" for kissing in public. On January 23, 1987, hundreds of lesbians took to the streets in protest of the police aggression against the two women and engaged in an act of public kissing, *la besada pública,* thus producing a visibility for lesbian sexuality that had otherwise been negated (Llamas and Vila 206). For Aliaga, the continued weakness of gay and lesbian liberation movements in Spain is due to the emphasis on tolerance—"a tolerance that is nothing more than pure façade" ("Como hemos cambiado" 41). A survey from 1988 showed that 50 percent of all Spaniards still believed that homosexuality should be condemned, and only 16 percent said that homosexual relations were acceptable (Pérez Cánovas 27). Aliaga interprets the early signs of liberation as replicating the stereotypes advanced under the Franco regime. The proliferation of magazines in kiosks such as the Barcelona *Party* "continued to form part of the territory of the inconfessable, of that which could not be said, of denial" ("Como hemos cambiado" 36). His pessimistic tone is corroborated by other Peninsular scholars in the incipient field of gay and lesbian studies in Spain. Xosé M. Buxán, for example, provides a succinct overview of the vicissitudes endured by scholars such as Ángel Sahuquillo and Alberto Cardín, among others, who have had to justify their intellectual endeavors to those who considered them of no interest or significance.[11]

The use of the epistolary mode by Fernàndez reflects an ambivalent portrayal of contemporary gay and lesbian subjectivities and their relationship to identity politics, offering its readers a sobering palliative to the more celebratory constructions of gay and lesbian liberation in Spain. In his study, Josep-Anton Fernàndez convincingly argues that *L'anarquista nu* vindicates gay identity and its public expression at the same time that it underscores the limitations of transgression as a political strategy of emancipation (133–34). Although he briefly notes the resonances of anarchism in the novel's approach to gender and sexual politics, *L'anarquista nu*'s relationship to the history of anarchism in Spain—and how anarchism relates to the novel's representation of contemporary gay and lesbian politics and sexual dissidence—remains to be adequately traced. The title's reference to anarchism brings to the fore the utopian revolutionary stance that characterized the anarchist movement in Spain, particularly in the 1930s. The novel unveils, "nude" before the reader, that the anarchistic notion of a self-governing community in which property is shared by the people and solidarity produces social cohesion is an impotent approach to political change: the Valencian gay community depicted in the novel is divided and in disarray. In the course of the novel's letter exchanges, the characters' inabilities to achieve a necessary level of consciousness of their subjection to a normative law functions as the basis for a critique of radical leftist emancipatory narratives. Sexual dissidence is thus portrayed as an unsuccessful revolutionary tactic because of the reinscription of the norms that such strategies profess to displace. So too the discourses of gender and transsexuality in the novel: the crossing of gender, linguistically through the adoption of feminine names and surgically through sex-reassignment surgery, simply adopts opposing norms without a conscious reflection on the political ramifications of such actions. *L'anarquista nu* tirelessly reinforces the same message in multiple manifestations: the failure of gay and lesbian liberation on a political plane is a reflection of a more profound failure on a psychic one. Although anarchistic thought offers a utopic escape from the power of the state and the normative function of the law, the novel reveals the extent to which sexual politics fail because of the subject's profound attachment to the law. While on the surface the characters appear to escape the letter closet by overturning the dynamic of shame inherent in confession examined in previous chapters, their outrageous expressions of sexuality reveal that the majority of them continue to function under concepts of homosexuality inherited from the Franco period.

Although the only explicit mention of anarchism is found in the title, the novel establishes an implicit parallel between the sexual and cultural politics of the anarchist movement of the 1920s and '30s prior to the Spanish civil war and the political circumstances of gays and lesbians during the transition to democracy. It is widely held that the fascist victory in the civil war spelled the virtual end of Spanish anarchism as a viable political force: the war exacerbated the differences between the anarchists, whose intention was to overthrow political structures, and the socialists and communists, whose goal was to form a popular front in opposition to fascism. The regime's Civil Guard attempted to eliminate the last vestiges of anarchism—the Juventudes Libertarias (Libertarian Youths) in Barcelona (Velázquez and Memba 33). Nevertheless, anarchism's continued existence—internally in Spain and in exile—throughout the Franco period played a significant role in the shifting terrain of sexual politics and youth culture during the early years of the transition to democracy. In the postwar years, the Spanish anarchist movement remained internally divided and practically paralyzed, in particular due to the exile of many of its members. Given the exiled position of the protagonist of *L'anarquista nu,* it is important to understand that anarchism never quite died but instead remained in exile. The movement evolved during that period, at times reinforcing the original positions of attempting insurrections from within the nation against the dictatorship, at others suffering from internal divisions and languishing abroad. In the 1970s the anarchist movement underwent an evolution, manifested most saliently in the organization of the Iberian Liberation Movement (Movimiento Ibérico de Liberación, or MIL). The MIL advocated violent revolution and departed from the classic definition of anarchism in order to align itself with some Marxist revolutionaries in a common battle against the dictator and capitalism (Alberola and Gransac 313). In particular, the 1974 execution of one of the members of the MIL, Salvador Puig Antich, a young Catalan anarchist, which resulted in public demonstrations to denounce the Franco regime, underscored the struggle between totalitarian forces and the anarchist revolution that continued to the very end of the dictatorship.

The execution of Puig Antich was the symptom of a revival of anarchism between 1974 and 1977. A burgeoning youth culture, influenced by members of the Generation of 1968 and well versed in the rhetoric of the sixties, turned to anarchism as a revolutionary platform for individual emancipation. The working class and the veteran leftist radicals were distrustful of the rebellious younger generation, and the latter favored rebellion and individualism in the face of the authoritarianism of some Marxist quarters. José Luis Velázquez and Javier Memba have recently argued that the anarchist youth culture had little place within the older frameworks of the radical left. The leftist groups saw the anarchist youths' interest in individual freedom as a form of bourgeois ideological contamination. In particular, listening to English punk rock music, wearing jeans and having long hair, smoking joints or being homosexual—all of which were associated with anarchist youth—were considered by leftist organizations as symptomatic of liberalism and bourgeoisification (66).

As Velázquez and Memba note, the revolutionary fever that had erstwhile dominated leftist politics soon ended. The death of Franco did not produce a revolutionary break with the Francoist political machinery but rather a politics of consensus between the moderate leftist groups—the PSOE and Partido Comunista Español (Spanish Communist Party, or PCE) primarily—and the former Francoist politicians. Not unlike the political situation during the civil war, in the initial years of the post-Franco era reformism prevailed over revolution: the struggle between the left and the right during the early years of the transition to democracy—a tug of war between *ruptura* and *reforma*—forced both the right and the left to assume a politics of consensus. Hence, the negotiated break with the past, or *la ruptura pactada,* as the agreement between the left and the right was known after the Moncloa Pacts, in which both sides shared power and responsibility for overturning the Francoist policies as a way to ameliorate the differences between them and secure their place in the fledgling democracy, left little space for anarchist thought. Significantly, Velázquez and Memba argue that the outlet for the energetic youth culture that had embraced anarchism as an individualist ideology was the sudden explosion of nightlife and countercultural practices that dominated Spain in the late 1970s and early '80s. In other words, one could argue that the politics of consensus that dominated these early years inadvertently reinforced normative concepts of sexuality ultimately rooted in Francoism. Hence, as a reaction against the disillusionment with politics, or *desencanto,* produced by *la ruptura pactada,* youth culture embraced the rhetoric of "sex, drugs, and rock 'n' roll" in urban centers, thereby garnering the sexual and cultural freedom they did not perceive themselves to have within official leftist politics. In short, anarchist politics became anarchic culture.

This history is never explicitly evoked in the novel. Reducing it to a narrative backdrop, *L'anarquista nu* draws from the cultural climate around leftist politics during this period in order to transform the utopian model of revolutionary action into a postmodern *anarchy* of chaos and confusion, delight and debauchery. "Anarchism" in this sense takes on a colloquial notion of a lack of order in which the vision of solidarity for social organization is, like Aureli, all too absent. Two concepts of anarchism are thus intimately intertwined in the text: one utopian, the other postmodern, in which the latter is portrayed as a "degenerate" version of the former. In particular, a hyperbolic, if not parodic, femininity and camp are the vehicles used to communicate this postmodern vision. Most of the letters are written by gay men, others by drag queens and transsexuals (Pipi Iaguer, for example, is a brash gay man who works as a transvestite call girl), yet almost all the letter writers' signatures are in the feminine as a form of linguistic drag.

This "degenerate" version of anarchism also figures saliently in the structure of the novel and the conventions of the epistolary genre. The formal use of letter writing, as a mode of self-disclosure and intimacy, reveals a world that had previously been denied any voice. The voices that emerge in these letters are, with some exceptions, far less equivocal about their sexuality than the protagonists of Villena's *Amor pasión* and Riera's "Jo pos per testimoni les gavines." The letter form allows each character to compose and construct reality from his or her point of view, providing intimate details not otherwise accessible to the reader. At the same time, the use of the letter form in Fernàndez's text disrupts a coherent notion of narrativity. In contrast with the back-and-forth correspondence of multiple voices in epistolary novels such as *Clarissa* and *Les liaisons dangereuses*, *L'anarquista nu* shows an astonishing lack of correspondence between the letter writers. Consequently, there is hardly a plot, the letters recount loosely narrated adventures, and the relationships between the various characters are difficult if not impossible to reconstruct. The epistolary genre traditionally places a heavy burden on the subjective representation of protagonists, whose personalities are often developed in their letter writing, but the absence of Aureli's letters means that he has little to no substance as a character; the only information about him must be culled from his interlocutors' correspondence. In this sense, Aureli functions simply as the absent knot that binds together all of the other characters' letter writing. The collection of letters and other fragments of writing functions as a mélange of texts that can only allude to a full narrative form that will never be reconstructed. As Lev rightly argues, Fernàndez undermines any sense of narrative authority since the novelistic center is a "void or tear" ("Redressing" 265–66). As a postmodern mode of writing, heteroglossic epistolarity becomes a form of anarchy itself, with a cacophony of voices proclaiming sexual freedom.

Letter novels are indexes on a formal level of the fractured solidarity that defines human relations on a social level. The modern epistolary mode generally denotes a private missive addressed to another person in a supposedly intimate, personal space of communication. However, writers have also drawn on the letter's capacity to communicate over distance as a means of initiating a political critique. As Mary Favret argues in an illuminating analysis of the political use of the letter by Romantic women writers, "Fictions of correspondence began to color political discourse itself. The genre of the familiar epistle, from its roots in classical rhetoric, had emerged at the end of the century as the medium of collective political activity" (30). The canonical concept of epistolary fiction has tended to emphasize the use of the sentimental letter. While works such as Richardson's *Clarissa,* Rousseau's *Julie,* and Goethe's *The Sorrows of Young Werther* are generally called to mind, other works of the eighteenth century often deployed letters in the service of social and political critique. For example, Montesquieu's *Lettres persanes* (*Persian Letters,* 1721) or José Cadalso's *Cartas marruecas* (Morrocan Letters, 1789) diverge from the canon of the amorous or intimate missive by employing the epistolary mode for moral or political purposes.[12]

Even within the genre of sentimental epistolary fiction, works such as Laclos's *Les liaisons dangereuses* oscillate between both uses of the letter. The corrupt manipulations of Valmont and Merteuil and their eventual destruction—Valmont's death in a duel with Danceny, Merteuil's social ostracism and physical disfigurement due to the publication of her letters—can be read as a commentary on the political corruption of Louis XVI's court (Favret 36). The rape of Clarissa Harlowe is also not without its political dimension. Terry Eagleton has argued that her sexual violation at the hands of Lovelace, which leads to her death, remains intimately linked to form: in *Clarissa,* the very act of writing is a dangerous enterprise that opens the protagonist to charges of inappropriate behavior. In short, the very act of opening herself to Lovelace by letting him read her letters and write to her becomes symbolic of the sexual act itself. Clarissa, the naïve reader who has believed in the transparency of language and the sincerity of intentions, uses her death to make a political statement about gender and power. Eagleton argues that "the public nature of Clarissa's death is the whole point: her dying is in a profound sense a political gesture, a shocking, surreal act of resignation from a society whose power system she has seen in part for what it is" (74).

In this respect, *L'anarquista nu* is closer to works that employ the sentimental and confessional letter forms but whose content moves beyond the individual to the political sphere. Whether the characters refer directly to the shifting terrain of national politics or to the private space of sexual encounters, the combined effect of their correspondence is the articulation of a political message. The postmodern anarchist platform of sexual emancipation recounted in the letter writers' epistolary correspondence invariably alludes to the history of sexual liberation in anarchistic thought, although no explicit reference is ever made. In the 1920s and '30s, Spanish anarchists established a more detailed agenda designed to overturn structures of power such as the Catholic Church and to establish a mode of society free from the constraints of capitalism and the state. Part of their emphasis on altering norms lay in confronting reigning dogma on sexuality. In terms of sexual freedom, anarchism promoted its own brand of ethics beyond bourgeois moral values—abolishing church weddings, legalizing abortion, and so forth. Anarchists involved in this intellectual project promoted open discussion of sexuality in order to remove the veil of silence and oppressive morality that has traditionally marked the topic in Spain. For some anarchists, the principle of self-improvement included sexual liberation as a significant component of revolutionary social reform. Anarchists such as Federica Montseny, who as minister of health legalized abortion in 1936, promoted sexuality freed from procreation and religious orthodoxy. For others, however, anarchism endorsed traditional views on gender roles, and heterosexuality was the only legitimate form of sexual orientation. One of the chief advocates of sexual liberation associated with anarchism, Félix Martí Ibáñez, described sexuality as "that manifestation of life that tends to perpetuate the human race through the use of the voluptuous union of two members of the opposite sex" (Nash 292). His heterosexism is most apparent in his frank discussions of homosexuality, which ultimately advocate the eradication of homosexual desire altogether (Cleminson 98). Furthermore, the topic of sexuality and liberation did not play a central a role in the strategies for a social revolution. Mary Nash has argued that those Spanish anarchists who dedicated themselves to reforming sexual norms were a peripheral minority, never fully integrated into the main core of the anarchist movement (289).

In spite of anarchism's heterosexism, its emphasis on individual freedom in the face of state oppression clearly resonates with the emancipatory desires of Spanish gays and lesbians in the 1970s. Fernàndez's novel implicitly evokes the programs being developed in the early post-Franco years, as most of the letters in the novel portray homosexuality in a liberationist rhetoric; an emphasis on sexual emancipation is directly addressed on a political level in several manifestos embedded in the letters. The novel's publication follows on the heels of gay liberationist statements that began to appear in 1977, most notably the FAGC Manifesto that situated revolutionary action within a post-Marxist model. In 1975, for example, the Movimiento Español de Liberación Homosexual (Spanish Homosexual Liberation Movement), originally named Agrupación Homófila para la Igualdad Sexual (Homophile Group for Sexual Equality), which appeared in 1972 in Barcelona, changed names again to become the FAGC and aligned itself with the Front d'Alliberament Homosexual del País Valencià (Homosexual Liberation Front of Valencia, or FAHPV) and the Front d'Alliberament Gai de les Illes (Gay Liberation Front of the [Balearic] Islands, or FAGI) in order to produce the basic platform of what would become the 1977 Manifesto. Gay and lesbian emancipation first emerges in Catalonia, then it quickly extends to Madrid, where the Frente Homosexual de Acción Revolucionaria (Homosexual Revolutionary Action Front) disseminated a manifesto against the Law of Social Dangers in April 1977, which was signed by various organizations, including the Frente de Liberación de la Mujer (Women's Liberation Front) and the Confederación Nacional del Trabajo (National Confederation of Labor, or CNT).

Fernàndez's novelistic depiction of manifestos thus invokes implicitly the emancipatory programs being developed in the early post-Franco years and parodies the ties these would share with the strong revival of nationalism. The alliances being formed between emerging gay and lesbian organizations such as the FAGC, FAHPV, and the FAGI were a fundamental part of a larger process of democratic change linked to nationalism. Indeed, in the early 1980s, organizations such as Nacionalistes d'Esquerra (Nationalists of the Left), Partit dels Socialistes de

Catalunya (Socialist Party of Catalonia, or PSC), and Partit Socialista Unificat de Catalunya (United Socialist Party of Catalonia, or PSUC) published a series of manifestos or programmatic statements in support of gay liberation as part of a broader nationalist platform (Mirabet i Mullol, *Homosexualitat avui* 344–51). For example, the 1982 "Programa de l'Assemblea de Gais de Nacionalistes d'Esquerra" states "this gay movement is coordinated with the members of the Catalan Countries, as a front to fight for a triple liberation [from legal, ideological, and social oppression]" (Mirabet i Mullol 348). Although prior to these events, the novel anticipates the link between sexual politics and nationalism. Early in the novel, an orgy is held at El Puig, symbolic of Valencian nationalism as the site from which King Jaume I launched the attack to take control of Valencia during the Christian reconquest. The characters engage in a wild night of sex and drinking, with a dose of camped-up liberationist rhetoric and a "cha-cha-cha" version of "Els segadors," the Catalonian national hymn. At the end of the evening, Lulú relates to Aureli that one of the participants, whose name F.A.C. may be an ironic twist on the FAGC, proclaimed: "'Beloved queens from all parts of Valencia . . . Fellowship makes for strength, a strength delicate and divine. Gathered together like this our strength exceeds that of the air force . . . indeed we are,' (She actually said this.) 'a giant aerodynamic plume conquering the frontiers of liberty'" (51).[13] Lulú writes Aureli with a sense of fulfillment and accomplishment that their sexual excess was the sign of an emancipation from the past: "Half dead we rolled out of the grand mansion, assured that we had won a war—and if not a war an important strategic battle" (51).[14]

Yet nationalism, like the concrete history of anarchism, also takes a back seat to the general discourse of sexual liberation. The most notable manifesto is composed by Eugeni in which he advocates an anarchism sui generis that extols the potential of sexual excess to disrupt social norms. Utopic in tone, the text begins with a condemnation of reason's repressive capacity and of the value of "excess" in all its myriad forms to subvert the status quo: "Shouldn't we make of our bodies living manifestos of sexual fulfilment—manifestos which would flaunt themselves daily, brazen 'banners' of erotic exuberance?" (59).[15] Attacking conformity with chaos, Eugeni promotes an anarchist platform of total destruction of norms; Josep-Anton Fernàndez writes, "he is commited to the destruction of all morals and to the activation of a perpetual disruption" (152). The construction of bourgeois culture as a capitalist commodity fuels his belief that only by visibly displaying homosexuality, imposing it as an "enlightened" state, can true political revolution take place. Weaving between reason and chaos, simulacrum and repression, Eugeni's manifesto advocates the use of sex as a form of weapon and promotes promiscuity in order to wreak havoc. Sex, reduced to penetration, becomes a mechanical act for Eugeni designed to shatter the subject in the passive position, a strategy strikingly similar to arguments made by the French author Guy Hocquenghem. Writing in the aftermath of 1968 and drawing from Deleuze and Guatarri's *Anti-Oedipus*, Hocquenghem argues that homosexuality is decidedly radical in its disturbance of the social sphere, through the introduction of desire as a form of "schizophrenic pick-up machine" (131). Hocquenghem sees the revolutionary value of desire for its destructive, *anarchic* power to disrupt civilization. He does not promote an integration into society or a justification of homosexual desire but rather a "dissolution of the human." Forging a similar path, Eugeni's technological use of the body leads him and several others to attack gay men who are closeted in daily life in order to prove his theories. Fashioning themselves as "urban guerillas," Eugeni and his followers kill their victims with electric dildos in a brutal act of high-voltage anal sex, a new form of the infamous anarchist "propaganda by deed."

Nevertheless, Eugeni's *mise en practice* of his theories certainly questions the *practical* validity of his "anarchist" vision. By "practice" I do not mean to suggest that what he relates actually takes place in the novel, for these episodes may well be a fantasy. Nonetheless, fantasy from a psychoanalytic perspective is not opposed to reality but, rather, an indication of how we desire. It is precisely Eugeni's theory of desire and sexuality—not whether he actually performs it—that concerns us here; the fact that he ends up hospitalized and eventually dies suggests that perhaps his actions did take place. Whether fantasy or reality, imagined or enacted, in the end he reinforces the dynamics of male dominance over an avowedly "weaker" figure: the freedom that he offers becomes an imperative enforced through violence. Eugeni plays "top" to the "bottom" position of his victims, paradoxically reproducing the top-down authoritarianism that his practice attempts to dismantle. The bodily boundaries that are seen as the embodiment of normativity are disrupted only through the imposition of a violent penetration. Eugeni, in penetrating his victims as a liberatory gesture, experiences not only sexual pleasure but a pleasure associated with domination, showing his own allegiance to the prohibitive power of the law. In a similar vein, Lulú later discusses the police rape of gays who have been imprisoned and how the officers take pleasure from the act even as they remain unstigmatized as homosexuals—the active, penetrating male is still perceived as heterosexual. In both Eugeni's manifesto and Lulú's anecdote, penetration becomes a sign of complicity with the law. Those in the passive position necessarily desire the active, penetrating role of the law. Given this argument, it is not surprising that Lulú's objection to police rape is not leveled at the act of rape itself but at the lack of consideration in not using a proper lubricant: it is the physical pain, not the dynamics of power, that bothers him, and hence the oppressive force is left unquestioned.

It is important to clarify at this point that two notions of "law" are operative here: a juridical concept in which the law functions as an interdiction or a proscriptive device, and a symbolic concept in which the law is a signifier that mediates any given individual's relationship to subjectivity. If the law as a juridical domain is a discursive construction that functions by prohibition, the law as a symbolic construction is perhaps best understood in psychic terms and functions by repression. While they may work in tandem, it is crucial not to conflate them. The legal interdiction of homosexuality and the symbolic prohibitions that structure desire are not wholly commensurate. Social forces and psychic repression are essentially contingent. In other words, the legal prohibition of homosexuality cannot be collapsed with its symbolic construction as a negated or disavowed form of desire. Hence, the elimination of legal repression is not tantamount to a psychic liberation, which, in the first volume of *The History of Sexuality,* is precisely what Foucault critiqued in certain strands of psychoanalysis in. Foucault argued against the notion that social suppression necessarily produced psychic repression in a unilateral, causal manner. This "hydraulic" model proposed by

Wilhelm Reich and Herbert Marcuse claimed that if the political circumstances were altered, then sexual oppression itself would cease to
exist (Lane, *Burdens* 4, 15). Political liberation would beget sexual freedom. While Foucault's purpose was to understand the function of power
as both prohibitive and productive, producing resistance to itself through
injunction, Lacan too drew a sharp distinction between symbolic law
and political law.[16] For Lacan, the political law functions on prohibition
in order to regulate desire while symbolic law creates desire by denying the very object that would complete the subject: the gap between
the subject and the object produces desire. Thus, regardless of historical or political context, psychic repression occurs even without the legal
suppression of certain forms of desire.

It is precisely the gap between political law and symbolic law—
their simultaneous imbrication and disjunction—that the epistolary
form articulates in this text: the relationship to the political sphere,
while mediated through the juridical construction of homosexuality, is
fundamentally predicated on psychic structures of desire. Herein lies the
fundamental paradox of anarchy rendered "nude" of its transgressive
clothing. Slavoj Žižek has argued that enjoyment only comes as a result
of the law, that enjoyment itself is something imposed: "when we enjoy,
we never do it spontaneously, we always follow a certain injunction.
The psychoanalytic name for this injunction, this imperative to 'Enjoy!'
is Superego" (*For They Know Not* 9–10). In *Totem and Taboo* Freud argued
that there were two fathers—one who enjoyed without prohibition and
the other who is the figure of prohibition. The latter father has come
to be associated with the law, the Name of the Father, while the former resides as the necessary supplement to that prohibition: the prohibition depends conceptually upon the potential for total pleasure. This
conceptual dilemma is more fully developed in Lacan's "Kant avec
Sade," where he argues that the ethical demand of the Kantian subject
finds its counterpart in the transgressive pleasure marked by crossing
the law in Sade. The prohibition of desire produces desire as an imperative. Sade, who advocates enjoyment without limitation, is thus held
by the injunction "Enjoy!": "You must experience pleasure!" Sade raises
pleasure to the level of a categorical imperative: he is the object of the
other's desire, jouissance for the other, always subject to the demand

of pleasure. Anarchism, in the sexual revolutionary guise adopted by Eugeni, becomes a Sadean categorical imperative united to the prohibitive imperative installed by Franco. As a result, the elimination of the law qua interdiction does not necessarily overturn the law qua symbolic injunction to desire.

In addition, Eugeni's version of anarchism brings to the fore several ambiguities of traditional anarchist thought. While anarchism bases its belief in violent revolution—though Kropotkin would move away from Bakunin's emphasis on violence—in order to produce a new social order, it has often been asked how that new order would emerge from the violence in which it was born. Although one could argue that the violence of revolution would produce a solidarity that might survive beyond its limited temporal scope, that solidarity would no doubt be of a different nature. Yet it is what we might call, after Lacan, the "Sadean" dimension of anarchist thought—the limit, as it were, of anarchism—that Eugeni exposes. The absolute adherence to individual freedom and the goal of social solidarity has long been a sticking point for anarchism. Eugeni's own story reveals a paradox underlying anarchism: the protection of the place of power so that no government may occupy its position is already the occupation of that place of power. The anarchist revolution is premised on the fundamental paradox that the implantation and consolidation of anarchism as a utopian community founded on self-governing solidarity depends on a locus of power whose purpose is to guarantee individual agency. Anarchism may not have advocated unabashed individualism with no restraint—a higher moral order was supposed to eliminate the need for state institutions and laws—yet that element consistently returned as a weak link. As Pere Joan i Tous writes: "Anarchism could not accommodate a Sadean discourse. It could not for obvious reasons, since it would have been necessary to remove its pathological charge" (174). Indeed, Bakunin struggled to negate the jouissance of violence that revolution would unleash: "unbridle that popular anarchy . . . let it loose in all its breadth, so that it may flow like a furious lava, scorching and destroying everything in its path . . . I know that this is a dangerous and barbarous way . . . but without it there is no salvation" (Thomas 289–90). Unfortunately, the revolutionary pretense of violence in Bakunin's thought simply inverted the dynamics of power without altering them fundamentally, or at least dismissed that question altogether by claiming that such pleasure in insurrection would cease after the revolution.[17]

While the revolutionary potential of sexual anarchy is questioned, its pitfalls are not corrected by another form of organized revolution. For all of the differences between anarchism and Marxism—the former negating all forms of state-controlled government, the latter advocating government as a necessary step to communism—neither is safe from the novel's acrid critique: the emancipation of desire is always expressed in relation to the law such that the law itself is never overturned. At the time of the novel's publication, Marxism in Spain was already undergoing a crisis. The aforementioned Moncloa Pacts in 1977 initiated a widespread disenchantment with revolutionary politics, and in 1979 the PSOE, under pressure from Felipe González, decided to no longer designate itself as a Marxist party (Lewis 181). Santiago Carrillo's support of the Pacts, with consulting members of the PCE, led to alienation and fragmentation in the party's ranks; in Valencia, the PCE, which only appeared there near the end of 1975, changed its name to the Partit Comunista del País Valencià (Valencia Communist Party, or PCPV). Written in this historical milieu, *L'anarquista nu* is highly ambivalent about Marxism. In the novel, Matilde Belda rejects Marxism as a viable platform and begins to circulate a manuscript called *Cómo casarse con un proletario* (How to Marry a Proletarian), an anthropological study of the gay urban world in Valencia based on all of the characters of the novel, in which he claims that homosexuals really desire a mild dictatorial regime of moderate fascism. In an ironic rewriting of the famous Francoist slogan, Belda is quoted as saying that homosexuals have never been treated better than under the dictator's regime (28). The power of the Francoist regime to oppress homosexuals also galvanized them in some ways, without leading to the overt politicization that Belda eschews; Aliaga argues, for example, that the Law of Social Dangers can be seen as the motivating force for gay liberation ("Como hemos cambiado" 30). Rosita la Patética reiterates this argument in another letter: "And now the pressure's on with all these democratic and liberal airs and graces we've come to adopt—I mean this fashionable cause of wanting to free ourselves from our condition as an exploited sexual

minority. The more I think about it, the more I think us queens were
better off under Franco. You'll be thinking what a cliché: 'We were
better off under Franco'" (172).[18] Belda's reactionary perspective sees
activism, "left-wing ideologues," and the overt politicization of homosexual desire as the true sources of exploitation. Citing the case of Cuba
and the Soviet Union, he claims that a Marxist revolution would only
oppress homosexuals even more (28).[19] Rather than take up the gaunt-
let of "Communist guerrilladom," he prefers to conform to power,
to accept the space of subjectivity offered by the regime; at one point,
Belda is referred to as "Franco's heroine" ("heroïna de Franco") (29).
In other words, Belda's critique of Marxist discourses is not directed
exclusively at Marxism but rather at the appropriation of Marxist tenets
in the emancipatory programs promulgated by such groups as the
FAGC. The impulse to activism and politics demanded by such groups
becomes, for Belda, indicative of how they too are in the final analysis
similarly authoritarian in their actions.

Matilde's theory is the most transparent example of how Marxism is
portrayed in the novel as a discourse that cannot fully attain its revolutionary program. But the novel's critique of Marxism is not directed
solely at the perceived weakness in its theoretical underpinnings. Part
of the problem lies with the characters' ignorance of Marxism itself.
The novel's portrayal of these characters' lack of awareness of their subjection implies that they might benefit from an awareness of Marxist
theory, as in the following example. Lulú, recounting "her" friend La
Bolchevique's purchase of *Capital,* says that "Carlos March was the
author, or someone like that" ("d'un tal Carlos March") (192), and his
description of the book reveals his ignorance of Marxism: he wonders
whether it might be nothing more than a cheap photo-novel anthology. Parodied and practically ignored, Marxism is ironically reduced
to a textual product—a book—that is reinscribed within a capitalist
system of commodity exchange. The irony is, of course, lost on La
Bolchevique, who does not even understand the pseudonym that he
dons. Moreover, the irony is compounded when he loses his money and
jewelry to a boyfriend, who deserts him, and he spends his time in a
peripatetic movement from bar to bar in search of another lover. Their
positions reversed—La Bolchevique occupying the bourgeois position

and his lover now the proletariat who "revolts"—he rejects Marxism altogether by refusing to read Marx and replaces his moniker with the name "la Bien Pagá" (evoking a camp version of the famous *bolero*). He takes on a younger man as his new lover, because "she says their distribution of labour is more equitable, nights being the time when he recharges her batteries . . . at a price!" (194, trans. mod.).[20] His revolutionary pretenses are empty as his new role as "sugar daddy" places him squarely in a capitalist economy in which he pays for sex.[21]

Against the revolutionary strategies of anarchism and Marxism, other characters in *L'anarquista nu* espouse the gender-bending performativity that dominated Anglo-American queer theory in the 1990s. Various forms of crossing gender—camp, drag, and transsexuality—are promoted in the novel as truly emancipatory gestures in which subjects can perform themselves out of subjection. The anarchist emphasis on individualism and the ascetic practice of self-improvement through will power finds its maximum expression in the possibility of radically altering one's own body: transsexualism is offered as the ultimate mode of liberation. While some characters change names and clothing, others change their bodies through sex-reassignment surgery. The vision of transgenderism portrayed in the novel is radically voluntaristic—an anarchist will to power, as it were—in that the individual is deemed to have absolute control over the body: the ultimate challenge to subjection would be the freedom to alter one's own body to become the other gender. This conceptualization of transgenderism opens itself up to various critiques made by psychoanalysis, chiefly, that the utopian notion of transgenderism is blind to the continued effects of sexual difference. While certainly not all transgendered subjects are guilty of such a claim, in *L'anarquista nu* the sex-change operation is portrayed as a utopic escape from the oppressive confines of gender. The belief that escaping the limitations of gender will in fact allow for true emancipation motivates Carles Besada to claim, referring to Àcrata Lys's and Anarquia Gadé's transitions before the sex-change operation, that transsexualism is "the only democratic option" ("l'única opció democràtica") (86). For Besada, transsexualism can give homosexuals what revolution cannot: individual agency for profound change. True revolution, he claims, would need to encompass gender, civil liberties, race, creed, and the rights of children to vote and choose their own sex, however improbable such a revolution might be. Control of sexual difference becomes the ultimate sign of individual agency: choosing one's sex denotes the final freedom from the dictates of the law.

In her reading, Lev underscores the subversive dimension of Fernàndez's portrayal of camp that upholds the right to pursue the gender identity that provides the subject with pleasure and meaning (270). At the same time, she acknowledges the limits of personal agency, that the granting of freedom to choose one's gender as a subversive democratic gesture does not guarantee that the very same gender norms will not be reiterated. Such is the case in *L'anarquista nu,* as transsexuality as a sign of "profound" change brings with it its own score of problems. Being a woman is reduced to the literal construction of the body. Àcrata writes: "You should see us now: our breasts bulge with their silicon implants—topless showgirls at last!—and we've a darling vagina each!" (187).[22] For while Àcrata and Anarquia fly to New York for their operation and to attend talks about transsexualism and class struggle, their vision of femininity is reduced to the *erotic* roles they may play as "women": "There's no stopping me as I flirt with myself, play the seductress, the exhibitionist, the courtesan, the impatient virgin. What fun it is, too, to play with my fanny and feel its feminine, rounded contours," writes Àcrata in a letter to Aureli (187).[23] Back in Valencia, they use their newly operated bodies to attend a presentation of literary awards with the sole purpose of securing a boyfriend; Anarquia provides a glimpse of her silicon phenomena, as she calls her breasts, to the delight of onlookers. The performance of the technologically enhanced Anarquia and Àcrata is presented as nothing more than surface, artifice, and vapid play. Their transformations do not lead to a new concept of transgendered subjectivity that would move between heterosexuality and homosexuality, masculinity and femininity, but instead they reproduce heterosexual relations in the form of clichéd gender roles such as "the seductress," "the exhibitionist," and "the courtesan." Like the other manifestos offered in *L'anarquista nu,* the utopian vision of transsexualism as a symbol of individual agency, in the guise of absolute control over the material body, can do little more than reproduce the norms it purports to displace. While one could certainly claim that this alone constitutes a modification of the system of gender and sexual norms, the lack of any consciousness on the part of Anarquia and Àcrata underscores the emptiness of their earlier claims to revolution.[24] The transsexual discourse offered herein transforms male homosexuals into copies of heterosexual women.

The gender inversions simply reinforce the idea that crossing and transgression do not alone constitute any subversion of the law, a point convincingly argued by Josep-Anton Fernàndez in his reading of the novel (139). To offer a final example, a small manifesto edited by the "Collective of feminist queens without vagina or clitoris" ("Col•lectiu de marietes feministes sense figa ni galló") and espoused by Matilde establishes the privilege of gay men as sexual objects for heterosexual men: "Faggots will be the true women of the race, a fact which, in any case, is ratified by history" (138).[25] In general, the characters in L'anarquista nu, in spite of their pleasurable insurrections, remain decidedly unaware (at least initially) of their subjection, of their repetition of norms that do little to alter their symbolic position. Their delirous sexual dissidence—either in radical sexual practices (Eugeni) or through transsexual surgeries (Àcrata and Anarquia)—only reaffirms their attachment to a prior set of norms that structure identity, devoid of any awareness of the complicity that such actions can invariably produce. In other words, the characters evince what Judith Butler has called a "passionate attachment" to power. For Butler, who follows the lead of Jacqueline Rose, there is an indissoluble tension between the unconscious as a product of power and the unconscious as an excess that would allow for a resistance to power. While the subject may exceed its discursive injunction, the unconscious is not necessarily a source of agency for resistance. As in her previous work on performativity, Butler still maintains a lingering optimism in the possibility that the terms by which discourses of identity operate may be resignified (Psychic Life 105). But she is less optimistic about a resistance to power and to the normalization that such subjection entails. Drawing on Freud, she argues that the subject is produced by power in such a way that the subject forms an attachment to subjection, desiring the very power that confers the subject an identity. To put it another way, we suffer from "passionate attachments" to power. In the end, Butler argues that the unconscious is not outside power but is rather "something like the unconscious of power itself" (104). This attachment to subjection—an attachment that is not at the conscious level of the ego but in the unconscious—is crucial for understanding why the mere exposure of the ideological forces behind homophobic discourses is not always sufficient to alter our relationships to those forces. In Fernàndez's text, pleasurable insurrections constitute minor skirmishes, not a sexual revolution that would fundamentally alter the very terms through which subjectivity is produced.

While the novel exposes the limitations of revolutionary solidarity within the individual letters, their compilation and collective publication suggests the search for an altogether different model for politics, one based on intimacy and community. Indeed, the exclusive focus on the sexual and political content of the letters runs the risk of occluding the importance of the letter form itself. The novel's use of the letter for political reflection pointedly suggests the limitations of an identity politics based on individual expression: the use of the epistolary form to break the silence of gay oppression under Franco gives voice not to liberation but to liberation's failures. Fernàndez's deployment of epistolarity—to underscore both the interconnectedness of these characters and their separation and distance—laments the loss of a cohesive community, one whose dispersal is rendered transparent through the exiled figure of Aureli. Anarchism can quickly fall into individualism, and perhaps no written form is better equipped to represent this individualism than the epistolary genre: each letter, representing a single voice, stands apart from the other letters even though they are collectively bound in a single volume. The novel's composition is based on the premise of an impossibility: the impossibility of political revolution is reflected on a structural level by the impossibility of the correspondence being reunited. "Community" and "solidarity" are perhaps inextricable terms. A community cannot be said to exist without some sense of solidarity. But the anarchistic sense of the word "solidarity" is not necessarily limited to a set of common interests that maintain group cohesion. As Crowder notes, what solidarity is and how to maintain it after the revolution is somewhat unclear in anarchist writings (154–55). While these characters constitute a loose community insofar as they share a solidarity based on sexuality, this solidarity is not of a political nature. The absence of community among the letter writers of Valencia's gay subculture is thus reflected in the novel's epistolary form as a collection of letters that remains linked by the absence of their shared interlocutor, Aureli.

In this respect, it is not insignificant that the identity of the editor of these letters—the person responsible for uniting them into a coherent whole—remains a mystery. Although the reader may presume it is Aureli, since they all were mailed to him, the inclusion of a telegram about his death and letters that were mailed after his death calls into question this assumption. In the end, there is no identifiable thread that logically binds these letters into a unified collection. The organization of these texts into a single text by an unseen and unidentified hand reflects on a formal level the novel's critique of subjectivity. The unseen force that binds the letters together is not an editor nor the addressee of the letters. It is rather that which remains outside the purview of the reality constructed in the letters—the *hors-texte* of these textual fragments—and thus beyond their knowledge. The binding force is, like the law that governs their desire, the law to which they remain passionately attached, beyond their control—a postal force whose ideological value rests precisely in the fact that its absence may go unnoticed by the reader. As such, the epistolary form exposes the political dimension of psychic attachments that structure our relationship to desire. It suggests that what makes a community is not only the law in juridical terms—the regulations and norms that explicitly govern, police, enforce, and punish certain types of behavior—but also the psychic dimension of subjectivity.

The need for intimacy and connection surfaces in the novel as a more melancholic tone invades the letters. The multiple mentions of cancer and death increase toward the end of the novel, and the various relationships developed begin to dissolve, forcing the characters to reflect on their quotidian affairs. Epistolarity, reflecting this dissolution of human connection and communication, becomes a failure, and letters suddenly become *dead letters:* Lulú's final letters never reach Aureli, and the telegram that serves as notice of Aureli's death never reaches Lulú, at least not within the temporal frame of the novel. When Lulú questions Aureli's silence in his final letters—a desperate call for an impossible response—this is little more than a vain cry of despair at the demise of the epistolary chain that has united them. The system of correspondence is fractured, yet the cause remains unknown. The author cannot communicate his own death in a letter; the silence of not corresponding is a form of death that cannot be corroborated except by a third person or information from another source. Of course, Aureli has been absent all along, virtually dead—at least, to the external reader. Lulú Bon's lack of awareness of Aureli's death takes on allegorical proportions as a failure to see that anarchism itself has died as a viable form of revolutionary thought—not because anarchism itself has failed, true as that may be, but because these characters lack sufficient awareness of their subjection to attempt to institute any fundamental change in social structures. Instead, the novel as a whole is composed of letters that do not conjure the image of a community or a revolutionary collective with political faith in change. Moreover, the epistolary disconnection underscores the effect of radical individualism that separates and distances these characters. As Thomas puts it: "Anarchism is not the solution to alienation but the maximization of a certain kind of alienation—alienation from the future prospect of genuine community" (350).

The failure of communication reveals the cracks in the edifice of their community, a disconnection that is likewise reflected in their failed search for love. Their failure to find love is the most significant index of their growing consciousness about their subjection to normative constructions of homosexuality. An unnamed letter writer, known only as a "stranger," sends Aureli letters sporadically. In them, he laments the failure of their relationship: "No encounter is more tragic than the romantic kind. I can tell you I had got myself into a right mess falling in love. My tacit links with *normality* were destroyed" (99).[26] Carles Besada engages in a series of encounters with the mysterious Àngel Donat (the reader only knows that his father has died and that he uses people to obtain money), who also associates with Loli "La Carajillo" and Lulú Bon. Near the end of the novel, Àngel becomes the figure who would seemingly provide everyone with love. Unfortunately, he always disappears at the last moment, passing as he does in the narrative from Carles to Loli and finally to Lulú. Lulú's account of his relationship underscores most clearly that Àngel represents the recuperation of love:

"This feeling of being in love has done me a power of good . . . I feel
as if I've recovered the love that until now I thought I had lost irrevocably on that fateful day you left for Amsterdam" (217).[27] By now,
however, the reader has learned to anticipate that the newly discovered
love will soon turn sour: two letters later, the final letter of the novel,
Àngel commits suicide, an act that leaves Lulú burdened with the belief
that his own actions provoked Àngel's self-imposed death.

Not only in the lives of these characters are love and sentimentality
mere mirages in an urban desert but fantasy also fails as a safety valve
for liberation. Vicent Montsomni writes a series of letters in which he
fantasizes about a straight married man who takes him on as his lover.
The fantasy quickly turns into a nightmare, however, as the fantasy wife
reasserts herself within the narrative and reclaims her husband. While
the virtual world of fantasy offers a utopian escape from reality, the
structures of domination are replicated within that fantasy world. In
the end, love becomes an impossibility since it can only be conceived
as a relationship of desire with the stereotypically masculine "straight"
male, in which gay men and women desire from the same position of
"insufficiency": "we [faggots and women] are not self-sufficient. Tragic
as it may be, we yearn for submission, slavery, the masterful domination
of an unbridled male. [. . .] Lying in our beds, wounded by unrequited
love, our asses await ultimate violation" (123–24, trans. mod.).[28] As
Aliaga rightly argues, this reductive association of homosexuality with
femininity reproduces a patriarchal paradigm of dominant masculinity
and passive femininity ("Como hemos cambiado" 69). Vicent's fantasy
of the inaccessible reveals his own internalization of homophobia and
the power of the law. He seems to experience a minor epiphany when
he recognizes that language and desire may be out of his grasp, that even
his fantasy could not be rightly called "his," insofar as the possessive
pronoun would symbolize a form of agency or control over his inner
thoughts. His brief epiphanic moment, nonetheless, cannot spur him
to any revolutionary reaction, and he remains impotent in the face of
homophobia. Vicent is hardly alone in his plight, however. Pipi Iaguer's
nymphomaniacal need for sex in public bathrooms, Eduard la Palletera's
tale about a homosexual being castrated by his mother, and Pamela
Tifus's own attempt to secure herself a married "straight" man all point

to the underlying problem that plagues these characters: they can only conceive of homosexual love in relation to the very object that would seek to oppress them, thus shoring up Matilde's earlier claim that homosexuals desire the law.

L'anarquista nu begins with Aureli's suicide note and ends with the news of Àngel Donat's suicide. Both of them—the anarchist and the angel, destruction and redemption—are eliminated in violent acts of self-annihilation, and the narrative comes full circle. In one of the unsigned letters, the letter writer describes both Aureli and himself in epistolary terms as "paragraphs alien to a text, yet intent on finding our place on the white page" (99).[29] The anonymously penned description not only underscores these characters' existences for each other as discursive constructs confined to letters but it also points up the impossibility of remaining solely on the margins: they are human texts that want to be on the page of society. His words are strangely close to those of the young Catalan anarchist, Salvador Puig Antich: "I have asked myself for a long time now what I was doing in this world where there is still no place for me" (Velázquez and Memba 25). Aureli's note at the beginning of the novel explains that he will be using suppositories to kill himself: death through the anus becomes an allegory of the fatality of homosexual desire. The failure of (letter) writing to traverse a distance, to establish connections, comes to stand for the limit of any political project based on absolute destruction of the state as a governing body. At the same time, Aureli's suicide suggests that it is precisely his voluntary decision—the ultimate anarchist choice—that reveals his awareness of the profound limitations of anarchism as a revolutionary platform, the reason why he is exiled from the world of his Valencian friends: death marks the ultimate escape from the law, psychic and juridical, the one space where the anarchist and the angel can in fact finally meet. Carles Besada, paraphrasing Aureli's letter, suggests precisely that the latter has achieved this awareness of the overwhelming power of subjection, that from his exiled vantage point he can better see "the reality that denigrates us because of our incapacity to hold on to what belongs to us and to change what holds us back. Incapable of a political, civic, supportive cohesion" (125, my translation).[30] The novel redoubles this message through the structural union of the anarchist and the angel. Àngel Donat's suicide underscores these characters' failure to achieve psychic liberation, their inability to find love outside the confines of a heterosexist vision of sexual relations.

L'anarquista nu offers a sobering counterpoint to the euphoric representation of post-Franco sexual politics. Fernàndez's critique of gay liberation suggests that what haunts these figures is the failure of revolution not only in political terms but, more importantly, in psychic terms. It remains for them to cease desiring the "passionate attachment" to the fascist regime's homophobic concept of gay identity to which they were formerly subjected. Trapped within the structures they set out to overturn, the Valencian letter writers remain tormented by the impossibility of homosexual love that can only exist for them as a love for the (phobic) law. The disjunction between political liberation and the symbolic realm of subjection suggests that sexual revolution can only occur in the radical restructuring of the latter. The hyperbolic practice of sexual dissidence and the dismissal of identity politics through camp and transgenderism, as represented by Fernàndez, are insufficient modes of emancipation. Fernàndez's novel does not advocate political activism, nor does it offer any programmatic solutions: it simply mourns the passing of revolutionary resistance.[31] Like the failure of the CNT to take full advantage of revolutionary possibilities during the civil war, the failed revolutionary potential of an anarchist sexual politics becomes the source of a post-Franco gay *desencanto,* one fundamentally linked to the larger sense that traces of Francoism continue to contaminate the newly established democracy. In other words, the novel acknowledges the pleasures of the apolitical hedonism of *la movida* and *el destape,* but critiques that pleasure as the sign of an unfettered sexuality that offers the illusion of a transitory emancipation. Although the novel was written before the repeal of the Law of Social Dangers in 1979, Fernàndez draws attention to the fact that homophobic constructions of gay sexuality persisted in the transition from dictatorship to democracy.[32]

Like the melancholic tone that pervades the final pages of *L'anarquista nu,* the stigma attached to homoeroticism continues to mark the ambivalent space of gay and lesbian subjectivity in Spain. Alberto Mira has argued recently against the value accorded to the absence of identity politics, rejecting that absence as a strategy of liberation. Instead, he suggests that the failure to produce a coherent discourse around gay identity has much more to do with "tendencies rooted in our culture that reject such an articulation at the level of discourse" ("De lo patológico" 255). Mira's assertion, which Fernàndez's novel confirms, is that we should not read the relative weakness of gay and lesbian politics as a queer critique *avant la lettre* of the avowedly cloistering space of identity. Instead, we would do well to interpret it as a sign of a prevailing homophobia that continues to exert a disabling force, in spite of the success of emancipatory efforts to overturn repressive legislation. Implicit within Mira's choice of words—"tendencies rooted in our culture"—is that the ties between contemporary gay and lesbian politics and the historical legacy of homophobia under Francoism remain unsevered.

There is a danger, of course, in seeing every instance of homophobia as a remnant of the Francoist past, of viewing each political impasse as the persistence of a historically rooted sexual oppression: such a perspective condemns gays and lesbians to an unassailable historical trap from which escape is impossible. As pessimistic as that may seem, it is difficult to deny that gay and lesbian politics have not entirely succeeded in escaping the homophobic laws and social norms of the past (Aliaga, "Como hemos cambiado" 48, 58). While Emilie L. Bergmann and Paul Julian Smith have argued that "Anglo-Americans" could learn about living in loosely defined "queer" communities from the Spanish context (12), the Spanish context also proves that the critique of identity politics is not always an escape from, but sometimes a capitulation to, ideological repression. As Pérez Cánovas bluntly states: "It's terrible to realize that the decriminalization of homosexuality has not led to its destigmatization" (77). The homophobic press catalyzed by *El caso Arny* in which homosexuality was equated with corruption of minors;[33] the widespread resistance to civil unions, especially from within the right-wing Partido Popular (Popular Party, or PP) currently in power (the Llei d'Unions Estables de Parella in Catalonia, which took effect in October 1998, is an exception to the national trend);[34] and the mediocrity of media images of gays and lesbians such as Pepelu, the gay caricature who appeared on the former Tele 5 program *Esta noche cruzamos el Mississippi* (Tonight We Cross the Mississippi) are but a few examples of the lack of ideological change in spite of the legal advances of gays and lesbians during the 1980s and '90s. If at the time of publication *L'anarquista nu*'s portrayal of the Valencia gay community was at the vanguard of a national literary trend, its message remains pressing even today: the relative weakness of gay identity politics cannot simply be interpreted as a queer liberation from overt homophobia or from various forms of subtle oppression still faced by Spanish gays and lesbians today. The prevailing ambivalence toward homosexuality depends not only on juridical reformations of the law but also, and perhaps more importantly, on ideological constructions of desire and sexuality implanted during the Franco dictatorship, which remain rooted in contemporary political practices of such parties as the Partido Popular. These specters of the past persist into the present and thus continue to shape, for better or worse, contemporary queer subjectivities.

CHAPTER 6

E-mail, AIDS, and Virtual Sexuality
in Lluís Fernàndez

A prevention campaign for AIDS in Spain, which aired on national and autonomous community television channels on August 12–31, 2003, begins with a man facing his computer and composing an e-mail with the subject line "I love you" in English. He hits the "send" button, and the advertisement moves quickly from one computer user to another, each one resending the message in turn. The voiceover states, "The AIDS virus is transmitted just like a computer virus: it can be given to you by the person you'd least expect." A "virus detected" dialogue box suddenly appears on the user's computer screen. The use of English connotes the sense of AIDS as a transnational health concern and invariably alludes to the "I Love You" virus that struck computer systems around the world on May 4, 2000, using terms of endearment to duplicate itself through address books and wreak havoc. Numerous other computer viruses (more accurately called "worms") such as "Anna Kournikova" or "Naked Wife" have since played copycat to the "I Love You" virus. While all seem to display a connection with sexuality, the "I Love You" virus stands out in the way in which human affection was used to disseminate an electronic "disease," if you will, one with the potential to eradicate a computer's contents, thus proving that the world of virtual space and electronic communication was just as vulnerable to contagion as material reality. Spain's Ministry of Health prevention campaign, playing on the "I Love You" virus's ability to masquerade itself as a message of love, transforms the transmission of an e-mail into the transmission of the HIV virus. By using "love" as its framework for connecting two or more individuals in a virtual space, both Spain's prevention campaign and the "I Love You" virus effectively evoke a discursive parallel between reading and sexual relations: the simple act of opening an e-mail is no longer an innocuous activity. Reading, like sex, becomes a form of contagious communication.

Published in 1998, Lluís Fernàndez's *Una prudente distancia* (A Prudent Distance) exploits the notion that reading can be a vehicle of contagion. Roberto Valencia has written a letter from Berkeley, California, where he has resided for the past twenty years, to his old friends in Valencia, Spain. Roberto's avowed goal is to produce a sociological tract on the effects of AIDS by accumulating a series of firsthand testimonials. For all of Roberto Valencia's presence as the epistolary catalyst of the novel, he is altogether absent. His virtual presence is felt on every page, but he is never seen, his words are never read. Only the symptoms of his presence are felt—in the reactions of his correspondents and in the few paraphrases they sometimes include within their own letters. In this respect, the novel evokes its predecessor, *L'anarquista nu,* in which Aureli Santonja was the primary addressee of the letters but whose own voice remained absent. *Una prudente distancia* is composed of twenty eight letters from various friends (Helio Trónica, Paqui-Tina), former lovers (Marnie la Ladrona, Pitita de Rancio Abolengo, Vic Toría), and enemies (Rojelia Stonewall, Melena Rubistein, Luis Alfredo Filigrana). It is also a roman à clef laden with thinly veiled references to real figures such as Carmen Alborch, the former minister of culture, and Alberto Cardín, a gay critic and activist who died of AIDS in 1992. As in *L'anarquista nu,* there is a lack of a developed plot line, with the letters reduced to snapshots of individual lives: the apparent lack of cohesion is itself a reflection of the disarray of the gay community. As a late-twentieth-century novel, it pushes the envelope, so to speak, of the epistolary genre: some characters compose messages on Apple laptops and send faxes or e-mails, while others resort to the more traditional epistolary technologies of pen and paper.

From the outset, the title draws on the discourse of safe sex and implies that issues germane to AIDS—safety and risk, infection and prevention, mourning and activism—will be at the forefront of this text.

Given the absence of any single narratorial voice, the novel does not spell out a uniform perspective on AIDS. Yet the accumulation of these letters into a single text—in spite of the wishes of many of the letter writers—obeys a deliberate editorial decision to expose the apathetic political and social response to the AIDS epidemic in Spain. In previous chapters, the use of epistolary writing has elicited ambivalent responses from the reader—whether it is the recognition of queer desire in Unamuno's and Martín Gaite's works, the ethical ambivalence of the knowledge of another person's sexuality in Villena's and Riera's texts, or the ambiguity of the politics of sexual dissidence that the reader perceives in having access to the letters of Fernàndez's earlier novel. In *Una prudente distancia,* Fernàndez exploits the confessional nature of letter writing by making the letter function primarily as a form of contagion, a communication that spreads, like a virus, throughout the fictional Spanish gay community. The prosthetics of epistolary writing (letters, e-mails, faxes) fail to provide a "prudent distance" from the disease of writing. In *Una prudente distancia* the risk that AIDS represents from physical contact is presented as an act of reading, in which the virtual space of the written word is by no means a safe space.

To speak of AIDS in terms of virtuality alludes first and foremost to the paucity of action on the part of both government health authorities and gay political groups in Spain in response to the virus. In 1995 Ricardo Llamas bluntly stated that one could infer from the lack of scientific and intellectual response that "in Spain no one has had or has AIDS" (xii). José Miguel G. Cortés, writing in 1993, notes the relative absence of straightforward and explicit educational campaigns for the prevention of AIDS, as most campaigns preferred a more oblique approach with such slogans as "Quiérete, quiéreme" ("Love Yourself, Love Me") and "Si queremos podemos parar el Sida" ("If we want, we can stop AIDS"). Even the more successful ones, such as the poster circulated by the Ministry of Health, "Sí da, no da" ("Yes it gives, no it doesn't"—a play on words, since AIDS in Spanish is SIDA), which did manage to communicate preventive measures in spite of the fact that human beings were represented as circles with legs, were hampered by limited diffusion (Cortés, "Silencio=Muerte" 98). Cortés is especially critical of the lack of campaigns directed toward gay men, in spite of the association of (and blame for) the virus with homosexuality (99–100). Although the information provided by the Ministry of Health has improved, the state of AIDS education and prevention campaigns can hardly be applauded. Among more recent campaigns in Spain are the December 2000 slogans "There are not risk groups, but risk situations" and "If you are in a risk situation and you don't take precautions, AIDS could cross your path." The limited success of AIDS education can be seen in the fact that a third of those diagnosed with AIDS in 2002 were unaware that they were HIV-positive before the onset of illness ("El sida disminuye").

Given the dearth of effective government campaigns, most direct poster campaigns designed for a specific audience emerged from within gay groups themselves, with the exception of two posters from the Comunidad de Madrid and the Generalitat de Catalunya. Cortés praises the work of Gais pers la Salut (Gays for Health) from Barcelona, and Coordinadora Gay y Lesbiana (Gay and Lesbian Coordinating Committee), although he does suggest that such representations are not nearly as explicit as those in France, Germany, and England. But even gay and lesbian political organizations were slow to respond to the epidemic (Lorenzo and Anabitarte 10). Ricardo Lorenzo and Héctor Anabitarte, writing in 1987, attribute part of the problem to Spanish attitudes toward sexuality: "we continue to experience sex with guilt and when it's about homosexuality, it induces terror" (13). Ricardo Llamas and Fefa Vila, adopting a different tack, point to the lack of action on the part of gay and lesbian political groups as a reflection of the "apolitical hedonism" of the Socialist years (1982–96) in which the first notices about AIDS were seen by gay communities as anti-gay propaganda (215). It was not until 1984 that a group of friends began to hand out their phone numbers as an early activist moment of disseminating information about HIV; these friends later formed the Comité Anti-SIDA de Madrid (Anti-AIDS Committee of Madrid), which gained legal status in 1986. In the 1990s, gay organizations such as La Radical Gai began to argue vociferously for the need for research for a vaccine and better drug therapies (218–19). Other organizations emerged such as El Proyecto 1 de Diciembre in Valencia and ACT UP in Barcelona. Until the formation of Lesbianas Sexo Diferente (Different Sex Lesbians, or LSD),

Llamas and Vila argue, the lesbian movement had not engaged directly in the debates on AIDS. In 1994, LSD engaged in its first act of spreading information about the relationship between sexual practices among lesbians and the transmission of HIV (220).

Similarly reticent to grapple with the epidemic, the Spanish media initially failed in its objective of presenting thoughtful and sensitive discussions of AIDS. Early in the epidemic, the media engaged in a number of dramatic violations of privacy. In 1986 an architect from Palma de Mallorca was revealed as HIV-positive in the daily press, which named both him and his partner (Sanz Cid et al. 83). In January 1987, a three-year-old HIV-positive child was expelled from a school in Durango, his name also revealed (Lorenzo and Anabitarte 26). A former minister of health, Ernest Lluch, announced that the "normal populace" did not have to worry about AIDS, foreshadowing the association that AIDS would have with IV-drug users and gay men (Lorenzo and Anabitarte 20). On March 11, 1993, María Consuelo Reyna, the director of the conservative Valencian daily *Las Provincias,* demanded in print to know why "drastic measures of isolation had not been adopted" (Aliaga, "El lenguaje" 23). It is not surprising, then, that few cultural and political figures have made their HIV-positive status public knowledge, preferring instead, along with artists and intellectuals, to maintain a high level of secrecy (Mira, "Esta noche SIDA" 153). Until December 1992, few programs that treated AIDS with seriousness and rigor had aired on Spanish television (Aliaga, "El lenguaje" 26), in spite of the fact that Spain has the highest relative number of AIDS cases in Europe. On Mercedes Milà's *Queremos saber* (We Want to Know) program, which aired November 17, 1992, not a single representative from gay and lesbian organizations was present to remark on the effect of AIDS on the gay and lesbian community. Instead, the show offered a space for Miguel Bosé to deny publicly the rumors that he had died from AIDS, which was in many respects a simultaneous denial of the rumor that he was gay. The suppression of information about the role that HIV played in the death of the gay Spanish poet Jaime Gil de Biedma in 1990 is yet another example of the reluctance in Spain to engage the topic openly.

The relative absence of governmental action and the bleak media representations of AIDS have found a discomforting parallel in the literary and artistic realm where Spanish artists and authors have been all too reticent about addressing the topic. With the notable exceptions of the artist Pepe Espaliú's 1992 "Carrying Project" and Juan Goytisolo's *Las virtudes del pájaro solitario* (*Virtues of the Solitary Bird*, 1988) the artistic response to AIDS can be described at most as impoverished. The first is an example of performance art, the second a novel that enfolds AIDS within a narrative of mysticism. Espaliú's work stands out, for it inspired several events that reproduced the performance and raised consciousness about AIDS. Goytisolo's work not only suffers from a limited reception but it also avoids naming AIDS directly. For Paul Julian Smith, both projects are representative of a predominant strategy of representation among Spanish artists that he dubs the "fatalist vision" of AIDS—"a reconciliation with death" that leads to an "obsession with decay and putrefaction" (*Vision Machines* 104). In many respects, and as Smith implies, the embrace of the spectacle of gay men who directly confront AIDS-related death harbors the possibility of colluding with homophobic discourses that can only see gay men as carriers of disease. Plausible and convincing explanations for this passivity and disinterest among intellectuals, writers, and artists are not easily found. The lack of public expression from the gay and lesbian community undoubtedly stems from a reticence around confession and testimony, particularly as they concern sexuality. As Llamas claims, there is still a certain "distrust" ("recelo") of studies "about 'intimate' questions such as disease and sexuality" (xv).

Given its explicit focus on AIDS, Fernàndez's text initially runs counter to the general trend of Spanish artistic responses to the AIDS pandemic. In contrast with Goytisolo's novel, the text does not employ an oblique mystical language; AIDS is clearly named as such. Yet if *Una prudente distancia* appears at first glance to avoid the pitfalls of these strategies of representation, its approach is not unproblematic in addressing the material reality of AIDS. The use of letter writing might elicit reader expectations of finding an autobiographical mode. In fact, the novel shares little in common with the genre of AIDS diaries and narratives—such as Hervé Guibert's *A l'ami qui ne m'a pas sauvé la vie* (To the Friend Who Did Not Save My Life, 1990), Eric Michaels's *Unbecoming* (1990), and Paul Monette's *Last Watch of the Night* (1994). The syndrome initially surfaces as the focal point of Roberto Valencia's investigations, but the reader is quick to realize that his purpose is not the avowedly innocuous and objective sociological project of soliciting information about AIDS. The fact that Valencia is HIV-positive is revealed in one of the response letters, yet the absence of his voice forecloses the possibility of a testimonial discourse in which the author, facing death, assumes an authorial voice as a mode of bearing witness to the effects of the disease.

Alexander García Düttmann, in a subtle analysis of AIDS writing, notes that the autobiographical mode—the retrospective of one's own lifetime—often determines the discourse on AIDS. AIDS provides the "occasion for autobiographical reflection, for witnessing, admitting, confessing" (11). Yet Düttmann questions the function of the autobiographical mode that characterizes the response to AIDS, for the confession of being HIV-positive, he argues, transforms the virus into the site of truth of the subject. The effect is that AIDS is, in a sense, spread by virtue of confession: "The admission, the confession, the urgent testimony that express contagion make it possible to survive oneself in language: perverse purification that consists of contagion" (13). On the other hand, the need to speak is fundamental to the subject living with AIDS. AIDS refashioned the closet, reinvesting it with fear and guilt, not only around sexuality and sexual practices but about HIV and the need to disclose one's seropositivity. In his powerful essay on coming to terms with queer desire and AIDS, "Dense Moments," the filmmaker and activist Gregg Bordowitz distinguishes between confession and testimony, the former motivated by guilt and sin that divests oneself of personal responsibility and gives it to a figure of authority, the second motivated by the need to bear witness as survivor to someone who listens but does not judge (25–26). For Bordowitz, the right to speak in a testimonial mode is key for undermining the stigma and guilt attached to AIDS and queer sexuality. At the same time, he recognizes that the distinction between confession and testimony—between bearing witness and seeking exoneration, between speaking to someone who listens and to someone who judges—is not an entirely stable line of demarcation. The precarious division between the two speech acts undermines the security of occupying one position (witness) without simultaneously occupying another (confessant).

Initially, then, one might interpret Valencia's refusal to discuss his sero-positivity as a denial of the confessional framework, a refusal to engage in a speech act motivated by guilt and remorse for one's actions.[1] Instead, the lack of any direct input from Valencia undermines the reader's capac-ity to ascertain the motives behind his writing, for contradictory pieces of information regarding his health are communicated in the course of the novel. Rojelia has been circulating the rumor that Valencia is a long-time survivor whose health has taken a turn for the worse. On the other hand, Helio relates in his final letter that Valencia's health is just fine, now that he has undertaken a cocktail drug therapy regime. Whether or not his motive for writing is due to his HIV status or im-periled health remains unclear since the information comes from sources whose reliability is suspect. The end result of Valencia's silence is that AIDS is represented as an invisible syndrome. In fact, no one with HIV ever speaks; their voices only appear in the third person, and then only by hearsay. There is no firsthand testimonial, no witness to the daily onslaught of the disease, no self-analysis or intimate reflection on death.

For all the novel's emphasis on the reality of Spain's political context during the 1990s, the reality of AIDS is kept at bay. For example, Helio Trónica, one of the few characters concerned with gay politics and political corruption, poignantly discusses the deaths of Gina, Herminia, and Tinín. Tinín was diagnosed in 1985, shortly after the deaths of some mutual friends involved in sadomasochism, and he himself died in 1992. The time of his death, references to his various publications, and the phonetic quality of his name imply that Tinín is a fictionalized version of Alberto Cardín. Helio recounts Tinín's fear of disease and the anger in being the only one of his friends diagnosed with AIDS while Helio and Roberto, among others, appeared to be healthy even though they had engaged in similar sexual practices. As Helio narrates it, Tinín's suffering dissolved their shared desire to sexually "conquer the world," for Tinín's own world was crumbling. The tragic denouement—Tinín's mother was indifferent during the funeral, no one collected his ashes—is perhaps the one moment of tender reflection that appears in the novel. Helio also conveys to Valencia that Gina went to live in New York, re-turning two years later with a boyfriend and HIV. Upon his death, the parents came to the funeral, ignored his boyfriend as if he too had AIDS, and used the funeral as an excuse to criticize the "sexual deviances and sins" of their son. Herminia's story is even less detailed. Embittered by the disease, he fell into oblivion, and Helio only received news of his death from a thirdhand source. In still another letter, Eustaquio Racionero reveals that Luis Filigrana's partner, Cenizo, also died of AIDS and that Cenizo's family did not allow Filigrana to see his partner's deceased body. Additionally, they altered his will to prevent Filigrana from being the beneficiary. In Helio's final letter he writes of another friend who died of AIDS, Klaus: the only thing that remains is a post-card of him and his boyfriend Sean, also dead, with their backs to the camera. This brief moment at the end of the novel stands out as a *mise en abîme* of the representation of AIDS in which those who suffer from the syndrome remain faceless, barely remembered, reduced to a fragment of superficial writing. AIDS, speaking only through hearsay and allusion, haunts the text in a spectral fashion, omnipresent yet virtually absent.

The novel's geographical alignment of AIDS with the United States—implied by Valencia's residence in Berkeley, California—is certainly not coincidental given the predominance of the United States in cultural responses to the pandemic. The fact that the majority of those characters who died from AIDS contracted the virus in the United States or died there reiterates a geographic framework in which the United States, not Spain, is associated with AIDS.[2] The text thus permits a retreat from the material reality of AIDS in Spain by seeing AIDS as belonging *elsewhere*.[3] As a result, in their brief testimonials the letter writers are less concerned with their friends' suffering from AIDS than with themselves; there is an absence of mourning in their accounts. Helio reveals that he left behind much of the promiscuity of the 1970s, horrified by the prospect of contracting venereal diseases and hepatitis; he and his boyfriend escaped the disease by limiting their sexual activities in saunas to superficial touches (130). This solipsistic concern for the self leaves its mark on another letter concerning Tinín. Devorah Coeur writes about Tinín's last months of life in which he threw his anger in their faces and then isolated himself completely: "It must be difficult to forget that you're going to die and everyone else will keep on living. God forgive me, but we were fed up with Tinín, and now I think that he did the right thing dying alone at home" (189).[4] Harsh words even as Devorah expresses his regret at Tinín's death—"He died, finally, like Gina, leaving a devastating black hole in our spirits" (189).[5] Yet any reflection on what has come to be known as "survivor's guilt" is left out of the letter. Instead, what is lost is a personal sense of freedom, as the day of Tinín's funeral marks the sudden awareness that *la vida loca* of promiscuous sex was now a lost utopia (191).

Ross Chambers concludes in his insightful study of AIDS diaries that "every reader must also face an awareness of the responsibilities of readerly survivorhood, which are those ensuring the survival of the text whose author is dead, and of prolonging its witness," and these responsibilities, he further notes, "are necessarily tinged with a sense of inadequacy and, almost as inevitably, with a sense of guilt" (22). In chapter 4, I analyzed how Riera's "Jo pos per testimoni les gavines" exhorts the reader to adopt a similar position in the face of the writer's loss of her lesbian lover to suicide. In this case, however, the reader's responsibility to those who have died from AIDS-related illnesses is cut short. The novel does not demand that the reader bear witness, at least not to the testimony of someone with AIDS. Rather, the reader's responsibility is directed elsewhere: to bear witness not to AIDS but to the moral corruption and political apathy of the gay community in Valencia, Spain. The relative absence of a testimonial mode of writing in the novel is, it turns out, consistent with Valencia's true goal for writing: he responds to the absence of critical voices on AIDS in Spain not by providing a space for people with AIDS to speak about their lives but rather by directly attacking what he perceives to be the attitudes toward AIDS that have fostered its virtualization as a kind of ghostly, invisible disease.

The letters from Valencia's interlocutors are remembrances of the frivolous, lost time that consumed their youth, a nostalgic look at the past from the perspective of the decadence into which they have ostensibly fallen. The first letter of response, signed by Rojelia Stonewall, sees through Roberto's feigned innocence and establishes the true purpose of his inquiry: "Even so, I think it's fabulous, this set-up of gathering together information about our generation and the changes that have taken place during these years of AIDS, political earthquakes and social stripteases, so you can get information about my life out of me" (16).[6] Rojelia notes that he's taking precautions by signing his name with a false one. In order to hide his identity and the fact that he was once gay, he has forged a "straight" image by marrying a lesbian (21, 33). Dated from 1994 and 1995, the letters reveal that the effervescent decade of the 1980s has now turned sour as socialist-dominated Spain is losing ground to the right-wing Partido Popular under the leadership of José María Aznar. The fall of the PSOE in the 1996 elections is clearly foreshadowed; in an anxious fax to Paqui-Tina, Rojelia Stonewall warns of the impending elections (31). Collectively, the letter writers convey the image of a debauched gay community that has begun to be devoured by its own material greed: they have sold out gay liberation for political and economic success. Rojelia is a prime witness to the machinations of his fellow gay men to climb the political and social ladder of the post-*movida*, socialist Spain of the 1980s and early '90s and the lack of cohesion among gay political organizations: "A pink mafia? With us queens as individualistic, evil, and lacking in solidarity as we are! I won't tell you how we slackers of local television are. To survive in this monstrous building, surrounded by ambitious women and insatiable faggots, is a true miracle, even for me, more 'survivor' than Gloria Gaynor" (19).[7] In their letters, the characters convey their crass materialism and backstabbing strategies to survive in "disillusioned" and "amnesiac" post-Franco Spain. Rojelia bluntly describes the 1980s as the era of "money, honey!" in which financial success was the only goal in life (17).

Sprinkled throughout the letters, published in chronological order, are isolated comments that lay bare the cruel intentions of Valencia's epistolary game. Responding to a fax from Rojelia Stonewall, Paqui-Tina warns of Roberto's return: "I think that his epistolary return should be interpreted as a long-postponed vengeance" (62).[8] From Pura Fantasía we learn that Roberto desires to know the "morbid" aspects of everyone's lives, a search for knowledge justified with "scientific pretensions." Finally, it is Helio Trónico who frankly declares that this is nothing more than an epistolary attack in order to take revenge on all of the gay men who apparently forced Valencia into exile. In spite of the fact that so many of them are aware of his intentions, that knowledge does not prevent them from confessing to him and thus falling prey to his machinations. Vic Toría reveals a clear awareness of the confessional nature of the epistolary enterprise, admitting that he responds to Valencia's letter "because I like to suffer, to expiate my guilt for my many sins committed in the past, and in confession I always find a healthy comfort" (101).[9]

Valencia's absence is a fundamental part of his strategy, designed to maintain a "prudent distance" from his interlocutors. A modern-day Valmont to Valencia's Merteuil, Roberto scavenges for salacious information under the pretext of "scientific pretensions" so that figures such as Rojelia Stonewall, Remedios Caseros, and Luis Alfredo Filigrana, to name a few, portray in their own words their moral and political decline. The success of the epistolary revenge depends not only on these characters penning their own failures, secrets, and sins but exposing their compatriots' debauched adventures as well. It becomes quickly apparent that Valencia needs only plant the seeds of discontent for several figures to come to his aid—Devorah Coeur and Paqui-Tina, among others, agree to provide him with secret information about other characters. For example, Paqui-Tina ignores Rojelia's demands to have his letters destroyed after reading them and passes them on to Roberto. Still others, such as Eustaquio Racionero, photocopy letters from one interlocutor to another and fax private missives to Roberto for inclusion in his "study." Yet even those who assist Roberto are similarly subject to his venomous attack, for he includes the letters that reveal their complicity with his project, thus exposing their betrayal to those who believe them to be friends. Bitchy cannabilists, they consume and devour each other, proving Roberto's thesis that they are all morally suspect. In the end, no one is safe from Valencia, not even his friends. In his final letter, Helio remarks that Roberto has sent him a photocopied packet of letters that contains all of the letters that form the novel. He writes a final letter, knowing that the publication of the letters will condemn all of them: "I can't avoid the idea that this letter, the one I'm writing now, will be a part of the fiction that you've created joining all of the letters together in this pack of photocopies that you've sent me" (234).[10] Aware that he himself is trapped in Roberto's epistolary enterprise, Helio offers a sweeping portrait of the collected correspondence: "I have never seen all together so much audacity, cowardice, baseness, mental impoverishment, dishonesty, immorality, nerve, indecency, disloyalty and betrayal as in these letters" (242).[11]

As a sociological tract, the collection of letters bears witness to the radical *lack* of importance that AIDS has for the gay community. For the most part, as these characters relate their memories of the past two decades, there are no reflections on activism, no mention of La Radical Gai or ACT UP, no explicit reproach of the paucity of government response, no discussion of sexual practices or access to health care. While most of the letter writers view Roberto's goal as a personal attack, one character, Enric Obrer, sees in Roberto's intentions the positive potential of clarifying the effects of AIDS and unveiling political corruption. Yet if Obrer's concern is how AIDS may have stunted the growth of gay liberation movements, the text does not respond to that concern. He instead advocates that Roberto pursue his exposé: "As you'll see, what we need in Valencia is an outing that puts each queen in his place and unmasks politically and sexually all those crooks still hidden in the closet" (71).[12] Indeed, Roberto sets himself up as a moral authority who, from the vantage point of Berkeley, casts judgment on his compatriots, portraying them as a collection of opportunistic queens who would do anything to succeed: political corruption and nepotism in the university system are only a few examples of their moral vacuity. To speak of "opportunism" within the context of AIDS is not incidental, however, for the text constructs their opportunism as a form of disease itself, as if their moral corruption were something like an opportunistic infection. Fernàndez's text implies that these characters' behaviors are responsible for the failures of HIV education and prevention in Spain.

Fernàndez's novel conveys this sense of indifference to AIDS and gay politics primarily through the language of camp. Camp and its avatars—frivolity, humor, melodrama—distinguish the novel from other writings about AIDS by authors such as Hervé Guibert, which often strike a melancholic chord. As a form of gay culture associated with Almodóvar, *la movida madrileña,* and the euphoric sense of liberation following the death of Franco, camp harkens back to that previous era and thus stands in opposition to AIDS. Rojelia writes to Paqui-Tina and describes a fantasy of slowly killing Roberto just as Bette Davis did to Joan Crawford in *Whatever Happened to Baby Jane?* (33). Pitita de Rancio Abolengo ends her letter declaring that she and a fellow friend have barred themselves from wearing Versace because it makes them look like Rosenthal cups (52). The second letter of the novel, signed "Melena Rubistein," is written by an overweight and balding aesthetician for fashion magazines who is traveling to a photo-shoot with the famous model Linda Evangelista. The details of his life, Melena tells Roberto, can be found in his updated autobiography, *Ladies Who Lunch* (119). Eustaquio Racionero likewise reiterates the sense of camp frivolity when he writes, "Excuse the levity of these slightly senile reflections. Let's blame the night and its campy charm" (224).[13] Even safe-sex practices are parodied with a wicked campiness. Paqui-Tina relates that Melena Rubistein stole her boyfriend's semen using a condom, not to practice safe sex but to save his semen for use as a facial moisturizer (90).

Melena stands out in the novel as the character whose camp sensibility bluntly portrays the lack of concern for AIDS that characterizes many of the letters. He describes a trip to New York in which he visits an old friend, La Pepisa, who had left the seminary in search of a boyfriend: "her boyfriend was HIV-positive and she played ignorant. I stopped her one day and said, 'Pepisa, we are both going to go now to the hospital in Manhattan and we'll take the Elisa test. Just to fuck with her! I knew mine would turn out negative. Which is what happened. But she turned pale. Her friends began to feel sorry for her" (28).[14] Clearly Melena does not figure among those friends, as his actions were designed to humiliate La Pepisa into divulging his seropositivity. As a result, the novel implies that many of these characters collude with the virus, by either turning their backs on those who are HIV-positive or, even worse, by tormenting them. As if to compound his emotional distance from his friend's seropositivity, Rubistein relays how drug addicts took La Pepisa's AZT for a quick fix—an anecdote that is delivered as a campy bit of humor without any awareness of its lack of sensitivity. Another interlocutor, Pura Fantasía, reveals the sexual awakening of someone by the name "Luis Gore," whose interest in flight attendants leads to the mention of "Gaetan Dugas," the mythic patient-zero of AIDS. Enfolded within a narrative of sexual promiscuity, the supposed origin of AIDS is left untouched as a mythic beginning and the possibility of contracting the virus in no way quells Luis Gore's sexual appetite. For Melena Rubistein and Luis Gore, AIDS is either a source of wicked pleasure in which knowledge of someone else's HIV status is information to be manipulated or a mere footnote on the page of one's sexual adventures.

In Valencia's project his interlocutors' letters become self-deprecating and destructive weapons designed to harm the hands that wield the pen. Sexual promiscuity is transformed into epistolary promiscuity, with all of them having "relations" with Roberto. Marnie La Ladrona's letter literalizes this figurative relationship by drawing an analogy between his letter and his penis: "In the fast times of fax and computers, you allow yourself to write a delicious handwritten letter, with a Mont Blanc pen and untrimmed stationery. I have it in my hands, just as I had your erect member in days gone by" (36–37).[15] The letter, as a material object, functions like Roberto's penis, and reading takes on the guise of sexual penetration. Epistolary correspondence replaces sex, or rather, pen and paper become dildonic tools that make sex a virtual reality. Letter writing, laden with confessional overtones, becomes the vehicle for contagion and language the source of infection. Valencia's epistolary foray becomes a metaphorically deadly enterprise as he disseminates—with all the connotations of that term—a viral-like letter throughout the Valencian community. His writing spreads throughout, each writer contacting and infecting the next with the knowledge that Roberto has returned. Valencia's intrusion into the gay demimonde, the sudden unexpected appearance of a lethal agent, takes on allegorical proportions of the viral intrusion of HIV into the lives of gay men. Chambers, in his study of AIDS diaries, notes a similar treatment of language: "A virus has been transmitted: not HIV but the virus of writing and reading" (8).

In this respect, *Una prudente distancia* falls in line with many of the critical and cultural writings that treat AIDS as a signifier within the comfortable terms of poststructuralist theory. Numerous critics—Paula Treichler, Susan Sontag, Simon Watney, and Cindy Patton—have commented on the ineluctible relationship between language and the virus; Aliaga similarly titles the introduction to *De amor y rabia* "language is a virus" (13).[16] In a rhetorical analysis of AIDS discourses, Lee Edelman has claimed that the virus breeds discourse, and the impossible position in which we find ourselves is that any discussion of the virus is, in some effect, also carrying the virus, or as he puts it, "the virulent germ of the dominant cultural discourse" (91). While we think of the AIDS virus in terms of language, Fernàndez's novel reveals how much, due no doubt in large part to AIDS, we think of language in terms of viruses, and how the increasing use of technology lends itself to viral terminology as a means of conceptualizing communication. The metaphors used to discuss the virus already draw from the language of epistolarity, such as when Treichler cites a 1987 *Scientific American* article that claims that "the envelope of the virus seems to be changing" (60). In *Una prudente distancia* the virtualization of AIDS—making it a sort of spectral entity and linking it to writing—extends the epistolary metaphor by treating AIDS more like a computer virus transmitted via e-mail than a physical one transmitted sexually. One of the implications of the novel is that conceptualizing the virus in terms of virtuality harbors its own dangers.

AIDS may be a virtual presence in the novel, but it is nonetheless given a material form insofar as Valencia's letter is handwritten. The careful calligraphy, the embroidered prose—mentioned by several interlocutors—harkens back to a time when letter writing was something of an art; in contrast, Paqui-Tina, who only sends messages from her e-mail address P@quit-Tina.es, proclaims that she has terrible penmanship now that she's become an "internet computer queen" ("mariquita informática internetizada") (86). Valencia's form of communication is almost passé, technologically behind the times, but the very antiquated quality is brought into stark relief for a reason. The use of postcards, the telegraph, and the tape recorder are examples of the ways in which technology rooted in epistolarity has supposedly evolved for the better, making improvements over the limitations of prior forms. The impact of those forms of technology is not to be underestimated, but it is undoubtedly e-mail that is most responsible for the renaissance of epistolary communication today. In part, the rise of e-mail would seem to be linked to its capacity to escape the limitations of standard mail—the rate of transmission, the need for postage, the materiality of ink and paper.[17]

Materiality is of course central to discussions of epistolarity: letter writing denotes the substitution of one form of materiality (paper) for another (the body). Pointing to the substitution of writing for the body, for example, Pedro Salinas describes the letter as a form of loving without caresses (29). All the more so in e-mail, where the materiality of the paper gives way to the virtual reality of the computer screen. The metonymic flow of letters and postcards spills, with all its metaphoric fluidity, back into materiality, as a letter recondenses upon arrival into paper, ink, and the hand that holds it; in contrast, e-mail purportedly keeps that materiality in check: communication remains fluid, in the form of computerized bytes of information that are easily deleted, forwarded, or saved.[18] Virtuality is deemed an improvement of technology and often connotes a positive, if not utopic, space since it supposedly allows for the ideological fantasy of enjoying bodily pleasures without bodies, or at least, without inhabiting our own bodies but those generated by a computer. Virtual spaces—cybersex, chat rooms—provide users a world detached from materiality, a fantasy realm that is not subject to the limitations of our quotidian existence. Providing an escape from our corporeality, sexuality takes on a heightened sense of liberation in virtual reality: we are not restricted by gender or place, and we can perform our sexual fantasies without fear of contagion. Virtual sex is thus for many "safe sex." In the novel, Melena Rubistein comments, "At times real sex is a burden. [. . .] Digital sex doesn't have problems with contamination" (117).[19] Indeed, there is no doubt that AIDS has had a tremendous impact on uses of technology for sexuality. Ellis Hanson has analyzed, for example, the role of phone sex in the era of AIDS in which bodies are reduced to voices and no physical exchange of fluids is possible. The interest in cybersex in which physical contact between bodies is avoided is certainly motivated in part by the specter of AIDS.

In his treatment of virtual reality and teledildonics, Howard Rheingold suggests that technology enables people to engage in sexual experiences without the concerns for pregnancy and sexually transmitted disease, and as a result, conventional notions of morality seem less pressing, less powerful, when the risks of sexuality are rendered virtual (351–52). The virtuality of letter writing and e-mail—the absence of the body, the distance between correspondents—grants a sense of freedom and security from the limits and dangers of corporeal pleasures. Valencia's project reveals the extent to which virtuality is no guarantee of freedom from contagion. Of course, diseases have long been associated with transmission by mail. In 1899 there was considerable anxiety in Spain about the spread of the bubonic plague through the postal system (with plans for fumigating the mail), and warnings about the transmission of flu viruses by letter were not uncommon ("La peste bubónica" 2243; "La gripe" 12); the transmission of anthrax in the United States in 2001 also fueled concern about the mail system. Computer viruses transmitted via e-mail have also shown time and again the vulnerability of computers to forms of contagion, that virtuality is by no means safe from contamination. In this respect, the virtualization of AIDS in the novel through letter writing unmasks the safety that virtuality purports to offer. The use of the basic technology of writing—dissemination through ink and paper, transported via the postal system—as a vehicle for contamination shadows forth the radically lethal dimension of technology and postal systems of all kinds, virtual or material. The letter writers who respond to Valencia's inquiries do so under the mistaken belief that writing functions as a prophylaxis: the distance and deferral inherent in letter writing provides a protective barrier between them. To speak of writing as a prophylaxis is somewhat ironic, however, for letter writing in turn fails in its prophylactic function for his readers. Quite the opposite: as a measure of self-protection, the letter places distance between Valencia and his interlocutors, thus making contagion and transmission possible and allowing him to expose their corruption to the reading public. The writing of AIDS is thus both prophylactic (protecting its author) and contagious (attacking its readers).

The "prudent distance" that writing would seem to allow offers the Valencian gay community no safe space but, instead, confirmation of its own implication in the epidemic. The avowed spirit of Valencia's project is, on the surface at least, laudable: he demands that his fellow gay men take responsibility for AIDS, to recognize that refusing to grapple with the issue is not a viable political platform. In this respect, Valencia's project resonates with one of the few political groups that emerged in Spain, El Proyecto 1 de Diciembre. This group's avowed purpose was to call attention to the prevailing attitudes around AIDS—"retrograde and insulting attitudes for any human being"—and to reveal how at

times society is just as deadly as the virus itself (Cortés, "Silencio=
Muerte" 105). For Cortés, the formation of El Proyecto 1 de Diciembre
was a response to the period of indifference and frivolity characteristic
of the 1980s (the assumption being that this attitude is partly responsible for the lack of response to AIDS, which Cortés leaves implicit) (105).

But Roberto's letter is not designed to shock his interlocutors into
activism. It is not a catalyst for producing a radical politics around HIV
prevention and education. Roberto's strategy is to deliberately engage
in, by way of confession, a violation of privacy, publishing their letters
in a public way that reflects, in some respects, the violations of privacy
that have taken place around AIDS in the Spanish context. For while
the novel refuses a specular and spectacular vision of AIDS, it focuses its
spectacular gaze on the HIV-negative gay men who eschew activism.
Roberto's sole purpose is to condemn them to social opprobrium.
Fernàndez's novel operates within a politics of shame—of shaming the
letter writers into seeing their own failures. The reader is meant to corroborate Roberto's condescending and hateful vision by laughing at the
characters, seeing their witty repartée as part of their willful ignorance
toward AIDS; Helio Trónica embodies the first reader position when
he describes the pleasure he will feel upon seeing his fellow gay men
"being crucified" with their own words (122). Such a reader would
view the text as a cutting indictment of the frivolous life of sex, drugs,
and rock 'n' roll that marked the newfound freedom of la movida and
other post-Franco cultural movements. Roberto's publication of these
letters is meant to portray a world in which frivolity and corruption
are the symptoms of a gay political apathy that functions as a form of
emotional innoculation against HIV, a means of disavowing it altogether. Both gay and straight readers may share this perspective, either
from a homophobic point of view that already sees homosexuality as a
frivolous, promiscuous "lifestyle" or from an identification with Roberto
Valencia's condemnation of political indifference. Their shame becomes
the reader's schadenfreude.

Not all readers will take a prurient pleasure in seeing these gay men
air their dirty laundry in such a public manner. Some readers may recognize that in the end Valencia effectively capitulates to a homophobic discourse that can only perceive gay men as shallow, empty, and self-hating,

and thus misses another possibility for the function and value of camp in the wake of AIDS. For while the humor of the text is meant in large part to confirm Valencia's view of the Spanish gay community, the recourse to camp implies something about the emotional anxiety that AIDS produces in its wake as well as the role that camp currently plays in contemporary gay communities. Missing in *Una prudente distancia* is the possibility that frivolity and activism, camp and political conscious-ness might go hand in hand. Fernàndez is hardly alone on this score, as several critics have postulated an antithetical relationship between AIDS and camp. For Fran Lebowitz, camp owes its demise to the AIDS epi-demic, and for Mark Finch and David Román, camp is a pre-Stonewall phenomenon (Flinn 26). In the context of U.S. theater, David Román acknowledges that camp's tendency toward superficiality and frivolity runs the risk of articulating AIDS in terms that are devoid of intimacy and emotional depth (212). But while it may be true that in many in-stances the characters in *Una prudente distancia* are indifferent to AIDS, the laughter evoked by the novel is not necessarily a laughter *at* AIDS. In some ways, the laughter exists *in spite of* AIDS. As Román also argues: "the pairing of AIDS and humor need not run counter to a politics of representation set forth by AIDS and/or gay activists" (206). The possibility certainly exists for camp humor to function as a strate-gic response to AIDS, one that can function as a cathartic tool. In 1977, Jack Babuscio wrote of camp in terms that could well apply to the con-temporary moment: "Camp can thus be a means of undercutting rage by its derision of concentrated bitterness. Its vision of the world is comic. Laughter, rather than tears, is its chosen means of dealing with the pain-fully incongruous situation of gays in society" (127).[20] So focused on petty vengeance, Valencia replaces the shame around sex with a shame around camp: their frivolity is presented as a form of "risky" behavior.

This sense of shame is by no means unique to the Spanish context. Michael Warner argues in *The Trouble with Normal* that shame has struc-tured the response to HIV in the United States as sex itself has been construed as something negative. As a result, many campaigns have pro-moted abstinence or monogamous sexuality within the context of mar-riage as a way of preventing the spread of HIV. In the United States Larry Kramer and Randy Shilts have scapegoated the gay community for its "self-destructive" behavior, making queer sexual practices responsible for the spread of AIDS. In more recent years, figures such as Gabriel Rotello and Andrew Sullivan have continued this mode of moralism, one that devolves into tendentious accusations of guilt and innocence without attending to other reasons behind the failure of gay communities to follow safe-sex practices. Douglas Crimp has been among the most trenchant critics of the onslaught of moralizing discourse in which gay men condemn themselves for not practicing safe sex, for not always taking an activist role. Crimp writes, mocking Sullivan's own words: "It turns out that the only reason gay men were shunned was that they were frivolous pleasure-seekers who shirked responsibility. Thank God for AIDS. AIDS saved gay men" (5). Sullivan's moralism projects that repudiation onto other gay men, refusing to see his own identification with them, blaming instead an entire generation of gay men (14). The moralistic stance nevertheless fails in its refusal to tackle the thorny questions of why sexuality invites risk, why it is that prohibition fails—because part of the attraction of sexuality is found in abjection, shame, and risk, all of which are bound up in sex and sexual desire.

In his famous essay "Mourning and Militancy," Crimp draws on Freud's "Mourning and Melancholia" to understand the difficulties that underlie the affective responses to AIDS. He sees a form of melancholy at work in the loss of a certain type of gay culture and sexual freedom caused by the discovery of HIV. Moralism resurfaces in our refusal to acknowledge and respect the range of emotional responses to AIDS, which is, in effect, "to deny the extent of the violence we have all endured" (146). *Una prudente distancia* is, in spite of its humor, a profoundly melancholic novel. If it is not a testimony about living with AIDS, it is a testimony about intellectual and political failure. Repeated references to Althusser, Lacan, Derrida, Marx, and Kristeva appear in the novel as symptoms of a loss of faith in the power of theory to effect substantial political changes. Alfonso Romo, in one of the last letters to Roberto, waxes nostalgically for the heady times of the transition to democracy, for an earlier moment of enthusiasm regarding the possibility of social transformation. In it, he sums up the entire novel's message in a single paragraph:

With just reason you argue that our rushed intellectual formation and ethical deficiencies have led us to this immoral situation from which we've
suffered long before the socialists rose to power, and which we continue
to cause, without too much reflection, with that enthusiasm born from the
guilty conscience of those who deep down yearned for revolutionary change
disguised as bourgeois democracy.[21] (220)

Although some readers may feel politically sympathetic to the spirit in
which Roberto denounces the apathetic attitude of the fictional Valencian gay community, his moralism strikes a rather hypocritical note.
Valencia's motives for attacking his former friends may stem from anger
or despair, but the absence of his voice provides no evidence; the reader
has no access to his psychological or emotional state, hidden behind
the voices of his interlocutors. It may be that the characters betray gay
liberation movements by seeking out a social respectability in the
socialist-dominated Spain of the 1980s and first half of the '90s, but
the moralism of Valencia's attack does not expose or question his own
implication in the very apathy that he condemns. Not only has he
abandoned Spain for the United States but he offers no evidence of
activism on his part, for he too, we learn from the letters, fully embraced
an apolitical sexual freedom in the early years of the transition to
democracy. As much as his plan may be designed to raise consciousness
about AIDS, in some ways he is really just settling old scores. Luis
Filigrana, for example, reveals that this is not the first time Roberto
has engaged in such an endeavor: his earlier publication of *El violador
del alba* (Rapist of the Dawn) was also a roman à clef that revealed the
sexual adventures of Roberto's fellow gay men in Valencia (55).

Roberto's venomous moralism, if not justifiable, is at least comprehensible in light of the AIDS-related deaths among gay men in Spain.
Yet his denunciation of the gay community carries with it even more
pathological overtones than the shame of one's past. For although the
novel strives to raise political consciousness about the failures of the
government and gay community to adequately address AIDS in Spain
and thus prevent HIV-related deaths, it ultimately duplicates the very
viral circuit against which it ostensibly argues. By making the letter
writers victims of their own confessions and portraying them as morally

corrupt individuals, Roberto charts a course similar to that treaded by
Andrew Sullivan and ultimately suggests that gay men infect themselves
out of irresponsibility, fulfilling a teleology that portrays homosexuality as lethal and reinforcing the dominant perception of gay men as har-
bingers of disease. From a phobic point of view AIDS has given a hor-
rifying literality to the psychoanalytic concept of the death drive, which
Freud theorized as a regressive and repetitive tendency that seeks to
establish the equilibrium in the subject, which existed prior to the subject's decentering and which Lacan reframed in terms of jouissance.
Desire continually searches for satisfaction, yet is never satisfied. The
death drive turns that dissatisfaction into a form of satisfaction itself. In
contrast, the phobic notion of a "death wish" suggests that homosexuals desire death—compelled by the guilt that afflicts them—and projects the heterosexual desire to see homosexuality eliminated onto the
homosexual figure so that the desire for death emanates from *within*
homosexuality. The desire for risk and the ambivalence regarding safe
sex, as signs of an internal struggle with the death drive, with the heady
risk of jouissance, are not an exclusively gay matter but form part of all
sexuality. Roberto's insistence on revealing publicly the hidden, secre-
tive corruption of the Valencian gay community—the evil they harbor
under the superficial masquerade of post-Franco Spain—depends fundamentally on a homophobic logic that condemns the homosexual as a
socially contaminating agent that must be brought to light and extir-
pated. Part of this moralistic bent is owed to the fact that Roberto's
attack is directed only at gay men and thus implies that the problems
of AIDS prevention in Spain rest solely with the gay community. There
are no heterosexuals, lesbians, government officials, sex workers, or intravenous drug users in the novel, nor even a sense that these categories
are not mutually exclusive. In so doing, his project replicates the common, pathological assumption that gay men suffer from a sort of "death
wish," in which the gay community, in Edelman's words, is "murderous
in its attachment to 'narcissistic' gratification" (107).[22]

Admittedly, Roberto's epistolary parry is meant to show that no one
is safe from AIDS: even with their knowledge of the purpose for his
return, even if they engage with him believing themselves safe from his
presence, the letter writers cannot protect themselves from his "viral"

attack. On the surface, the equation of the virus with reading and writing communicates a powerful message. There is, to be sure, a certain promise in the message that anyone can contract HIV, a promise of a collective solidarity that transcends sexual orientation, the possibility that if anyone can contract HIV, AIDS cannot be a gay disease. Yet the association of AIDS and gay sex has been so powerful, so predominant, that even heterosexual transmissions have reiterated conceptually the association of homosexuality and AIDS: early descriptions of heterosexual relations between a female prostitute and a male client portrayed viral transmission as an underlying homosexual activity, in which the previous male client's semen passed the virus onto the next client, with the female prostitute merely functioning as a vehicle for transmission (Treichler 49). The movement away from AIDS as something ghostly, nearly invisible, and pertaining only to gay men to something omnipresent and contractable by anyone, like a computer virus, signals, on the surface at least, an important and desperately needed shift. Yet Fernàndez's use of the epistolary form demonstrates that, just as e-mail does not necessarily escape the limitations of traditional epistolary writing, the shifts in how we rhetorically conceptualize the virus do not always bear out their promise to escape older, more insidious modes of thinking. The representation of reading as a form of contagion through the use of letter writing fails in the novel because the reduction of AIDS to a signifier that anyone can contract rests on an implicit association of contagion with homosexuality.

In Fernàndez's novel, the logic of communication and contagion depends fundamentally, as Marnie La Ladrona's treatment of Roberto's letter as a substitute phallus suggests, on the reiteration of another persistent and troubling discourse about homosexuality that manifests itself time and again: that speaking about homosexuality is, in effect, to promote it, even if the terms in which it is spoken are ostensibly prohibitive; that speaking about homosexuality is, to some degree, to participate in homosexuality. The notion that speaking about homosexuality is, to some degree, itself a homosexual act can of course have strategic political functions, where the speaking about homosexual desire is a refusal to keep it consigned to a realm of silence and illegibility.[23] But it can also just as easily treat language about homosexuality as a form of contagion.

Edelman notes that the prohibition on speaking about homosexuality granted it a seductive allure, that to name it would present something so attractive it would corrupt those who heard it spoken. "One corollary of this fear of seduction through nomination or representation is the still pervasive homophobic misreading of homosexuality as contagious" (87). A similar logic subtends the U.S. military's "Don't Ask, Don't Tell" policy. Judith Butler writes: "The ascription of magical efficacy to words emerges in the context of the U.S. military in which the declaration that one is a homosexual is understood to communicate something of homosexuality and, hence, to be a homosexual act of some kind" (*Excitable Speech* 21).[24]

The same argument cannot be made for heterosexuality. To speak of heterosexuality is not to engage in a heterosexual act; the concept of language as contagion holds strictly for homosexuality. As a result, the equation of the transmission of AIDS with the communication of language, of AIDS as a signifier, in which we can all contract some sort of virtual contagion through reading, subscribes to the homophobic logic that everyone can participate *virtually* in a homosexual act and thus runs the risk inherent in homosexuality as a lethal sexuality. Consider, for instance, an article from the Spanish daily *El País* that discusses computer viruses via Microsoft's Outlook e-mail program: "This attachment can be any type of computer application: from an innocent screen-saver to a simple program that erases the hard drive, entering through a virus that infects the system or through a Trojan horse that opens a back door ["puerta trasera"] that then grants the attacker access to the affected computer's files" (Barca). Similar language is used to describe the virus's operation: a "Trojan Horse" virus communicates its deadly agents by surreptitiously entering the subject under the masquerade of an innocent e-mail, or, in the case of AIDS, hidden in a helper T-cell (Treichler 59). But the phrase "back door" ("puerta trasera") is noteworthy since it refers not only to an entrance that remain unnoticed by the computer user but, in Spanish, as the *Diccionario* of the Real Academia Española reminds us, it is also a synonym for "anus" (1689). So too in English it functions as a slang term to refer to the anus, and by extension to anal sex: the very language used to describe the attack of an e-mail virus alludes to the homosexual practice most commonly assumed to be the primary source of transmission of HIV. Reading—the opening of the e-mail program and the downloading of the electronic missives into one's "inbox"—accrues a metaphorical value of receptivity and infiltration associated with anal sex. This rhetorical alignment between technologies of sexuality, AIDS, and homosexuality is recurring, as can be seen in Slavoj Žižek's explanation of the term "interface" by means of a homosexual encounter: "the very notion of 'interface' has its predigital precursors: is not the notorious square opening in the side wall of the restroom, in which a gay offers part of his body (penis, anus) to the anonymous partner on the other side, yet another version of the function of interface?" (*Plague* 151). The very idea of contagion—and contagion through technology—depends on the analogy of an anonymous homosexual encounter, where "interface" between computers is somehow understood as fucking through a bathroom-stall glory hole. The conceptualization of AIDS as a form of computer virus does not, in the end, provide us an escape from sexuality and the homophobic linkage between AIDS and gays. It becomes apparent upon closer inspection that the language used to describe computer viruses and virtual contagion merely replicates homophobic discourses around AIDS and homosexuality.

The lingering presence of phobic concepts in the discourses about AIDS means that those discourses do not implicate everyone equally and in the same manner. It bears repeating that there is, quite obviously, a difference between reading e-mail and contracting a virus, between cybersex on a computer and physical intercourse. As vexing as it may be to lose one's computer files, it is surely not the same as contracting a debilitating or life-threatening virus. Unlike computer virus programs that eliminate bugs with the touch of a button, no cure exists for HIV, rendering problematic the conceptual condensation of reading and downloading of viruses with physical (be it through blood, semen, or other bodily fluids) contraction. While we all live in a world that is subject to AIDS, there is a danger in asserting that we are all in some fashion living with the virus. This is not to deny a collective responsibility, but I do wish to emphasize that the evocation of this "we" is, of course, a loaded term, denoting a collective that, in the pursuit of solidarity, potentially undermines the all too physical and psychic suffering of those who do, in fact, live with the virus. This danger may be exacerbated further by the textual nature of literary criticism. In his analysis of Goytisolo's novel, Epps offers a trenchant critique of Linda Gould Levine's celebratory embrace of the notion of reading as a form of contagion in *Las virtudes*. He argues that her analysis both discards the material reality of those who do suffer from the virus and idealizes contagion, turning reading into an act of redemption (*Significant Violence* 439–43). Fernàndez's novel replicates this textual danger insofar as AIDS is presented as a virtual reality, as a text within a text, a series of letters, faxes, and e-mails bound together into a single volume.

By the same token, the novel's collection of letters—dated from November 6, 1994, to September 15, 1995, written in Valencia, and containing concrete references to political organizations such as the Socialist Party and veiled allusions to figures such as Alberto Cardín— invariably returns the reader to the reality of contemporary Spain. In 2001, Celia Villalobos, former head of the Ministry of Health, stated that AIDS was "under control" (Piquer 25). In the past five years, the number of new cases reported each year has decreased 64 percent since 1995. While rates of infection have continually decreased relative to previous years due to the arrival of retroviral treatments, the conclusion that AIDS is "under control" is suspect: the overall number of AIDS cases is still increasing, and Spain still retains one of the highest relative numbers of AIDS cases in Europe. Of the 243,000 cases of AIDS reported in Europe from the beginning of the pandemic until the end of 2000, nearly one quarter (59,466) were in Spain ("Al SIDA" 8). Numbers alone do not tell the whole story, however, for the relative percentages are also shifting in Spain. Intravenous drug use transmission rates are dropping, while the percentage for heterosexual transmission is increasing. In 1998, 64 percent of cases were intravenous drug users and 18 percent of cases involved heterosexual transmission ("El número"), while in 2003, the intravenous drug users dropped to 51 percent while rates among heterosexuals increased to 28 percent, with staggering increases among women ("El sida disminuye"). AIDS never was a gay disease, nor is it now.

In the final analysis, Fernàndez's *Una prudente distancia* seems to say that the more things change, the more they stay the same. On August

8, 2003, *El Mundo* published an article to announce the Ministry of
Health's "e-mail virus" prevention campaign. The article concludes,
using terms that should have been long surpassed, that the largest "risk
group" is now heterosexuals: "The group of greatest proportional risk
is today that of heterosexuals, to whom the new television spot is principally directed" ("El sida disminuye"). In spite of its intended audience, the ad campaign not only reflects a persistent sexual puritanism
surrounding AIDS by refusing more explicit approaches to sexuality,
but the association of AIDS with homosexuality resurfaces in an unanticipated, oblique way. In the commercial the chain of computer users
begins with a man sending a message of love to a woman. That woman
in turn sends it on to another man, that man sends it to two men,
and they send it to a woman who then receives the virus warning on
her desktop. The communication from one man to two men (who may
or may not be gay but nonetheless are the only "couple" represented)
is significant in that it is only after the transmission *between men* that the
next user, a woman, contracts a virus. The advertisement replicates, perhaps unintentionally, the association of sexual activities between men
as the source of HIV contagion. Heterosexual transmission is, in the
end, a homosexual, or at least bisexual, transmission. This is perhaps an
overly pessimistic reading, one that courts cynicism a little too closely,
but there is little comfort or solace about AIDS to be found either
in Fernàndez's novel or in the ad campaign. Singling out some people
more than others, both *Una prudente distancia* and the Spanish Ministry
of Health end up communicating not just an informative message about
AIDS but also a homophobic warning against the contaminating effects
of love between men.

Postscript

> The epistle . . . is not a genre, but all genres, literature itself.
>
> —JACQUES DERRIDA, *The Post Card*

In epistolary studies, it seems almost de rigueur to offer a postscript, as if the "p.s." of letter writing were somehow more appropriate than the standard "conclusion." Letter writing involves the inscription of past events, an action that gestures in turn toward a future moment of reading. Writing a conclusion about a genre that by its very nature resists such temporal closure is a difficult task. The study of queer desire in epistolary fiction in Spain could include additional works such as Miguel Espinosa's *La tríbada falsaria* (The Deceitful Tribade, 1982) and *La tríbada confusa* (The Confused Tribade, 1984), Miguel Àngel Riera's *Els déus inaccessibles* (The Inaccessible Gods, 1987), Olga Guirao's *Mi querido Sebastián* (My Dear Sebastian, 1992) and *Carta con diez años de retraso* (A Letter Arriving Ten Years Late, 2002), and Tomás Ortiz's *Te esperaré* (I'll Wait for You, 2000), all of which engage with issues of the communication of homosexuality via the epistolary mode. The study could also move beyond the boundaries of this book to include works from other national literatures. In Latin American literature, Jaime Bayly's Internet novel *Los amigos que perdí* (The Friends I Lost, 2000) stands out as an online experiment in epistolary fiction that engages with explicit representations of queer desire. Numerous texts from other literary traditions would likewise provide additional terrain for the exploration of how epistolarity conditions the representation of homosexual desire. But a postscript is not necessarily a conclusion; it functions as an addendum to writing, as a movement to something else. Rather than speculate on various other directions that this study could undertake or offer a definitive conclusion on the state of gay and lesbian sexuality in contemporary Spain, in these final remarks I would like to reflect briefly on the theoretical consequences for queer approaches to literature that emerge from this project.

The preceding analyses have taken the practice of queer reading as their point of departure. At the risk of redundancy, the first part was devoted to two queer readings to see how the letter functioned as a repository of desire, one that either generated a window into the psyche of the writer (Unamuno) or foreclosed that access as a reflection of the foreclosure of lesbian desire (Martín Gaite). The second part turned to the explicit representation of desire to articulate the ethical stakes of having access to someone's sexuality, either by making that knowledge public by disseminating a written confession (Villena) or by engaging in a public display of one's sexuality by writing a testimony meant to be disseminated (Riera). The third part engaged with how the acts of reading and writing reflected the fractured state of a gay and lesbian community in the aftermath of the death of Franco and currently during the AIDS epidemic (Fernàndez). While the social conditions under which contemporary gays and lesbians in Spain live on a daily basis have improved of course in the last three decades, the tenor of this study has remained suspicious of a narrative of liberation. The opposite approach to an affirmative outlook is the wholly pessimistic view that little has changed in any significant manner; such pessimism likewise overstates its case. This book has attempted instead to chart a course between this version of Scylla and Charybdis, attending to the increasing explicitness and freedom of expression—to the letter's movement from intimate, private exchanges to public spaces—without claiming such expression to be always and necessarily emancipatory.

No doubt one could ask whether the exclusive focus on the epistolary form has precluded other literary modes that may not emphasize confession, privacy, secrecy, and stigma. The ambivalence toward homoeroticism that appears in Unamuno's and Martín Gaite's texts is perpetuated in the stigma that imbues Riera's and Villena's characterizations of homosexual love affairs, and is reiterated in turn in the ambivalence

toward gay and lesbian liberation politics in Fernàndez's 1979 novel and
toward the response of the gay community to AIDS in his 1998 sequel.
Is the concern with confession attributable to the epistolary form alone
or does the recourse to the epistolary form reflect a broader concern
with the guilt, stigma, and secrecy that have marked homosexuality in
Spain? Other representations of gay and lesbian sexuality may reflect a
more optimistic outlook, and it is certainly plausible to argue that the
formal constraints of the epistolary novel necessarily inflect the representation of sexuality in a particular way. Be that as it may, the continual presence of epistolarity in contemporary Spanish literature is, to my
mind, the sign of an ongoing engagement with the characteristics that
lend to letter writing a confessional mode of speaking about desire and
which continue to structure and condition queer sexualities.

In the final analysis, the question that *Confessions of the Letter Closet*
raises is whether queer studies can move beyond a confessional mode
of sexuality—or, at the very least, beyond a type of queer reading that
reinforces a confessional dynamic. Although we associate the contemporary understanding of identity with confession, the Spanish context
demonstrates that the power that confession exerts on subjects persists
in spite of their ambivalence toward identity categories. By extension,
it questions the notion that "queerness" as a political posture of refusing
identity and identification is an effective escape from the power dynamics that confession exerts on sexual identity. Yet it would hardly be an
overstatement to claim that sexuality as it is understood and lived in
Spain is not unique in its relationship to confession. The need to move
beyond a confessional approach to sexuality has motivated two recent
assessments of the field of queer literary studies: Eve Sedgwick's introduction to *Novel Gazing* and Christopher Lane's afterword to *The
Burdens of Intimacy*. Both authors respond to the proliferation of queer
studies of literature and to the concepts and modes of reading that dom-
inate its practice. Sedgwick and Lane, adopting different perspectives
with divergent solutions, call into question queer theory's tendency to
privilege narrative enigmas and opacity as signs of queer desire, to treat
the literary text as a sort of secret message about sexuality that the critic
can simply extract and decipher.

In her assessment of queer studies as a critical discipline, Sedgwick argues that a particular mode of reading has become institutionalized. Suspicion and paranoia are now common stances in queer studies, conceiving homosexuality as a secreted desire to be discovered. Queer approaches to literary studies have often operated on a logic of exposure, revealing queer desire that has remained latent, undisclosed, or even deliberately suppressed. The political power of this mode of queer reading rests in the unmasking of the oppressive force of heteronormativity to render expressions of homosexuality invisible and unintelligible. In this respect, the "queering" of literary studies is a politically motivated practice that attempts to rectify the historical legacy of silence that surrounds homosexuality. As laudable and politically necessary as such an enterprise may be, according to Sedgwick, exposure operates by turning paranoia into an epistemological strategy. The transformation of paranoia into a critical methodology, she argues, turns queer reading into a constant and ever-vigilant process of exposing where gender norms break down, where the law of sexual difference fails, or where identity becomes fractured and troubling for the self. Exposing sexual difference as a fallacious masquerade or heteronormativity as a repressive force that fails to repress homosexual desire, a paranoid epistemology of exposure offers the security that somehow we are more equipped to resist and overturn the ideological forces that shape queer subjectivities, as if exposing the hidden sites of desire were sufficient to alter the way homosexuality is conceptualized.

Working with Victorian literature, Lane similarly notes that sexual secrets are too often interpreted as signs of repressed homosexual desire. He suggests that critics are misreading those enigmas and ambiguities because of a fundamental misunderstanding of the psychic life of the subject. Lane summarizes his project when he writes: "the unconscious reminds us that the desires, acts, and relationships we invoke as elements of our sexual identity are never quite the same as the contradictory psychic impulses of which this identity consists" (228). His advocacy of psychoanalysis is thus designed to underscore the instability of sexual identity—that the very phrase "sexual identity" is in fact oxymoronic when we take into account the radical split between our conscious understanding of sexuality (the ego) and its inner workings (the unconscious). The exposure of secrets and enigmatic desires is thus a flawed methodology not because it is paranoid, as Sedgwick argues, but rather because it fails to understand the ways in which all subjects—heterosexual and homosexual—struggle with the enigmatic function of unconscious desire.

I agree, in essence, with their respective positions. The chief value of Sedgwick's and Lane's arguments resides in their laudable attempts to move beyond the confessional mode of locating any and all instances of queer desire in literary texts—to treat all literature as a form of closet—that dominates current practices of queer reading. Both want to avoid the normalizing practice of finding homosexuality and attributing identities that, following Foucault, arose from the secular expansion of confession. Where Sedgwick emphasizes amelioration and pleasure over guilt and shame, Lane highlights the instability of the unconscious over ego-identifications. The solutions that they present, however, underscore the very difficulty of overcoming the limitations each one avers in queer studies.

Sedgwick advocates that critics turn away from paranoia and exposure and adopt a "reparative" stance that emphasizes not the oppression and loss that characterize the world in which we live but rather the possibilities of finding pleasure and joy in spite of those circumstances. Demystification, denaturalization, and exposure are the hallmarks of a "hermeneutics of suspicion," whereas the reparative stance takes the position that the motives for reading may be pleasure and amelioration (22). Sedgwick calls for a shift in the motives behind our reading practices, so that we might move beyond paranoia and suspicion and focus on queer experiences that are not necessarily forged by those two oppressive forces. In short, she promotes a mode of reading that seeks not to expose the ideological forces that are the sources of our subjection but the "many ways in which selves and communities succeed in extracting sustenance from the objects of a culture—even of a culture whose avowed desire has often been not to sustain them" (35). Sedgwick thus suggests that queer scholars should forsake the vast array of theorists that have until now heavily informed queer work. In particular, she singles out Freud (and Lacan, to a lesser extent); Foucault, in a much more limited fashion, also seems to fall under the category of thinkers associated with a hermeneutics of suspicion.

In making her argument, Sedgwick is forced to expose in previous critics' writings (to her credit, she includes her own work) the workings of this hermeneutics of suspicion. In exposing the critical practice of exposure, however, her writing itself seems to take on a paranoid tone when it comes to Judith Butler's work, anticipating at several turns any potential criticism. From the outset she declares that her use of Butler's *Gender Trouble* (as well as D. A. Miller's *The Novel and the Police*) as exemplary of a paranoid hermeneutic should not be read as a critique of Butler since that particular book is no longer representative of her more recent work (9). That caveat alone would perhaps not suggest any sort of paranoid stance on Sedgwick's part if it were not repeated in different guises. In her discussion of psychoanalysis, for example, Sedgwick chastises psychoanalytic critics for the certainty with which they deploy such terms as "sexual difference" and "the phallus" and asserting their "inexorable, irreducible, uncircumnavigable, omnipresent centrality, at every psychic juncture" (11). Yet she is quick to mitigate her claims as they apply to Butler, claiming that she is "very far from the most single-minded" of theorists who deploy psychoanalytic terminology such as "the phallus" or "sexual difference" (11). A page later, she writes parenthetically: "I don't want to suggest, in using the word 'mimetic,' that these uses of psychoanalytic gender categories need be either uncritical of, or identical to, the originals: Judith Butler, among others, has taught us a much less deadening use of 'mimetic'" (12). Sedgwick's own theorization of paranoia confirms her own argument that paranoia is, to some extent, contagious. Something like paranoia ends up permeating her own discussion of earlier approaches to queer studies insofar as she exposes the ways in which their own texts operate according to a paranoid hermeneutics of exposure, and at the same time she attempts to preempt any possible criticism of her remarks about Butler.

In *How to Do the History of Homosexuality*, David Halperin makes an incisive point about Sedgwick's earlier claim in *The Epistemology of the Closet* that previous sexual paradigms were not simply superseded by later ones. Halperin claims that her argument, in attempting to move beyond the debates between essentialism and social construction, replicated the very problem that she criticized in social construction theories of sexuality: "In a gesture exactly congruent with the one she criticized, she structured her project in such a way that 'the superseded model then drops out of the frame of analysis'" (11). Sedgwick replicates the very same maneuver by trying to supersede "paranoia" with a "reparative" approach: where Sedgwick once proposed to bracket essentialist arguments in spite of their historical foothold (and their capacity to reemerge in contradictory and unanticipated ways in contemporary understandings of homosexuality), she now wants to bracket "paranoia" and "exposure" as outdated modes of undertaking queer studies. Sedgwick, I would argue, draws too stark a line between exposure as paranoia and exposure as a necessary engagement with older forms of thinking that even reparative approaches may themselves conceal or in fact produce. In fact, Sedgwick's treatment of Butler offers an example of exposure as reparative: in trying to move away from psychoanalysis, in attempting to "repair" the state of queer criticism, Sedgwick ends up exonerating psychoanalysis by arguing that Butler's use of Freud and Lacan does not necessarily reproduce what Sedgwick sees as a "mimetic" and thus "deadening" use of theory. Not only can exposure be reparative, as her treatment of Butler suggests; Sedgwick's call to focus on pleasure over paranoia does not necessarily guarantee that we have escaped a hermeneutics based on exposure: one person's intimacy is someone else's voyeurism. As epistolary fiction reminds us, even when we shift our attention to affects such as sentimentality and love, we may still be operating within a confessional framework by *exposing* the ways in which sentimentality functions in relationship to categories of sexuality. Lauding pleasure as a narrative of reparation and amelioration potentially falls prey to an unquestioned and uncritical belief in pleasure as liberatory. To dismiss suspicion altogether for the sake of pleasure is the very definition of ideology.

In contrast with Sedgwick's argument that thinkers such as Freud have branded queer studies with suspicion and paranoia, Lane's work demonstrates that the use of psychoanalysis is not necessarily constrained to a paranoid hermeneutical project. At the end of his afterword, Lane exhorts critics to grant the ineffable the place he claims it deserves in our studies. He emphasizes that we cannot interpret the sexual identity of authors or characters with any certainty. Lane does not deny the influence of social norms of sexuality, but he argues that sexual identity is contested by both the political sphere *and* the unconscious (228). He admirably charges critics with ignoring issues of doubt, uncertainty, and the ineffable, yet by virtue of his object of study, Victorian literature, Lane implies that the representation of sexuality as "a secret or not-yet-palpable enigma" is the only form of doubt that sexuality raises. His use of psychoanalysis to demonstrate that psychic concerns about desire need not always be the sign of repressed homosexuality is persuasive: not all forms of queer reading are about outing. What remains untapped in this formulation are the ways in which contemporary works whose representations of sexuality are decidedly explicit present other types of doubt about the meaning of sexuality and characters' desires. Studies of late-twentieth-century literature are not necessarily faced with the task of deciphering whether sexual enigmas are heterosexual or homo-sexual when the text clearly establishes the presence of same-sex desire. By equating the interpretive difficulties that literary texts pose for queer reading with the representation of sexuality as an enigma to be decoded, Lane overlooks the fact that the explicit representation of sexuality may raise other difficulties or uncertainties, ones that may or *may not* involve the unconscious, that emerge as a result of knowing a given character's sexual practices.

One of the risks of equating ineffability and doubt with unconscious desires is that critical doubts about the meaning of sexuality are suppressed by a critical certainty about the role of the unconscious. Marshaling psychoanalysis as a corrective for queer studies may have the unintended effect of advancing a critical shift from "from finding the homosexual" to finding the effects of the unconscious. In reference to D. A. Miller's work on Roland Barthes, for example, Lane writes: "[W]e could use biography to explore subjective instability, not ontological veracity" (242). Rejecting the centrality of Foucault in queer studies, Lane affirms the instability of identity over any notion of ontological consistency. Psychoanalytic appeals to the unconscious, on the one hand, and a social construction view of sexuality, on the other, might therefore be seen as sharing the same fundamental goal of loosening the essentialist binds that tie down subjectivity. In other words, both psychoanalysis and queer theory purport to offer a theoretical path that escapes a view of subjectivity as something fixed and stable. Any notion of a coherent identity is consistently overturned by the supposed fluidity of gender and sexuality or because of the undeniable role of the unconscious in our psychic lives. At root, we might argue, is a belief in the capacity to advance theoretically beyond a confessional mode of conceptualizing subjectivity—beyond the frameworks of identity and sexuality that Foucault traced as a secularized extension of confession as a religious practice. Yet the critical task of scrutinizing literary texts in search of evidence of the unconscious potentially reinscribes a different version of the confessional framework. Lane asserts that "every identity must struggle with internal constraints" (228), but in so doing the hermeneutic impulse potentially changes the object of analysis from a single, fixed truth known as identity to a single, fixed truth that sexuality is unstable due to the "internal constraints" of the unconscious. Literature, as a result, becomes less a repository of transparent sexual meaning than a place marker for the unconscious that cannot be represented.

Moving between Foucault and psychoanalysis, between suspicion and reparation, this study has drawn inspiration from both approaches, emphasizing the ways in which exposure leads to doubt and ineffability and, at the same time, gesturing toward the affirmative value of giving voice to same-sex desire. Letters that convey homoerotic desire, either because their contents communicate strong feelings of affection or because they allow for two interlocutors to connect in unanticipated ways (chapters 1–2), raise questions of doubt about sexual identity because they are fragments of an individual's subjectivity, written in a specific time and place, and destined for a particular reader. When letters connect two members of the same sex, they do not necessarily offer definitive answers about the writers' relationships to queer desire. The explicit confession of homosexual desire likewise does little to dispel the sense of doubt that surrounds the act of corresponding; to write about one's homosexual desire, relaying it to another, does not alone make sense of it. Confessions of desire confuse and confound readers because they are not simply confessions of desire or even admissions of one's own failure to love (chapters 3–4). Letters demand responses to conscious and unconscious wishes, they are requests for something that often remains ineffable and unspoken. The response engages the boundaries between public and private spaces and remains open to interpretation. As a result, the response to a letter, in light of the responsibility a letter entrusts to its reader, is a difficult one to provide: is the reader meant to uphold or affirm the confession, adopting the position of moral authority, or to read and accept the confession as a form of testimony that demands not a response but recognition? When faced with correspondence exchanged between multiple writers rather than a single missive, the reader confronts a profound sense of disruption, chaos, and discord (chapters 5–6). Epistolary works composed of multiple writers convey the fractures and fissures of a network of interlocutors who pour their thoughts into the space of a sealed envelope, with the faith that letters will overcome the distance that separates writers from their addressees. Viewed as a totality, a polyvocal epistolary novel often portrays a different image than the individual accounts offer, requiring the reader to deduce the meaning of each letter in relation to the collected correspondence as a whole.

By emphasizing the interpretive difficulties that epistolary texts pose for the reader, *Confessions of the Letter Closet* has argued, in essence, for an approach to queer desire that refutes the traditional sentimental parameters of letter writing and the genre of epistolary fiction. Epistolary works grant the reader access to intimate expressions of sentimentality, passion, and love—but almost exclusively between members of the opposite sex. The genre's formal and historical constraints enable queer desire by allowing for the intimate expression between correspondents who might not otherwise share such thoughts, but they also constrict that expression: queer mail, associated with confession and confidentiality, struggles to articulate a concept of homosexual desire not stained by stigma, shame, and guilt. The foregoing analyses have repeatedly returned to several topics: the tenuous border between friendship and eroticism; the absence, loss, and melancholy inherent in epistolary relations; the role of memory in fashioning a coherent discourse about the self and its affective relations. The letter as a form of closet writing in this study has taken the form of a confidential exchange, a testimonial declaration, a multifaceted portrait of a community of interlocutors, and a malicious tool of revenge. Future manifestations of epistolary fiction will no doubt continue to modify the genre's formal and discursive parameters, advancing unanticipated representations of queer desire. Whether our theoretical approaches to literary texts can move beyond the confessional framework that has shaped and conditioned the study of homoeroticism and homosexuality remains to be seen. Although this study comes to a close, its project remains unfinished. The task of re-dressing the limitations of our critical reading practices begins anew with every *envoi* of a queer letter.

NOTES

Introduction

1. David Bergeron's study of homoeroticism in the letters of James I and Rictor Norton's volume of "gay love letters" from antiquity to the present are two more examples of this conceptual trend. In these critics' works, the letter functions as an open closet—or at least, a door to the closet—to recuperate, at moments ahistorically, queer subjectivities from the past.

2. I have taken my cue from Robert Adams Day, who argues that "the writing, receiving, suppression, and discovery of letters [. . .] should have more than merely mechanical importance" (158).

3. In her seminal work, *The Epistemology of the Closet,* Eve Sedgwick criticized Freudian psychoanalysis for avowedly reducing differences between individuals to reductive and normalizing categories such as "*the* other" or "*the* oedipal" (23–24).

4. For example, the meaning of the unconscious for Foucault differs from that for psychoanalysis. According to Arnold Davidson, Foucault rejected the psychoanalytic interpretation of the unconscious as sexual (211). For Joan Copjec, Foucault's historicism construes the unconscious as a socially constructed category, rather than a gap in the symbolic (19). Judith Butler, for her part, has argued that the unconscious may not be determined in its entirety by social and cultural forces, but neither is it entirely divorced from that cultural and social dimension, for its effects can only be seen within that domain (*Psychic Life* 88). Rather than see the unconscious as an ideological anchor that oppresses *or* as a site of pleasure and emancipation from prohibition, Jacqueline Rose posits that it ought to be considered as "something that hovers uncomfortably in between" (12).

5. Foucault treated sexuality as a discourse, which is not the same as saying that he saw sexuality as only discursive. In *How to Do the History of Homosexuality,* David Halperin argues that critics overlook the fact that Foucault's arguments do not

apply to what people felt or desired personally (29). Foucault, in focusing on discursive and institutional practices, does not offer a theory of desire.

6. Christopher Lane's *The Burdens of Intimacy,* for example, dissents from an
exclusively Foucauldian view of sexuality during the Victorian era and marshals
psychoanalysis as the primary theoretical lens. He advocates an "anti-identarian"
perspective, affirming the value of the unconscious and of psychic fantasy as that
which consistently troubles any coherent identity at the level of ego.

7. For example, Ellis concludes his study with the affirmation of an increasingly positive trajectory for gay autobiographical writing in Spain (139).

8. For a discussion of the terminological difficulties posed by the study of
homosexuality in Spain, see Aliaga, "Como hemos cambiado," 43–47, and Martínez
Expósito, 6.

9. For a nuanced discussion of the distinctions between identity, subjectivity,
and morphology as they pertain to sexuality, see Halperin, *How To Do the History
of Homosexuality,* esp. 37–42.

10. In Spanish, the verb *sellar* ("to stamp") means not only "to leave an impression for identification" but also "to cover or hide." As Pedro Salinas notes, the word
sello ("stamp") is derived from the Latin *sigilo,* meaning "secret" or "silence" (37).

11. Psychoanalytic models of the subject reiterate this epistolary focus. Nicolas
Abraham, working with Maria Torok, refers to the ego as the Envelope, which
Lane notes is suggestive of messages that are sealed or "entombed" ("Testament"
9). For his part, Slavoj Žižek labels the Lacanian definition of the unconscious as
"the dead, uncomprehended letter" (*Sublime Object* 43). In *The Post Card* Derrida
argues that, in effect, Freudian psychoanalysis is a theory rooted in epistolarity and
the post (41). Derrida's view of the postal system continues his interrogation of the
metaphysics of presence: letter writing, and the postal system that enframes its
practice, offers the illusory promise of a coherent subjectivity and relationship with
others. For a brief analysis of the ways in which letter exchanges emulate psychoanalytic exchanges between analyst and analysand, see Carlos Pérez.

12. Godfrey Singer, at the end of *The Epistolary Novel,* asserts that Spain's
national literature may be the only one fundamentally dependent upon letter writing. For his part, Charles Kany attempts to rectify the lack of importance granted
to Spanish literature in the development of the epistolary novel. Turning to Juan
de Segura's (1548) *Processo de cartas de amores (Process of Love Letters),* he writes that
it is the first modern novel made entirely of letters, and he notes furthermore that
Spain has yet to be given its due in epistolary discourses (x, 72).

13. For a listing of foreign works in translation and their dates of publication in
nineteenth-century Spain, see Montesinos.

14. Pagés-Rangel argues that the nineteenth-century public, and especially
women readers, had an insatiable appetite for published letters and letter-writing

manuals, but the majority of letters published at this time were not in the form of a single author's correspondence (9, 12).

15. Rueda notes that eighteenth-century epistolary fiction also emphasizes privacy, whereby interlocutors demand that their letters be burned or kept private, a demand that invariably guarantees the opposite effect (*Cartas* 31).

16. I would further speculate, following Gold's arguments, that in Spain the association of letters with confession as a didactic and moralizing practice may have contributed to the weakness of novelistic uses of epistolarity in the nineteenth and early twentieth centuries. The association of letters with confession—particularly the confession of illicit desires—may have carried a didactic association that effectively proscribed their use in narrative works. Rueda also notes that many of the works adopt a moralistic or didactic purpose, which she attributes to the dominant presence of Catholicism (40, 78).

17. See Ocón for an overview of the consistent concern about the politics of the mail system, its insufficiencies, the lack of personnel, and the impoverished state of its services.

18. José María Castán Vázquez notes that there are, however, many exceptions to the right to secrecy including the rights of parents, teachers, and medical doctors over the epistolary correspondence of their charges (23–25).

19. Rueda notes that both of Galdós's works draw attention to the porous borders between private and public spaces, between fiction and reality ("El poder" 376).

20. "mudando sólo los nombres propios, para que, si viven los que con ellos se designan, no se vean en novela sin quererlo ni permitirlo" (137).

21. "le escribo siempre como si estuviera de rodillas delante de usted a los pies del confesionario" (222).

22. "¿cómo penetrar en lo íntimo del corazón, en el secreto escondido de la mente juvenil de una doncella, criada tal vez con recogimiento exquisito e ignorante de todo?" (149).

23. "Como quiera que sea, dejando a un lado estas investigaciones psicológicas que no tengo derecho a hacer, pues no conozco a Pepita Jiménez" (150).

24. "Usted me ha enseñado a analizar lo que el alma siente, a buscar su origen bueno o malo, a escudriñar los más hondos senos del corazón, a hacer, en suma, un escrupuloso examen de conciencia" (153).

25. "No imagines, sin embargo, que la afición de Luis y Pepita al bienestar material haya entibiado en ellos, en lo más mínimo, el sentimiento religioso. [. . .] Luis no olvida nunca, en medio de su dicha presente, el rebajamiento del ideal con que había soñado" (350).

26. "Te cuento todos los fenómenos que se van sucediendo en mi alma, porque eres mi confesor y nada debo ocultarte" (84).

27. Part of the concern with confidentiality is that Infante is preoccupied with public opinion and his place within society. His letters reveal his insecurities and his opinions of others, offering him a way to express his concerns in a manner that speech—and public speech, in particular—would not allow. For an analysis of the conflict between private and public perception of events in relation to Infante's fears of breaking social conventions, see Delgado.

28. "los obstáculos permanentes de su carácter, de muy difícil solución" (67).

29. "Bien podía ella, pues, revelármela [la verdad], que yo la oiría como un confesor y la encerraría en mí como en un sepulcro" (177).

30. "pero yo voy creyendo que en este caso la fatalidad existe, y que Federico no adelanta porque se lo estorba alguna fuerza interior incontrastable, y también circunstancias externas independientes de su voluntad" (68).

31. Homosexuality does appear at one point in the novel: Infante refers to Malibán, a sort of dandyesque figure, as a *marica* ("faggot") (166).

32. "Hágame la merced y otórgueme la honra de aceptar para siempre la franca, y pura, y desinteresada, aunque inútil, amistad de este su humilde servidor, y amigo, y hermano, y padre, y . . . todo lo que V. quiera, menos novio."

33. "Sr. Don Pedro Lasso, frustrado amor mío: ¡Acabáramos, hombre, acabáramos! . . . ¡Nada! Que me da vergüenza del bromazo que he corrido con mi amor postal, y que no sé si suicidarme, ó soltar la carcajada."

1. Archival Resurrections of Queer Desire in Miguel de Unamuno

1. "Don Sandalio es un personaje visto desde fuera, cuya vida interior se nos escapa, que acaso no la tiene . . . ¿pero es que mi Don Sandalio no tiene vida interior, no tiene conciencia, o sea con-saber de sí mismo, es que no monodialoga?" All Spanish citations are from the *San Manuel Bueno, mártir y tres historias más* edition. I have used Kerrigan's translation for English quotations; however, Kerrigan does not include Unamuno's prologue.

2. "para mejor representarse y a la vez disfrazarse y ocultar su verdad" (96).

3. Barthes does not address letter writing in "The Death of the Author," but one can infer from his comments about autobiographical forms such as diaries and memoirs that the letter writer suffers the same linguistic "death" as any other author: "The author still reigns in histories of literature, biographies of writers, interviews, magazines, as in the very consciousness of men of letters anxious to unite their person and their work through diaries and memoirs" (143). Unamuno was also acutely aware of the author's lack of control over his writing, as Frances Wyers has convincingly argued, but his position was much more tormented than that of Barthes (330).

4. For a brief overview of the many points of intersection between Unamuno's other writings and this story, see Lowe.

5. "Veo delante de mí muchos problemas, muchos ojos que me aprisionan. El fantasma que vive en nosotros y que nos odia me empuja por el sendero. Hay que andar porque tenemos que ser viejos y morirnos, pero yo no quiero hacerle caso [. . .] y sin embargo, cada día que pasa tengo una duda y una tristeza más. ¡Tristeza del enigma de mí mismo!"

6. For a powerful analysis of the function of the letter's relationship to the closet, see José Quiroga's "The Mask of the Letter" in his *Tropics of Desire*. Quiroga demonstrates that Latin American writers have employed the letter in coded ways for the expression of homosexuality. He suggests that the coded representations of homosexuality are less a reflection of reticence and concern with privacy, although that is true in some instances, than an acknowledgment that the secret was already out in the open and therefore did not need to be named (37).

7. "la imagen de Don Sandalio me seguía a todas partes" (68).

8. "Está visto que necesito a Don Sandalio, que sin Don Sandalio no puedo ya vivir" (69).

9. "sueño con él, casi sufro con él" (73).

10. "Te digo, Felipe, que este Don Sandalio me vuelve loco" (76).

11. "Y además, me entretenía tanto en la cama, ¡se me pegaban tan amorosamente las sábanas!" (76). I have occasionally modified the published translations in order to reflect more accurately, in my opinion, the literal meaning of the original quotation. All such modifications are indicated as such parenthetically.

12. "me ha metido en el hondón del alma" (73).

13. "este suceso imprevisto cambiaba totalmente el giro de mi vida íntima" (80). On the intertwining of the seductive play of chess with the letter-writing practice, see Rueda, "*La novela de Don Sandalio.*"

14. "¿Por qué de pronto ha invadido una negra congoja y me he puesto a llorar, así como lo oyes, Felipe, a llorar la muerte de mi Don Sandalio? Sentía dentro de mí un vacío inmenso" (84).

15. "Yo creí, señor mío, que había usted cobrado algún apego, acaso algún cariño, a Don Sandalio" (88).

16. For an analysis of the homoerotic implications of the male couple in *Bouvard and Pécuchet,* see Orr.

17. For an extended analysis of Freud's difficulty in distinguishing sexuality from sociality, see Lane, "Freud on Group Psychology."

18. See Michael Lucey's chapter on *Corydon* for an analysis of the text's struggle to contain its own homophobia, and in particular, disdain for lesbianism.

19. "Si el homosexual normal—expresión de Gide—es el llamado casto, es que no se trata más que de un amigo; todo lo amigo que se quiera, pero sólo amigo. No nos atrevemos a ver más que amistad entre dos hombres que se quieran, se ayuden y no puedan vivir, incluso el uno sin el otro, pero que no se entreguen a

prácticas homosexuales. A nadie se le ocurriría llamar 'homosexuales normales' a dos hombres que se quisieran tiernamente, como hermanos, sin que entre ellos mediara nada pecaminoso."

20. Marañón's prologue is an "anti-socratic" dialogue with the editor in which he refutes Gide's arguments about the normality and naturalness of homosexuality. Where Gide conceives homosexuality as a higher stage of evolution, Marañón claims that it is an evolutionary defect that, over time, will be lost. His dialogue stages, in essence, a refusal to write a prologue that endorses the book.

21. An exception to this trend is Pamela Bacarisse's reading of *San Manuel Bueno, mártir* in which she analyzes convincingly how the novel poses but does not answer the ambiguous question of desire and the "secret" that is shared between the narrator's brother, Lázaro, and San Manuel Bueno.

22. Hoyos's letters to Unamuno are archived in the Casa-Museo Miguel de Unamuno in Salamanca. *El hombre que vendió su cuerpo al diablo* first appeared in 1915 but was republished in 1917 with Unamuno's prologue as the seventh volume in a series that also included Hoyos's *El martirio de San Sebastián* with a prologue by Jacinto Benavente.

23. On the relationship between dandyism and homosexuality, see Sinfield. He argues that dandyism becomes associated with homosexuality after Wilde, its ambivalence once serving as a mask that allowed for both same-sex and cross-sex relations (71). For an analysis of the early discourses around homosexuality that are closely linked to the Spanish *modernismo* and dandyism, see Mira, "Modernistas, dandis y pederastas."

24. The cross-gender paradigm for conceptualizing homosexuality, often associated with Freud and in the Spanish context with Marañón, was prevalent but not exclusive. See Marañón's *La evolución de la sexualidad y los estados interesexuales* (The Evolution of Sexuality and the Intersexual States), which followed nineteenth-century sexologists in this area and treated male homosexuality in terms of inversion. In the 1920 version of *Three Essays on the Theory of Sexuality,* Freud conceded that there were male homosexuals who were completely masculine and whose only difference from other men was the selection of a male object of desire rather than a female one.

25. Unamuno tended to link sexuality with procreation: sex, leading to reproduction, served as an extension of the self, with the subject perpetuating himself through his children. In *Del sentimiento trágico de la vida (The Tragic Sense of Life in Men and Nature,* 1913), for example, he argues that love always involves a sexual element whose function is to reproduce oneself (181). As a result, works such as *La tía Tula, Nada menos que todo un hombre* (Nothing Less than a Whole Man, 1920) and *Abel Sánchez* (1917) dramatize issues of paternity over erotic relations.

26. In a letter to his close friend Juan Arzadun, dated December 18, 1890, shortly before the marriage to Concha, Unamuno rejects romance and conjugal happiness

and expresses instead his hope for having children. Unamuno also mentions that Concha's presence will regenerate his ideas (Baeza and Reyes 64). In either case, Concha appears reduced to her procreative capacity as wife or generative catalyst for Unamuno's other offspring, namely, his writing.

27. "Tú has echado de menos en toda esta mi correspondencia una figura de mujer y ahora te figuras que la novela que estás buscando, la novela que quieres que yo te sirva, empezará a cuajar en cuanto surja ella. ¡Ella! ¡La ella del viejo cuento! Sí, ya sé, '¡buscad a ella!' Pero yo no pienso buscar a la hija de Don Sandalio ni a otra ella que con él pueda tener relación" (91).

28. Letter XXII and the enigmatic letter in which the writer watches a young woman on the beach appear to have been added after the initial composition of the book. The original manuscript, housed in the Casa-Museo Unamuno, is written in black and blue ink. I can only speculate that Unamuno added Letter XXII to provide a more detailed explanation for the rejection of the woman.

29. "No sé qué escritor de estos obstinados por el problema del sexo dijo que la mujer es una esfinge sin enigma. Puede ser; pero el problema más hondo de la novela, o sea del juego de nuestra vida, no está en cuestión sexual, como no está en cuestión de estómago" (91).

30. Max Nordau's *Degeneración*, published in Spanish in 1902, singles out Oscar Wilde as a central figure in the decline of aesthetics at the fin de siècle. Pompeyo Gener's *Literaturas malsanas* (Unhealthy Literatures, 1894) also diagnoses several "infirmities" in literature. On the influence of Nordau and Gener in Spain, see Fernández Cifuentes 52, and Krauel 148–49.

31. "Puede ser que haya esfinges sin enigma—y éstas son las novelas de que gustan los casineros—, pero hay también enigmas sin esfinge" (91). As Unamuno uses the term "novel" he refers not only to a text but also to the "authentic" life of a human being (La Rubia Prado 59).

32. The oft-quoted statement from *Three Essays on the Theory of Sexuality* (1905) suggests that for Freud, homosexuality was not a perversion and that it is present in all psychic development: "All human beings are capable of making a homosexual object-choice and have in fact made one in their unconscious" (145n). Paul Robinson argues that "in Freud's psychic universe, homosexuality is everywhere, insinuating itself into the psychic lives of the most impeccably 'normal' and presentable individuals. Indeed, no one has done more to destabilize the notion of heterosexuality than Freud" (93).

33. On the extensive commentaries and footnotes appended to Richardson's *Clarissa* in an attempt to foreclose certain interpretations and maintain authorial control, see Eagleton, *The Rape of Clarissa,* and Castle, *Clarissa's Ciphers.*

34. One example would be the critical treatment of Freud's epistolary correspondence with Wilhelm Fliess. Freud's friendship with Fliess lasted from 1887 until 1904, ending in a quarrel over theories of bisexuality. For an overview of the

homoerotic resonances of their letter writing, see Garner. Some time after their friendship had ended, Garner notes, Freud wrote to Salvador Ferenzi that he had overcome his homosexual attachment to Fliess (87).

2. Specters of Lesbian Desire

1. To suggest that it may have been a lesbian love letter runs the risk of "filling in the blank," so to speak, and duplicating the very critiques made by Derrida of Lacan and by Barbara Johnson of Derrida, a duplication that is perhaps inevitable. In his reading, Derrida accuses Lacan of making the lack of meaning of the letter into the meaning of the letter as lack. Johnson astutely notes that Derrida takes his attack a step too far by filling in the lack himself with the term "castration," which Lacan never uses (116).

2. See Bergmann's "Letters and Diaries as Narrative Strategies in Contemporary Catalan Women's Writing."

3. Kay Turner has suggested that letters have been the primary written evidence of lesbian culture (9).

4. I have used Helen Lane's translation, with occasional modifications. When references are not accompanied by a quotation, page numbers are given first for the English translation followed by those of the Spanish edition.

5. "Es una carta larga, de letra apretada, dirigida a mí, no tiene fecha, mi cuerpo tapa el lugar donde debe venir la firma, rectifico mi postura, presa de curiosidad y queda al descubierto una inicial borrosa, indescifrable, la tinta aparece corrida como si se le hubiera caído encima una lágrima" (20).

6. "es un hombre porque los adjetivos que se refieren a él vienen en masculino" (21).

7. "¿Era Ud. lesbiana?" (192).

8. "un desván del cerebro, una especie de recinto secreto lleno de trastos borrosos" (91). Andrew Bush has argued recently that Martín Gaite's back room maps out a psychic topography that adopts a Freudian model, albeit with significant changes regarding women and daughters (161). Blas Matamoro was one of the earliest critics to note the association of the back room with the Freudian unconscious.

9. "Tenía un nombre aquella tela, no me acuerdo, todas las telas lo tenían, y era de rigor saber diferenciar un shantung de un piqué, de un moaré o de una organza, no reconocer las telas por sus nombres era tan escandaloso como equivocar el apellido de los vecinos" (12).

10. In a similar vein, Žižek notes that the return of the repressed is not a return to the past but a "back to the future": what was disrupted and sutured over for the sake of subjectivity is constructed retroactively through the lens of the present (*Sublime Object* 55–58).

11. "Podría decirle que la felicidad en los años de guerra y postguerra era inconcebible [. . .] superponer la amargura de mis opiniones actuales a las otras sensaciones que esta noche estoy recuperando" (69).

12. See Scanlon, 320–56, for an overview of the influence of the Women's Section of the Falange and the transformations that the economic evolution of the regime had on women's lives.

13. The December 1931 constitution allowed women to vote and hold government positions, and a February 1932 package of progressive social reforms granted women, among many opportunities, the right to divorce.

14. "las locas, las frescas, las ligeras de casco andaban bordeando la frontera de la transgresión" (125).

15. "no me atrevía a confesárselo a nadie" (125–26).

16. "Historias de chicas que no se parecían en nada a las que conocíamos, que nunca iban a gustar las dulzuras del hogar apacible con que nos hacían soñar a las señoritas, gente marginada, a la deriva, desprotegida por la ley" (152).

17. Stephanie Sieburth has admirably demonstrated the ways in which Martín Gaite's text marshals mass-cultural objects and texts as "vehicles of feeling" that open up previously forbidden spaces (194).

18. As Janice Radway has argued, the traditional romance novel depends upon the marriage resolution as one of the precepts for a successful narrative; a failed romance is often based on the failure of the man and the woman to consummate their love in matrimony.

19. "al hombre descalzo ya no se le ve" (23).

20. "«quiero verte, quiero verte», con los ojos cerrados: no sé a quien lo digo" (24).

21. "Lo más terrible de las cartas viejas—dice el hombre pensativo—es cuando ha olvidado uno dónde las guardaba o no sabe si las guardaba siquiera y de pronto reaparecen. Es como si alguien, desde otro planeta, nos devolviera un trozo de vida" (45).

22. "salí al parque y la estuve releyendo, era totalmente literario, el destinatario era lo de menos, me embriagaba de narcisismo" (53).

23. "Pero si desaparece o no ha existido nunca ese «tú» ideal receptor del mensaje, la necesidad de interlocución, de confidencia, lleva a inventarlo. O, dicho con otras palabras, es la búsqueda apasionada de ese «tú» el hilo conductor del discurso femenino, el móvil primordial para quebrar la sensación de arrinconamiento."

24. "La literatura de misterio tiene mucho que ver con las cartas que reaparecen [. . .] También con las que desaparecen" (45–46).

25. "porque ninguna chica modosa y decente de aquel tiempo tendría la audacia de escribir una carta así" (53).

26. "sería un buen momento para dar un quiebro y hablar de la literatura epistolar a ver qué salía, parece estarme invitando" (190).

27. "¿y si las hubiera escrito ella y no se acordara? le parece que nunca le ha gustado escribir cartas y menos de amor, pero puede estar equivocada, ¿qué sabe nadie de sí mismo?" (170).

28. "¡Qué ganas tenía de pedírselo!" (166).

29. Magazines devoted to the postal system in Spain regularly published brief articles that lamented the loss of amorous letter writing as a specialized practice, blaming the technological advances of the telephone and telegraph (Valverde 9; Cupido 7; García Vásquez 15).

30. "Me gustaría que fuera usted la de las cartas." "A mí también me gustaría serlo. Ojalá" (173). Martín Gaite repeats a similar letter exchange in *Nubosidad variable* (*Variable Cloud*, 1992), an epistolary novel in which two friends, Sofía Montalvo and Mariana León, write each other for solace and affection in face of their failed relationships with other men. In contrast with C. and Carola, Sofía and Mariana are successful in their attempts to contact each other through letters.

31. Lanser argues that the elimination of sex and/or gender markers in an auto-diegetic narrative in the form of paralepsis can be seen as a mode of "queering" narratology. The erasure of sex, or at least its ambivalent status in a narrative, erases the presupposition of a heterosexual plot, thereby allowing for alternative readings of sexuality (254–55).

32. "Me quedo callada, qué difícil es contar todo esto sin hablar del prodigio principal, de que ella, después de muerta, sigue volando conmigo de la mano, es un poco espeluznante" (183).

33. "le tenía sorbido el seso" (191).

34. As Heather Findlay notes, Freud delayed publishing Dora's case history (345n. 1). It eventually appeared, after much revision, under the title "Fragment of an Analysis of a Case of Hysteria."

35. For a nuanced discussion of "queer" versus "gay and lesbian," see Halperin, *Saint Foucault*, 62–67. Halperin notes, especially with regard to lesbianism, the possibility of "sexual despecification," in which "queer" becomes synomyous with "gay" at the expense of lesbians (65).

36. The polarization of the domains of identification and desire has come under attack in feminist and queer theory. As Diana Fuss notes, by virtue of their supposed mutually exclusive status in Freudian psychoanalysis, same-sex desire cannot exist, since one cannot possibly identify with his or her own sex and desire it at the same time (11). All homosexuality is thus rewritten as a form of latent heterosexuality, in which one of the partners is identified with the opposite gender. On the precariousness of the distinction between identification and desire in the context of Freud's treatment of lesbianism, see Fuss, 67–72.

37. "Pero las palabras «invertido» y «lesbiana» no las aprendí hasta muchos años después, en Madrid, y me costó trabajo hacerme cargo de su significado, no tenía un lugar preparado para recibir aquellos conceptos" (192).

38. See Brooksbank Jones, 1–39, for an overview of the advances women's liberation movements have secured.

39. My argument has benefited from Annamarie Jagose's lucid discussion of memory and homosexuality in Freud's writings. See her *Inconsequence*, 77–100.

40. "No, no se me ocurría tal cosa. Sólo se puede ser lesbiana cuando se concibe el término, yo esa palabra nunca la había oído" (192).

41. "Yo una fugada, eso sí que tiene gracia. Nunca me habían dicho cosa semejante."

42. "No se lo habrán dicho, pero es evidente" (123).

43. "Me embriaga la sospecha de haber podido merecer esa calificación, siento sobre la piel, como un estigma, la atribución de esa identidad insospechada, «fugada, loca». . ." (146).

44. See my "Corresponding with Carmen Martín Gaite: The Death of the Letter Writer" for an extended analysis of the author's reaction to my original essay.

45. "siempre da en el clavo" (55).

46. "Lo que pasa es que entiendo de literatura y sé leer entre líneas" (196).

47. For a history of the figuration of lesbianism as a ghostly presence that haunts the text and a discussion of the theoretical and political consequences of this model of literary representation, see Castle, *The Apparitional Lesbian*.

48. "Esta noche pienso que mis lecturas no andaban descaminadas: se ha pasado usted la vida sin salir del refugio, soñando sola" (196).

49. For Welles, the turn to dialogue as the search for a true self is both a narcissistic enterprise, in which the interlocutor serves as a mirror for the self, and a regressive one, in which a unified image is nothing but a mirage (202–05).

50. Freud's distinction between psychoanalysis and confession attempts to acquit the former of charges of replicating the oppressive gestures of power and subjection. For Freud, what is "confessed" in analysis is not reduced to some essential core of the subject but instead points to an unassimilable remainder produced as a residue of subjection (Tambling 182).

3. The Ethics of Outing in Luis Antonio de Villena

1. "En realidad este relato no es otra cosa que una confesión."

2. In his analysis of Antonio Roig's autobiographical writings, Ellis cogently remarks on Roig's awareness of the difficulty of producing an identity free from guilt when appealing to a confessional discourse (38).

3. On the influence of the Catholic Church on discourses of homosexuality in Spain, see Martínez Expósito, 109-21.

4. Confession by letter did have, nevertheless, official status in the Catholic Church at the Centro de Consulta Oral y Religiosa in Rome whereby people could make "official" confessions in writing and receive a response by mail ("Podemos confesarnos" 13).

5. "uno de esos espléndidos momentos de comunión, de comunicación profunda, que sólo una buena, una honda amistad deparan."

6. "que si yo era tan amigo tuyo como me sentía (y me siento) era mi obligación deshacer tales *puntos oscuros*."

7. "Y dirás, ¿era un niño afeminado? ¿Es de un chiquillo con aires de niña de lo que me estás hablando? No, naturalmente que no. Ambiguo lo era por lo adolescente, no por femenino. Aquel chico no recordaba en nada y para nada a una mujer."

8. "Prometí rozar muy poco la fisiología del amor. Y así haré."

9. "Es evidente que no te cuento todo, ya dije. Pero quisiera contártelo."

10. "Ser su amigo (no su hermano mayor, ni su tutor), su amigo, su compañero."

11. "era como si su presencia me rejuveneciese o más exactamente me adolescentizase."

12. "compañero, amigo, camarada, joven guerrero que recibe la tutela del mayor."

13. José Miguel G. Cortés, for example, advocates, uncritically at times, the speech act of *salir del armario* for the political affirmation of queer identities ("Acerca" 118–25).

14. "De repente, al verle distinto, yo me había dado cuenta que amaba a Sixto, que lo quería, que le había querido desde la primera y lejana vez."

15. John Rajchman argues that Foucault, even as he remained suspicious of the location of desire as the source of our moral obligations, saw in Lacan a similar investigation of the relationship between the truth and the subject, namely, what is the cost one has to pay in order to speak the truth about oneself (14).

16. In "Insólitos y exquisitos" (The Unusual and Refined Ones) Villena extols the virtues of being "banal." He uses the term to describe a dandy figure, someone who takes pleasure from leisure time: banality, in this essay, refers to the pleasure of quotidian activities.

17. See Kopelson's *Love's Litany*, 1–3, for a brief discussion of the absence of love in studies of queer desire.

18. One of the ways in which heterosexuality has projected its own illusory status onto homosexuality is through the discourse of narcissism. Michael Warner has astutely deconstructed the assumed narcissism of homosexuality by demonstrating that modern heterosexuality has obscured the narcissistic dimension of all sexual desire—namely, that desire is a "self-reflexive erotics of the actual ego measured against its ideals" ("Homo-Narcissism" 206).

19. "Pero si todo era el amor (un amor apasionado, fuerte, excluyente de casi todo lo otro) ¿por qué no lo había sabido antes, y por qué sólo me daba cuenta cuando ya acababa? Ese era el indudable enigma."

20. "Yo no era como él, y aunque presumía de no tener prejuicios tampoco me agradaba la mezcla."

21. "Era una mera fantasía sexual, que muy poco tenía que ver con mi propio y real sentimiento."

22. In his reading of Lacan's "Kant avec Sade" in *Tarrying with the Negative*, Žižek argues that the Kantian ethical subject is always uncertain, stricken by the doubt that the ethical duty or obligation was never fulfilled "for the sake of duty itself" but rather was motivated by some "pathological" desire. For Žižek, then, the Kantian subject only remains ethical by virtue of holding onto that uncertainty.

23. "No quiero parecer un moralista adusto y sentencioso. Pero tampoco se me ocurre ningún otro camino."

24. "la inmensa felicidad no existe." This is a recurring theme in Villena's fiction and essays. In *La tentación de Ícaro* (The Temptation of Icarus) Villena argues in a series of essays that true, complete happiness is impossible.

25. In the 2000 edition of the book, Villena eliminated definitively the final chapter from César and confirmed that he was never certain about its addition (129). Villena does not give a reason for his decision, except to say that it did not add anything to the story. I believe that Villena is mistaken; his suppression of César's response draws the reader's attention to the ambivalent role it plays in the novel.

26. Hence I would qualify Angel Loureiro's recent claim for autobiography that "no other genre's thematics and strategies are so dependent on, and determined by, its addressees" (xiii).

27. "Y naturalmente correspondió a mi confidencia (que, al fin, era lo que yo esperaba)."

28. "ofrece íntimos y valientes detalles (que agradecí y estimé en el amigo)."

29. "La carta de Arturo que acabo de transcribir, ciertamente no me sorprendió como él temía."

30. Spaniards' distrust of the postal system gave rise to a curious practice of writing postcards and letters in a form of personal, quasi-poetic code. In the Museo Postal y Telegráfico in Madrid are nearly fifty "encrypted" letters from the 1930s, '40s, and '50s that had to be deciphered before they could be delivered. Many of the letters were written in poems or with hieroglyphs. An entire department of *Correos* was dedicated to the deciphering of these letters until the practice was banned in 1955 by Franco, and it became punishable by law to post a letter without an address that followed codified norms (Gutiérrez Llamazares 993).

31. Llanos y Torriglia notes that Spanish intellectual property laws at that time were not clear on the rights concerning publication of private letters. The restrictions on publishing private letters whose intimate details would tarnish the writer's reputation were more moral than legal (8). In 1956 Calvo Hernández argues that Spanish jurisprudence has generally focused on violations of correspondence, and hence there persists a lack of clarity concerning the distinction between the

material letter and its contents, and thus whether those contents merit protection from dissemination (5–6).

32. *Intimidad* and privacy are not precise synonyms. Spanish legal scholars have debated the validity of a concept of *privacidad* as opposed to *intimidad*. I have opted for the phrase "right to privacy" as the most approximate translation for *derecho a la intimidad*. For an overview of the terminological debates between *intimidad* and *privacidad* in contemporary Spanish law, see Herrán Ortiz, 42–51.

33. My thanks to García Sánchez for providing me with a copy of his unpublished essay and granting permission to cite from it.

34. "Fraudulent letters," as they were known, were not protected by the inviolability of correspondence because they included illegal items. Yet, paradoxically, in order to determine whether a letter was fraudulent, it had to be violated. The postal system justified opening letters with the term "inspection" ("Cartas fraudulentas" 3).

35. "Y Arturo quería conservar su fracaso, poder recordar—bellamente—la gloria." The nostalgic and retrospective point of view recalls Foucault's argument in an interview with James O'Higgins that because of the lack of extensive courtship rituals between gay men, "it is the recollection rather than the anticipation of the act that assumes a primary importance in homosexual relations" ("Sexual Choice" 297).

36. "poner el punto final a esta historia."

37. Duyfhuizen notes that in epistolary fiction the distinction between confidants and lovers is often blurred such that the normal pairings of candor with friendship and coquetry with love are conflated and confused (8).

38. Gay liberation organizations in Spain have never fully embraced outing as a political strategy. In 1995 Leopoldo Alas outed a number of high-profile figures in an article published in the newspaper *El Mundo* (Bruquetas de Castro 31). For a discussion of the ethical concerns around outing as a gay political strategy, see González and Pons. For a recent history of outing, with a list of various figures who have been outed or have declared their homosexuality publicly, see Bruquetas de Castro.

39. Antonio Sabater Tomás, one of the designers of the Law of Social Dangers, explains that it was meant to offset the limitations of the criminal code, which focused on specific, isolated acts, and to allow the law to exercise control over those who engaged in homosexual practices habitually (Domingo Lorén 124). As he puts it, the law was originally designed to "penetrate an individual's mind and attempt to verify the 'whys' of his conduct, the reasons for his behavior" (123).

40. Vivas Marzal focuses exclusively on male homosexuality, arguing that lesbianism is less present and remains completely hidden, and hence is less of a "danger" than male homosexuality. He adds, by way of evidence, that none of the cases before the supreme court has dealt with lesbianism (7).

41. Whereas in the British context the 1885 Labouchère amendment criminalized both public and private homosexual acts, in Spain the law emphasized the impossibility of policing those acts that took place behind closed doors.

42. Vivas Marzal mentions a small number of court cases from the 1950s and 1960s in which the supreme court ruled that the sexual acts had not been publicly divulged and thus were not prosecuted under the law.

43. "Porque quizá el *amor*—quizá—tampoco nos pertenezca."

4. A Witness to Mourning

1. "Pens que tal volta aquesta història meva, corregida per vostè, reescrita si vol, pot interessar a la gent que ha llegit el seu llibre, com a testimoniatge d'uns fets reals."

2. Whereas gays were subject to numerous legal attacks on the basis of "public scandal," lesbians were not. Llamas and Vila claim that there is little evidence of legal repression against lesbians in spite of the fact the laws were written in such a way as to include them (194). Anabitarte and Lorenzo Sanz note that of sixty-four homosexuals prosecuted under the Law of Social Dangers in 1974, and of eighty-eight in 1975, only one was a woman in each year (19).

3. The gesture of effacing herself reiterates a longstanding association of women's letter writing with discretion (Salinas 72). The writer's concern with discretion also resonates with the laws against "public scandal" that, as we saw in chapter 3, criminalized acts "contrary to decency or discretion" ("pudor") with someone of the same sex (Vivas Marzal 15).

4. "Perquè el record més bell, aquell que hauria bastat per donar plenitud a la meva vida, fou un record esguerrat, incomplet, per culpa meva."

5. For a brief account of the use of letter writing in a number of Riera's works, see Glenn, "Las cartas de amor."

6. See Riera's Grandeza y miseria de la epístola" for a discussion of the letter as a seductive tool that, like literature in general, reflects the need to connect with another. Riera emphasizes the use of the word *epístola* over *carta* as the former denotes a mode of writing with literary intentions, and she acknowledges the predominance of epistles in her literary oeuvre.

7. In "Confesión general" ("General Confession") the narrator is a writer who parodies the conventions of confession by apologizing for the woes that have befallen her literary characters (such as brain cancer and car accidents), thus taking responsibility, with a large dose of irony, for such fictional acts.

8. On the lack of attention given to Catalan literature and culture on the part of many scholars of Spain, see Resina.

9. In her interview with Dupláa, Riera comments, "To me, it's incomprehensible that people still don't understand that Catalan is a Spanish language, like

Castilian" (59). For a compelling argument for the need for Castilian literary histories to include Catalan authors and for Catalan literary histories to include Catalan authors who write in Castilian, see Santana.

10. In some texts, such as *Qüestió d'amor propi*, the translations erase the linguistic ambiguity of the Catalan texts. See Epps, "A Writing of One's Own," 146n. 1.

11. On the play of ideological and market forces in translations from Catalan to Castilian, see Parcerisas. One of the dilemmas of the market force of Castilian, he notes, is that a "successful" Catalan writer is one whose works are translated into Castilian.

12. Maryellen Bieder also points to how Catalan and Castilian are often presented in rather complex and intertwining ways, without one dominating the other. For Bieder, Riera's use of Catalan is not meant to point up a univocity but a diversity of perspectives on how language unites and disunites those in Catalonia (71).

13. Luisa Cotoner's 1991 Castilian translation of both of Riera's volumes under the single title *Te dejo el mar* follows the original Catalan version in that the stories are separated by several other tales and the framing letters are reinserted.

14. In her interview with Glenn, Riera suggests that the differences in translation are owed in part to the fact that Castilian and Catalan constitute different linguistic registers for her (47).

15. On the hybridity of the testimonial novel and the inherent tensions between testimony and fiction, see Lucille Kerr, 46–64, and Doris Sommer.

16. "Li sabria greu que començàs aquesta història amb paraubles manllevades?"

17. "Tancar els ulls amb la son suficient per a somniar-te un altre cop tan sols i lliurar-te després com a una ofrena, no penyora, no mar, a l'oblit necessari on tants de cops t'he esperada."

18. "Pronunciar amb aquests llavis tristos, que encara cremen quan lletregen un nom, la darrera paraula; que pus mai més ningú no n'escrigui ni un sol comentari, ni digui que em conegué o la conegué a ella. Ni canviï la fi per fer-la feliç i que acabi com cal, com li agradaria que acabés perquè s'ha identificat un punt massa amb la història" (11). María Pilar Rodríguez and I concur in many respects that the latter tale is a revision of the first, one that chastizes Riera, albeit mildly, for her identification with the narrator and for altering the denouement. For comparative analyses of both stories, see Rodríguez, who sheds light on the pedagogical dimension of the lesbian relationship; Camí-Vela, who focuses on the sense of exile the protagonists feel being in Barcelona rather than Mallorca and their rejection of bourgeois morality; and Servodidio, who analyzes the correspondence and contiguity between the two stories in the 1980 Castilian translation.

19. The final revelation of lesbian love in the name "Maria," in the words of Geraldine Nichols, "compels readers to reevaluate the whole experience: the story

and their facile acceptance of the heterosexist assumptions that overdetermined their (mis)reading of it" (342).

20. "Sense salvació, car aquella era l'única manera de salvar-nos, perquè allà baix, al regne de l'absolut, de l'inefable, ens esperava la bellesa, que es confonia amb la teva-meva imatge quan em mirava a l'espill de la teva carn" (25).

21. See Mirabet i Mullol's *Homosexualitat avui*, 327–36, for an overview of the tension between homosexuality and the Catholic Church in Catalonia in light of the rise of gay Christian groups that sought to reconcile homosexuality with religious faith.

22. "Certament vaig passar tota la nit amb tu. A estones la ploma sobre el paper escrivia amb tanta morositat, tan delicadament que era com si t'acaronés en silenci" (32).

23. In some respects the first letter was also a last will since she asks to name her child after her lover. Rodríguez describes the first story as testamental, the second as testimonial (136).

24. "Sé que estas notas nunca llegarán a publicarse y, pese a ello, continúo escribiendo."

25. "La memòria ho és tot per a mi. Gràcies a ella visc encara pendent del somriure més bell de tota la terra, quan em puc recordar del seu perfil."

26. "Barataria totes les hores que em resten de la meva vida per reviure aquella, per repetir-la gaudint amb fruïció, però, cada instant, tot i sabent-ne la fugacitat deletèria."

27. "I el record me la retorna palpable, real: apareix davant meu adolescent, bella."

28. "Fantasmes que m'assetgen sense poder més, fins a fer-me cirdar com a una boja."

29. "dret inalienable de continuar patint una neurosi massa depressiva."

30. In *Stanzas* Giorgio Agamben relates fetishism to melancholia, claiming that for both processes the object is possessed and lost at the same time (21).

31. For a critique of the viability of psychoanalysis for theorizing lesbian desire in light of de Lauretis's work, see Grosz.

32. For a critique of Butler's use of Freud's theories of melancholia, see Žižek, *Ticklish* 269–73, and Restuccia. Both authors argue that Butler conflates melancholic loss with Lacanian lack: whereas for Butler the loss that originates the subject is one of gender, thereby instituting a melancholic identification with one's own sex, for Lacan the primordial lack that gives rise to the subject is what produces sexual difference in the first place; that original lack is not gendered.

33. "Em dol sobretot de justificar-me davant vostè ara que ja m'és impossible corregir, esmenar tants d'errors."

34. In contrast, John Beverley maintains a distinction between *testimonio* and

literature insofar as the former, because it involves a real-life referent, engages the reader in ways that traditional narrative fiction does not (82–86).

35. "Les he vistes, ho jur i en pos per testimoni les gavines."

36. For a compelling analysis of witnessing and narrative authority in slave testimony, see McBride, 85–102. McBride addresses several of the key concerns around testimonial writing—the authority of the witness, the unknowability of the witness's actual experience, the role of the reader who witnesses the impossibility of bearing witness—that obtain as well in Riera's text.

5. Pleasurable Insurrections

1. All citations are from the 1990 English translation by Dominic Lutyens, with occasional modifications.

2. The normalization of the language under the direction of Pompeu Fabra, codified in the *Gramàtica catalana* (Catalan Grammar) from l'Institut d'Estudis Catalans in 1932, included the collaboration of numerous grammarians from Valencia such as Josep Giner and Manuel Sanchis Guarner (Cuenca 81).

3. Regarding the resistance to the name *català*, Fuster also remarks on the resistance in Catalonia to the Valencian and Mallorcan forms and rejects a project of linguistic normalization that would lead to a uniformity based on the Barcelonese form of Catalan (Cucó and Cortés 242).

4. Fernàndez does not offer any explanation for the novel's lack of interest for scholars of Spanish literature and culture. I can only hypothesize that perhaps its rather melancholic portrayal of sexual emancipation, in opposition to the celebratory mood of the period associated with Almodóvar and embraced by critics, has condemned it to relative obscurity.

5. For an overview of Fernàndez's work, see Lev's "Lluís Fernàndez," in which she notes that his works share a common "camp poetics and politics that, while allied with Anglo-American camp strategies, are also specific to peninsular sociohistorical concerns" (65).

6. In a persuasive analysis of the ways in which post-Franco authors have negotiated the repression of homosexuality, Dieter Ingenschay argues that prior to Franco's death a large body of work dealing explicitly with homosexuality had not been produced, in large part because of the repressive force of censorship during the dictatorship (157, 162). Ingenschay similarly associates Fernàndez's novel with *la movida* due to its use of camp and linguistic experimentation (172).

7. While the gay movement in Spain has been documented, the lesbian movement has been uncritically subsumed under feminism and remains understudied. In fact, lesbian politics and feminism in Spain are intimately linked, but it would be inaccurate to collapse the two as homologous movements. The organization of lesbian groups begins to take place, first in Catalonia with the Coordinadora de

Organizaciones Feministas del Estado Español (Coordinating Committee of Feminist Organizations of the Spanish State, or COFEE) and then in other urban centers, at the beginning of the 1980s. According to Llamas and Vila, lesbian liberation groups suffered from their focus on ideological issues around difference and equality and the internal struggles of lesbian feminists with homophobia from heterosexual feminists. The result at the end of the '80s is that only small groups are left in large urban centers (208). See Escarío et al., *Lo personal es político,* for a brief review of the development of lesbian political movements in Spain.

8. See Llamas and Vila, who note that internal ideological divisions among the leftists groups and between these groups and social-democrats have marked the gay and lesbian liberation movement, which has led to the dissolution of many organizations. In *Homosexualitat avui,* Antoni Mirabet i Mullol, citing remarks made in an October 1982 *Infogai,* also questions the alliance between political parties and gay liberation groups (351).

9. The FAGC platform is somewhat ambivalent on this point, for it simultaneously desires the elimination of roles and the recognition of homosexual desire. The desire to abolish all roles is predicated on the notion that these roles impede an individual from "becoming aware of his/her sexual identity" (Likosky 205). For his part, Oscar Guasch interprets the platform in a slightly different light from Ellis, claiming that the thrust of the FAGC Manifesto was the desire for increased visibility *as gays and lesbians* (Guasch 82). Guasch notes moreover that overwhelming presence of drag queens in the 1977 gay demonstration in Barcelona emphasized visibility as homosexuals.

10. Ingenschay writes that as recently as 1995 police in Valencia still had a social danger record on file for a gay Valencian man, who finally managed to have the record destroyed nearly twenty years after the law had been lifted (184).

11. Sahuquillo had to defend his study of homosexuality in works by Lorca and other Generation of 1927 poets from the reproach of colleagues. Cardín was denied access by the Consejo Superior de Investigaciones Científicas (Superior Council of Scientific Investigations) to holdings in the anthropology section of their library for his study *Guerreros, chamanes y travestis: Indicios de homosexualidad entre los exóticos* (Buxán 20–22).

12. The letter as moral vehicle or as essay has several examples in Spanish literature, such as Antonio de Guevara's *Epístolas familiares* (*The Familiar Epistles,* 1539), Benito Jerónimo Feijoo's *Cartas eruditas y curiosas* (Erudite and Curious Letters, 1742–60), and Angel Ganivet's *Cartas finlandesas* (Finnish Letters, 1898). *Cartas marruecas* testifies to the use of the familiar letter whose contents are not limited to the particularities of the relationship between Gazel and Ben-Beley, but rather they are used as a platform to articulate a critical commentary on the nation-state. Antonio Domínguez Olano's 1974 *Carta abierta a un muchacho "diferente"* (Open

Letter to a "Different" Guy) employs the epistolary form to discuss homosexuality with six imaginary interlocutors, each one named "Manolo." The text's express
purpose is neither to condemn nor to proselytize but rather to inform readers about
homosexuality. For an analysis of the various types of "Manolos" represented in the
text, see Martínez Expósito, 43–45.

13. "Minyones, boniquetes marietes de totes les contrades del País Valencià . . .
La unió fa la força! Una força delicadament divinal. Totes plegades som més que
l'exèrcit de l'aire, som . . . —i ho digué—més que una ploma gegant ultrapassant
les fronteres de la llibertat" (48).

14. "totes mig mortes ixquérem de la gran mansió, segures d'haver guanyat, si
no una guerra, sí una batalla important" (48).

15. "¿Què no faríem dels nostres cossos pamflets porno-linguístics, impossibles
d'amagar, mostrant-se diàriament pel canal misteriós com a cimbells de la nostra
exuberància eròtica?" (58).

16. In *Vital Signs,* Charles Shepherdson points out the similarity between
Foucault's and Lacan's views of law and transgression (172–77). Foucault sees power
as producing its own resistance, so that transgression itself is a product of the law,
already engendered from the outset. Lacan makes a similar argument when he
posits jouissance as a by-product of the law, the intense pleasure that we lose as a
result of our subjection to the law. Yet that pleasure is an effect of the law, the law
that compels us to enjoy that which we can never quite obtain.

17. Ironically, Bakunin makes this very argument against Marx in *Statism and
Anarchy.* Bakunin argued strongly against Marx's notion of the "dictatorship" of the
proletariat, claiming that in its hegemonic position it would create another class to
oppress in order to maintain that position. It could be argued, nonetheless, that
both shared a similar weak link: revolutionary power would not eliminate oppression but simply change hands.

18. "Perquè si les coses continuen així, prenent aquest caire democràtic i d'alliberament de les autoanomenades minories eròtiques explotades, mos quedem a la
lluna de València! Mona, crec que la dictadura mos afavoria, a les marietes. Vaja,
que «con Franco estábamos mejor»" (157–58).

19. Consensual male homosexuality was interdicted in 1934 under Stalin. The
Cuban revolution obtained by Fidel Castro on December 31, 1958, certainly allowed
no space for homosexuality and systematically attempted to either eliminate homosexuals or "retrain" men to fortify their masculinity. It should be noted, however,
that the revolutionary government that emerged from the Bolshevik Revolution
of 1917 abolished laws that proscribed homosexuality (Petty et al. 41). On the other
hand, Marx and Engels's correspondence reveals their phobic opinions about homosexuality (Kennedy 69–96). Kennedy argues that Marx used Bakunin's alleged love
for the Russian Nechaev to have the anarchists expelled from the First International

in 1871; whether or not the rumors were true, they were fueled by the widespread belief that the majority of anarchists were homosexuals (87–89).

20. "perquè la relació capital-treball que té amb el xulo és d'allò més equitativa, i . . . recuperen força de treball . . . a força de nits, que ja és mèrit!" (175–76).

21. In this respect, one could argue that the narrative plays out the Marxist critique of the anarchist failure to accommodate or account for economic factors in social revolution. Marx and Bakunin fought bitterly in the First International over differing conceptions of revolutionary action. One of the crucial distinctions is that the anarchists saw the state as the main target, while Marxists attacked capital and class antagonism between capitalists and wage-earners. Social revolution must come before the elimination of the state, Engels maintained, because without any change in economic conditions, social relations between people would not be fundamentally altered (661). Marx likewise criticized anarchism's blindness to economic conditions: "the basis of Bakunin's social revolution is the *will*, and not the economic conditions" (149).

22. "Hauries de veure'ns. Silicona als pits, com unes *topless*, i un forat preciós" (169).

23. "Em mire a l'espill tocant-me els mugrons, les mamelles, el clotet; . . . grontxant-me; seduint-me; coquetejant-me; provocant-me; erotitzant-me; enfigant-me! Quin gustet, quan em furonege la cloxineta amb lo dit!" (169).

24. Llamas and Vila observe that in the early years of gay and lesbian emancipation, no political group was ever organized by transvestites or transsexuals, who only came to be iconic of the gay and lesbian movement due to the mass media representation of pride parades. Not until the 1990s, they claim, did transsexuals begin rallying for recognition of the specificity of their identity (204).

25. "La marieta serà dona de debò, puix que s'ho mereix històricament" (128).

26. "No hi ha cap trobada més tràgica que la de l'amor! M'havia clavat en un bon bolic: enamorat! Trencava els fils secrets que em lligaven a la normalitat" (91).

27. "Estimar-se ha tornat a ésser una sensació de benaurança tan gran com reviscoladora [. . .] pense que a la fi he retrobat l'amor que tu t'endugueres a tan llarg i impossible exili" (195).

28. "Una dona, com un a marieta, no és autosuficient. Aquesta és llur tragèdia! Desvergades, necessitades, patixen l'esclavatage de l'home violador de consentiments. [. . .] Ferides al llit de l'amor, llurs culs destronats esperant la darrera investida" (114).

29. "paràgrafs desconeguts cercant-nos per la pàgina blanca" (91).

30. "la realitat que mos denigra per la nostra incapacitat de conservar allò que mos pertany i canviar ço que mos atura. Incapaços d'una cohèrencia política, cívica, solidària" (116).

31. The rhetoric of anarchism resurfaces in gay and lesbian communities in

Spain. In her study of male homosexuality in Valencia, Begoña Enguix Grau mentions the existence of "Radio Klara," self-described as "libertarian and anarchist-inspired" ("libertaria y de inspiración ácrata"), which broadcast a radio program for a gay audience at the time of her publication (137).

32. At least as early as 1982, representatives of gay liberation organizations began to express similar concerns. Jordi Petit, spokesperson for the FAGC at the time, remarked that in Catalonia the official persecution of homosexuality had given way to a repressive tolerance (Mirabet i Mullol, *Homosexualitat avui* 357). In this respect, the novel also foreshadows the division in gay and lesbian politics during the 1980s between "reformists" and "revolutionaries," in which the former emphasize the need to initiate legal reforms to seek a more equitable space for gays and lesbians and the latter tend to critique identity politics by emphasizing the repression that persists under the guise of tolerance (Enguix Grau 140–41).

33. *El caso Arny* was the 1996 investigation of an alleged case of corruption of minors in el Arny, a gay pub in Sevilla, which led to a virulent outpouring of homophobic journalism that equated homosexuality with prostitution and corruption of minors. See Juan Vicente Aliaga's account in *Bajo vientre,* in which he argues that the journalistic rhetoric is reminiscent of language used during the Franco dictatorship (47).

34. According to Llamas and Vila, Valencia's parliament was the first legislative body to grant rights to adoption for gay and lesbian couples (209). See Mirabet i Mullol, *Homosexualitat à l'inici del segle XXI,* 119–29, for an overview of the legal changes around homosexuality in Catalonia, with specific reference to the 1998 law on civil unions. The PP has impeded past efforts by the PSOE and Izquierda Unida (United Left, or IU) to allow for civil unions for gays and lesbians. The entrenched position of the PP is based on opposition to the possibility of gay and lesbian couples adopting children. Nevertheless, it is important to recognize that the 2004 election of the PSOE candidate, José Luis Rodríguez Zapatero, as prime minister potentially marks the beginning of a new chapter in the history of gay and lesbian sexuality in Spain. On October 10, 2004, the Spanish government approved modifications to the current laws governing marriage in order to legalize same-sex marriage, placing Spain at the forefront of gay and lesbian liberation. It remains to be seen if the passage of such a law, and the same-sex marriages that will emerge as a result, will engender any critical discussion of gay and lesbian politics similar to the debates produced among legal scholars, gay and lesbian activists, and queer theorists in the United States.

6. E-Mail, AIDS, and Virtual Sexuality in Lluís Fernàndez

1. On the tension between HIV-seropositivity and negativity early in the epidemic, see Odets. He recounts the criticism he faced for addressing the needs of

HIV-negative men while many were dying from AIDS. "Denied or not," he writes, "being gay and being uninfected is now a condition, not the absence of one" (15).

2. Alberto Cardín and Armand de Fluviá's *SIDA: ¿Maldición bíblica o enfermedad letal?* (SIDA: Biblical Curse or Lethal Disease?, 1985) is a collection of essays, the majority from U.S. writers, whose express purpose was to inform the Spanish populace about the syndrome. The relatively few pieces by Spanish writers gives the impression that AIDS is a phenomenon closely tied to the United States.

3. For an astute analysis of the geographic alignment of AIDS and the shifts between tropical and epidemiological thinking (the former posits an essential link between a disease and the place where it "resides," the latter sees the possibility of spreading indiscriminately and tries to quarantine the disease), see Patton, 27–50.

4. "Debe de ser muy duro olvidarse de que uno va a morirse y de que los demás seguirán con vida. Dios me perdone, pero acabamos hasta el gorro de Tinín, y ahora creo que hizo bien en morirse solo en su casa."

5. "Murió, finalmente, como Gina, dejando en nuestro ánimo un agujero negro desolador."

6. "Así y todo, me parece estupendo el montaje ese de recopilar datos sobre nuestra generación y los cambios fundamentales ocurridos durante estos años de sida, terremotos políticos y estriptíes sociales para que te suelte información sobre mi vida."

7. "¿Mafia rosa? ¡Con lo individualistas, malignas e insolidarias que somos las mariquitas! No te cuento cómo somos las maltrabajas de la *televisón* local. Sobrevivir en este edificio monstruoso, rodeadas por mujeres ambiciosas y mariquitas insaciables, es puro milagro, incluso para mí, más «superviviente» que Gloria Gaynor."

8. "creo que su vuelta epistolar debe interpretarse como una venganza aplazada largo tiempo."

9. "porque me gusta sufrir, expiar mi culpa por mis muchos pecados cometidos antaño y en la confesión encuentro siempre un saludable consuelo."

10. "No puedo sustraerme a la idea de que esta carta, que ahora escribo, formará parte de la ficción que has creado reuniéndolas todas juntas en esta gavilla de fotocopias que me has enviado."

11. "Nunca vi reunidas tanta desfachatez, cobardía, bajeza, pobreza mental, deshonestidad, inmoralidad, descaro, indecencia, deslealtad y traición como en ellas."

12. "Como verás, lo que necesitamos en Valencia es un outing que coloque a cada loca en su lugar y desenmascare política y sexualmente a todas esas sinvergüenzas todavía escondidas en el armario."

13. "Excusa la levedad de estas reflexiones un tanto seniles. Echémosle la culpa a la noche y su hechizo camp."

14. "su novio era seropositivo y ella jugaba a hacerse la ignoranta. Yo la cogí un día y le dije: «Pepisa, ahora las dos nos vamos al hospital de Manjatan y nos

hacemos el Elisa. ¡Por joder! Yo sabía que el mío saldría negativo. Como así sucedió. Pero ella se quedó lívida. Sus amigos comenzaron a compadecerla."

15. "En tiempos veloces de fax y ordenadores, tú aún te permites escribir una deliciosa carta a mano, con pluma Mont Blanc y papel barba rasposo. La tengo entre mis manos, como antaño tuve tu enhiesto miembro."

16. "el lenguaje es un virus." Epps argues for a similar relationship of contagion and communication, of language as a virus, in his reading of Goytisolo's *Las virtudes* (*Significant Violence* 394).

17. Although an e-mail message is broken into numerous packets, routed through several servers, and recomposed upon delivery, e-mail remains tied to standard epistolary concepts. E-mail programs employ the signs of the postal system and of traditional letter writing such as mailboxes, stamps, envelopes, etc. Furthermore, e-mail's supposed ability to deliver instantaneously only creates the illusion that technology can overcome the deferral inherent in writing. Like the postal system, servers can be slow or even fail to deliver messages.

18. William Decker, for example, views e-mail as a hybrid between letter writing and telephone conversations, since it often functions much more spontaneously and there is no permanent written record unless the correspondents print their messages (236).

19. "A veces el sexo real es un agobio. [. . .] El sexo digital no tiene problemas de contaminación."

20. For a powerful analysis of the value of laughter and "the ridiculous" in the context of art and activism, see Bordowitz, "The AIDS Crisis Is Ridiculous."

21. "Con justa razón arguyes que nuestra apresurada formación intelectual y carencias éticas nos han abocado a esta situación inmoral que padecemos desde mucho antes del ascenso a los socialistas al poder, que propiciamos, sin demasiada reflexión, con ese entusiasmo que nace de la mala conciencia de quienes, en el fondo ansiábamos un cambio revolucionario disfrazado de democracia burguesa."

22. In his famous "Is the Rectum a Grave?" Leo Bersani advocates the self-shattering jouissance associated with anal sex, a call to embrace, provisionally, the association between death and anality that dominant culture reiterates. For Bersani, sex is always a shattering of the self, in having the contours of the self come under erasure by accepting a certain powerlessness experienced during sex. Although Tim Dean emphasizes the role of the unconscious and the death drive in the desire behind risky and unsafe sexual practices, he nevertheless warns that the eroticization of safe-sex practices to promote disease prevention "inadvertently connects condoms with death—an assocation that not only may discourage their use but also may shroud AIDS-related death in an erotic patina" (*Beyond Sexuality* 145).

23. In Eduardo Mendicutti's *Siete contra Georgia* (*Seven against Georgia*, 1987), for example, seven queer characters tape-recorded "letters" addressed to the fictional

"Chief of Police of Georgia" that condemn anti-sodomy laws. The novel mounts an explicit attack against legal interdictions of sexuality through the explicit description in graphic detail of their various sexual escapades, attempting, in the process, to convince the chief of the pleasure that homosexuality generates. The desired effect, they claim, is that the listener of the tapes will become so aroused by their linguistic performance that he will instantly desire to have sex with one of his fellow police officers.

24. The rhetoric of contagion also appears in the Law of Social Dangers. The original 1954 law on which it is based included several articles on homosexuality, chief among them 6.20, which said that homosexuals must be absolutely separated from the rest of society. See Butler's comments on contagion as well in *Excitable Speech*, 110, 114, 124.

BIBLIOGRAPHY

Abellán, José Luis. *Miguel de Unamuno a la luz de la psicología: Una interpretación de Unamuno desde la psicología individual.* Madrid: Tecnos, 1964.

Abraham, Nicolas, and Maria Torok. *The Shell and the Kernel: Renewals of Psychoanalysis.* Translated by Nicholas T. Rand. Chicago: University of Chicago Press, 1994.

Agamben, Giorgio. *Stanzas: Word and Phantasm in Western Culture.* Translated by Ronald L. Martinez. Minneapolis: University of Minnesota Press, 1993.

Aguado, Neus. "Epístolas de mar y de sol: Entrevista con Carme Riera." *Quimera* 105 (1991): 32–37.

Alas, Leopoldo. *Leopoldo Alas: Teoría y crítica de la novela española.* Edited by Sergio Beser. Barcelona: Laia, 1972.

Alberola, Octavio, and Ariane Gransac. *El anarquismo español y la acción revolucionaria 1961–1974.* Paris: Ruedo Ibérico, 1975.

Aliaga, Juan Vicente. *Bajo vientre: Representaciones de la sexualidad en la cultura y el arte contemporáneos.* Valencia: Generalitat Valenciana, 1997.

———. "Como hemos cambiado." In Aliaga and Cortés, *Identidad y diferencia,* 17–107.

———. "El lenguaje es un virus." Introduction to Aliaga and Cortés, *De amor y rabia,* 13–29.

———, and José Miguel G. Cortés, eds. *De amor y rabia: Acerca del arte y el SIDA.* Valencia: Universidad Politécnica de Valencia, 1993.

———, and José Miguel G. Cortés, eds. *Identidad y diferencia: Sobre la cultura gay en España.* Madrid: Editorial Gay y Lesbiana, 1997.

"Al SIDA Ponle un . . ." *Dirección General para la Salud Pública.* 2003. Generalitat Valenciana Conselleria de Sanitat. December 7, 2003. http://dgsp.san.gva.es/. Path: Servicio del Plan del SIDA; prevención.

Altman, Janet. *Epistolarity: Approaches to a Form*. Columbus: Ohio State University Press, 1982.

Anabitarte, Héctor, and Ricardo Lorenzo Sanz. *Homosexualidad: El asunto está caliente*. Madrid: Queimada, 1979.

Aristotle. *Nicomachean Ethics*. Translated by Martin Ostwald. Indianapolis: Bobbs-Merrill, 1962.

Augustine, Saint. *Confessions*. Translated with an introduction by R. S. Pine-Coffin. Harmondsworth: Penguin, 1961.

Babuscio, Jack. "The Cinema of Camp (*aka* Camp and the Gay Sensibility)." In Cleto, *Camp*, 117–35.

Bacarisse, Pamela. "Will the Story Tell? Unamuno's *San Manuel Bueno, mártir*." In *Carnal Knowledge: Essays on the Flesh, Sex, and Sexuality in Hispanic Letters and Film*, edited by Pamela Bacarisse, 55–72. Pittsburgh: Tres Ríos, 1993.

Baeza, Ricardo, and Alfonso Reyes, eds. *Literatura epistolar*. Barcelona: Éxitos, 1960.

Balzac, Honoré de. *Histoire des treize: Ferragus & La fille aux yeux d'or*. Paris: Flammarion, 1998.

Barca, Héctor. "Un truco informático permite asaltar ordenadores con un simple correo." *El País* March 31, 2001, natl. ed.: 23.

Barthes, Roland. "The Death of the Author." In *Image, Music, Text*. Edited and translated by Stephen Heath, 142–48. New York: Hill and Wang, 1977.

———. "Introduction to the Structuralist Analysis of Narratives." In *Image, Music, Text*, 79–124.

———. *A Lover's Discourse: Fragments*. Translated by Richard Howard. New York: Hill and Wang, 1978.

Beebee, Thomas O. *Epistolary Fiction in Europe, 1500–1850*. Cambridge: Cambridge University Press, 1999.

Benstock, Shari. "From Letters to Literature: *La Carte Postale* in the Epistolary Genre." *Genre* 18, no. 3 (1985): 257–95.

Bergeron, David M. *King James and Letters of Homoerotic Desire*. Iowa City: University of Iowa Press, 1999.

Bergmann, Emilie L. "Letters and Diaries as Narrative Strategies in Contemporary Catalan Women's Writing." In *Critical Essays on the Literatures of Spain and Spanish America*, edited by Luis González-del-Valle and Julio Baena, 19–28. Boulder: Society of Spanish and Spanish-American Studies, 1991.

———, and Paul Julian Smith. Introduction. *¿Entiendes? Queer Readings, Hispanic Writings*, edited by Emilie L. Bergmann and Paul Julian Smith, 1–14. Durham, N.C.: Duke University Press, 1995.

Bersani, Leo. "Is the Rectum a Grave?" In *AIDS: Cultural Analysis, Cultural Activism*, edited by Douglas Crimp, 197–222. Cambridge, Mass.: MIT Press, 1987.

Beverley, John. *Against Literature*. Minneapolis: University of Minnesota Press, 1993.

Bieder, Maryellen. "Cultural Capital: The Play of Language, Gender, and Nationality." *Catalan Review* 14, nos. 1–2 (2000): 53–74.

Blanco Aguinaga, Carlos. *El Unamuno contemplativo.* Mexico: Colegio de México, 1959.

Bordowitz, Gregg. "The AIDS Crisis Is Ridiculous." In *Queer Looks: Perspectives on Lesbian and Gay Film and Video,* edited by Martha Gever, John Greyson, and Pratibha Parmar, 208–24. New York: Routledge, 1993.

———. "Dense Moments." In *Uncontrollable Bodies: Testimonies of Identity and Culture,* edited by Rodney Sappington and Tyler Stallings, 25–43. Seattle: Bay Press, 1994.

Bou, Enric. *Papers privats: Assaig sobre les formes literàries autobiogràphiques.* Barcelona: Edicions 62, 1993.

Bower, Anne. *Epistolary Responses: The Letter in Twentieth-century American Fiction and Criticism.* Tuscaloosa: University of Alabama Press, 1997.

Brooks, Peter. *Troubling Confessions: Speaking Guilt in Law and Literature.* Chicago: University of Chicago Press, 2000.

Brooksbank Jones, Anny. *Women in Contemporary Spain.* Manchester: Manchester University Press, 1997.

Bruquetas de Castro, Fernando. *Outing en España: Los españoles salen del armario.* Madrid: Hijos de Muley-Rubio, 2000.

Bush, Andrew. "Dwelling on Two Stories (Carmen Martín Gaite, María Zambrano)." *Revista de Estudios Hispánicos* 36, no. 1 (2002): 159–89.

Butler, Judith. *Excitable Speech: A Politics of the Performative.* New York: Routledge, 1997.

———. "Imitation and Gender Insubordination." In *Inside/Out: Lesbian Theories, Gay Theories,* edited by Diana Fuss, 13–31. New York: Routledge, 1991.

———. *The Psychic Life of Power: Theories in Subjection.* Stanford, Calif.: Stanford University Press, 1997.

Buxán, Xosé M. Introduction. *ConCiencia de un singular deseo: Estudios lesbianos y gays en el estado español,* edited by Xosé Buxán, 11–27. Barcelona: Laertes, 1997.

Cadalso, José. *Cartas marruecas; Noches lúgubres.* Edited by Joaquín Arce. 7th ed. Madrid: Cátedra, 1978.

Calvo Hernández, Bienvenido. "La carta en el mundo del derecho." *Revista Técnica y Profesional de Correos* 16, no. 175 (1956): 11; 16, no. 179 (1956): 5–6; 16, no. 180 (1956): 7–8.

Camí-Vela, María Antonia. *La búsqueda de la identidad en la obra literaria de Carme Riera.* Madrid: Pliegos, 2000.

Carbó, Ferran, and Vicent Simbor Ruig. *Literatura actual al País Valencià (1973–1992).* Valencia: Institut Universitari de Filologia Valenciana; Barcelona: Publicacions de L'Abadia de Montserrat, 1993.

Cardín, Alberto, and Armand de Fluvià, eds. *SIDA: ¿Maldición bíblica o enfermedad letal?* Barcelona: Laertes, 1985.

"Cartas fraudulentas." *La Valija*, May 1977: 3.

"Cartas violadas." *La Valija*, April 1977: 21.

Castán Vázquez, José María. *El derecho al secreto de la correspondencia epistolar.* Madrid: Instituto Nacional de Estudios Jurídicos, 1960.

Castillo, Debra. "Never-Ending Story: Carmen Martín Gaite's *The Back Room.*" *PMLA* 102, no. 5 (1987): 814–28.

Castle, Terry. *The Apparitional Lesbian: Female Homosexuality and Modern Culture.* New York: Columbia University Press, 1993.

———. *Clarissa's Ciphers: Meaning and Disruption in Richardson's* Clarissa. Ithaca, N.Y.: Cornell University Press, 1982.

Chabran, Rafael. "Miguel de Unamuno." In Foster, *Spanish Writers on Gay and Lesbian Themes,* 167–70.

Chambers, Ross. *Facing It: AIDS Diaries and the Death of the Author.* Ann Arbor: University of Michigan Press, 1998.

Chartier, Roger, Alain Boureau, and Cécile Dauphin. *Correspondence: Models of Letter-Writing from the Middle Ages to the Nineteenth Century.* Translated by Christopher Woodall. Cambridge: Polity, 1997.

Cleminson, Richard. *Anarquismo y homosexualidad: Antología de artículos de la* Revista Blanca, Generación Consciente, Estudios e Iniciales *(1924–1935).* Madrid: Huelga & Fierro, 1995.

Cleto, Fabio, ed. *Camp: Queer Aesthetics and the Performing Subject: A Reader.* Ann Arbor: University of Michigan Press, 1999.

Constanzo y Vidal, Julio. *Repertorio epistolar y ramillete de amantes: Manual moderno de estilo general de cartas.* Valencia: Juan Mariana y Sanz, 1878.

Copjec, Joan. *Read My Desire: Lacan against the Historicists.* Cambridge, Mass.: MIT Press, 1994.

Cortés, José Miguel G. "Acerca de modelos e identidades." In Aliaga and Cortés, *Identidad y diferencia,* 109–98.

———. "Silencio=Muerte: Los grupos activistas españoles frente a la moralización del SIDA." In Aliaga and Cortés, *De amor y rabia,* 93–108.

Cotoner, Luisa. Introduction. *Te dejo el mar,* by Carme Riera. Translated by Luisa Cotoner, 11–34. Madrid: Espasa-Calpe, 1991.

Cousineau, Diane. *Letters and Labyrinths: Women Writing/Cultural Codes.* Newark: University of Delaware Press, 1997.

Crimp, Douglas. *Melancholy and Moralism: Essays on AIDS and Queer Politics.* Cambridge, Mass.: MIT Press, 2002.

Crowder, George. *Classical Anarchism: The Political Thought of Godwin, Proudhon, Bakunin, and Kropotkin.* Oxford: Clarendon, 1991.

Cucó Giner, Alfons, and Santi Cortés, eds. *Llengua i política, cultura i nació: Un epistolari valencià durant el franquisme.* Valencia: Edicions 3 i 4, 1997.

Cuenca, Maria Josep. *El valencià és una llengua diferent?* Valencia: Tàndem, 2003.

Cupido. "Cartas de amor." *Carteros y Subalternos,* July 1967: 7.

Cvetkovich, Ann. *An Archive of Feelings: Trauma, Sexuality, and Lesbian Public Cultures.* Durham, N.C.: Duke University Press, 2003.

Davidson, Arnold I. *The Emergence of Sexuality: Historical Epistemology and the Formation of Concepts.* Cambridge, Mass.: Harvard University Press, 2001.

Day, Robert Adams. *Told in Letters: Epistolary Fiction before Richardson.* Ann Arbor: University of Michigan Press, 1966.

Dean, Tim. *Beyond Sexuality.* Chicago: University of Chicago Press, 2000.

————, and Christopher Lane, eds. *Homosexuality and Psychoanalysis.* Chicago: University of Chicago Press, 2001.

Decker, William Merrill. *Epistolary Practices: Letter Writing in America before Telecommunications.* Chapel Hill: University of North Carolina Press, 1998.

De Lauretis, Teresa. *The Practice of Love: Lesbian Sexuality and Perverse Desire.* Bloomington: Indiana University Press, 1994.

Delgado, Luisa Elena. "Pliegos de (des)cargo: Las paradojas discursivas de *La incógnita.*" *MLN* 111, no. 2 (1996): 275–98.

De Man, Paul. *Allegories of Reading: Figural Language in Rousseau, Nietzsche, Rilke, and Proust.* New Haven, Conn.: Yale University Press, 1979.

Derrida, Jacques. *The Post Card: From Socrates to Freud and Beyond.* Translated by Alan Bass. Chicago: University of Chicago Press, 1987.

————. *Demeure: Fiction and Testimony.* In *The Instant of My Death,* by Maurice Blanchot, translated by Elizabeth Rottenberg, 13–103. Stanford, Calif.: Stanford University Press, 2000.

Domingo Lorén, Victoriano. *Los homosexuales frente a la ley: Los juristas opinan.* Esplugas de Llobregat: Plaza & Janés, 1977.

Donato y Prunera, Emilio. *Homosexualismo (Frente a Gide).* Madrid: Javier Morata, 1931.

Dupláa, Cristina. "Interview with Carme Riera." In Glenn et al., *Moveable Margins,* 58–62.

Duyfhuizen, Bernard. "Epistolary Narratives of Transmission and Transgression." *Comparative Literature* 37, no. 1 (1985): 1–26.

Eagleton, Terry. *The Rape of Clarissa: Writing, Sexuality, and Class Struggle in Samuel Richardson.* Oxford: Blackwell, 1982.

Edelman, Lee. *Homographesis: Essays in Gay Literary and Cultural Theory.* New York: Routledge, 1994.

Ellis, Robert Richmond. *The Hispanic Homograph: Gay Self-Representation in Contemporary Spanish Autobiography.* Urbana: University of Illinois Press, 1997.

Engels, Friedrich. "Letter to Theodor Cuno." In *The Marx and Engels Reader,* edited by Robert C. Tucker, 660–61. New York: Norton, 1972.

Enguix Grau, Begoña. *Poder y deseo: La homosexualidad masculina en Valencia.* Valencia: Generalitat Valenciana, 1996.

Epps, Brad. "La fragilitat de l'escriptura." In *El mirall i la màscara: Vint-i-cinc anys de ficció narrativa en l'obra de Carme Riera,* edited by Luisa Cotoner, 73–95. Barcelona: Destino, 2000.

———. *Significant Violence: Oppression and Resistance in the Narratives of Juan Goytisolo, 1970–1990.* Oxford: Oxford University Press, 1996.

———. "Virtual Sexuality: Lesbianism, Loss, and Deliverance in Carme Riera's 'Te deix, amor, la mar com a penyora.'" In Bergmann and Smith, *¿Entiendes?,* 317–45.

———. "A Writing of One's Own: Carme Riera's *Qüestió d'amor propi.*" In Glenn et al., *Moveable Margins,* 104–52.

Escarío, Pilar, Inés Alberdi, and Ana Inés López-Accotto. *Lo personal es político: El Movimiento Feminista en la transición.* Madrid: Instituto de la Mujer, 1996.

Eslava Galán, Juan. *Historia secreta del sexo en España.* Madrid: Temas de Hoy, 1991.

Favret, Mary A. *Romantic Correspondence: Women, Politics, and the Fiction of Letters.* Cambridge: Cambridge University Press, 1993.

Felman, Shoshana. "Education and Crisis, or the Vicissitudes of Teaching." In *Testimony: Crises of Witnessing in Literature, Psychoanalysis, and History,* edited by Shoshana Felman and Dori Laub, 1–56. New York: Routledge, 1992.

Fernàndez, Josep-Anton. *Another Country: Sexuality and National Identity in Catalan Gay Fiction.* London: Maney Pub. Modern Humanities Research Association, 2000.

Fernàndez, Lluís. *L'anarquista nu.* Barcelona: Edicions 62, 1979.

———. *The Naked Anarchist.* Translated by Dominic Lutyens. London: GMP, 1990.

———. *Una prudente distancia.* Madrid: Espasa Calpe, 1998.

Fernández Cifuentes, Luis. *Teoría y mercado de la novela en España del 98 a la República.* Madrid: Gredos, 1982.

Findlay, Heather. "Queer Dora: Hysteria, Sexual Politics, and Lacan's 'Intervention on Transference.'" *GLQ: A Journal of Lesbian and Gay Studies* 1 (1994): 323–47.

Flinn, Caryl. "The Deaths of Camp." In Cleto, *Camp,* 433–57.

Foster, David William, ed. *Spanish Writers on Gay and Lesbian Themes: A Bio-Critical Sourcebook.* Westport, Conn.: Greenwood, 1999.

———. "Christianity and Confession." In *The Politics of Truth,* edited by Sylvère Lotringer and Lysa Hochroth, 199–235. New York: Semiotext(e), 1997.

Foucault, Michel. *The History of Sexuality.* 3 vols. Translated by Robert Hurley. New York: Pantheon, 1978.

———. "Sexual Choice, Sexual Act: Foucault and Homosexuality." In *Michel Foucault: Politics, Philosophy, Culture: Interviews, and Other Writings, 1977–1984,* edited by Lawrence D. Kritzman, 286–303. New York: Routledge, 1988.

Franz, Thomas R. *Valera in Dialogue/In Dialogue with Valera: A Novelist's Work in Conversation with That of His Contemporaries and Successors.* New York: Peter Lang, 2000.

Freud, Sigmund. *The Ego and the Id.* 1923. Translated by Joan Rivière. Edited by James Strachey. New York: Norton, 1960.

———. "Fragment of an Analysis of a Case of Hysteria." 1905. *Standard Edition (SE)* 7: 1–122.

———. *Group Psychology and the Analysis of the Ego.* 1921. Translated and edited by James Strachey. New York: Norton, 1959.

———. "Mourning and Melancholia." 1917. *SE* 14: 237–48.

———. "Psycho-analytic Notes." 1911. *SE* 12: 1–82.

———. "The Psychogenesis of a Case of Homosexuality in a Woman." 1920. *SE* 18: 145–72.

———. *The Psychopathology of Everyday Life.* 1901. Translated by Alan Tyson. Edited by James Strachey. New York: Norton, 1965.

———. "The Question of Lay Analysis: Conversations with an Impartial Person." 1927. *SE* 20: 183–258.

———. *The Standard Edition of the Complete Psychological Works of Sigmund Freud.* Edited and translated by James Strachey. 24 vols. London: Hogarth, 1953–74.

———. *Three Essays on the Theory of Sexuality.* 1905. *SE* 7: 135–72.

———. *Totem and Taboo.* 1913. Translated and edited by James Strachey. New York: Norton, 1989.

Fuss, Diana. *Identification Papers.* New York: Routledge, 1995.

Fuster, Joan. *Nosaltres, els valencians.* 1962. Barcelona: Edicions 62, 1977.

García Düttmann, Alexander. *At Odds with AIDS: Thinking and Talking about a Virus.* Translated by Peter Gilgen and Conrad Scott-Curtis. Stanford, Calif.: Stanford University Press, 1996.

García Lorca, Federico. *Obras VI, Prosa I.* 6 vols. Edited by Miguel García-Posada. Madrid: Akal, 1994.

———. *Epistolario completo.* Edited by Christopher Maurer and Andrew A. Anderson. Madrid: Cátedra, 1997.

García Sánchez, Jesús. "El secreto de la correspondencia y la violación del derecho a la intimidad durante la dictadura franquista." Unpublished essay, 1997.

García Vásquez. "Cartas amistosas o 'voces' que vuelan." *La Valija,* April 1978: 15.

Garlinger, Patrick Paul. "Corresponding with Carmen Martín Gaite: The Death of the Letter Writer." *Revista de Estudios Hispánicos* 36, no. 1 (2002): 191–208.

Garner, Shirley Nelson. "Freud and Fliess: Homophobia and Seduction." In *Seduction and Theory: Readings of Gender, Representation, and Rhetoric,* edited by Dianne Hunter, 86–109. Urbana: University of Illinois Press, 1989.

Gide, Andre. *Corydon*. 1925. Translated by Richard Howard. Urbana: University of Illinois Press, 2001.

Gil-Albert, Juan. Prologue to *Oscar Wilde*, by Robert Merle. Translated by Juan Gil-Albert, 11–16. Valencia: Fomento de Cultura, 1956.

Gilroy, Amanda, and W. M. Verhoeven, eds. *Epistolary Histories: Letters, Fiction, Culture*. Charlottesville: University Press of Virginia, 2000.

Glenn, Kathleen. "Las cartas de amor de Carme Riera: El arte de seducir." In *Del franquismo a la posmodernidad: Cultura española 1975–1990*, edited by José B. Monleón, 161–69. Madrid: Akal, 1995.

———. "Conversation with Carme Riera." In Glenn et al., *Moveable Margins*, 39–57.

———. "Reading and Writing the Other Side of the Story in Two Narratives by Carme Riera." *Catalan Review* 7, no. 2 (1993): 51–62.

———, Mirella Servodidio, and Mary Vásquez, eds. *Moveable Margins: The Narrative Art of Carme Riera*. Lewisburg, Pa.: Bucknell University Press, 1999.

Glick, Thomas F. "Psicoanálisis, reforma sexual y política en la España de entreguerras." *Estudios de Historia Social*, 1981, 7–25.

Goethe, Johann Wolfgang von. *The Sorrows of Young Werther*. Translated by Michael Hulse. London: Penguin, 1989.

Gold, Hazel. "From Sensibility to Intelligibility: Transformations in the Spanish Epistolary Novel from Romanticism to Realism." In *La Chispa '85: Selected Proceedings*, edited by Gilbert Paolini, 133–43. New Orleans: Tulane University, 1985.

Goldsmith, Elizabeth C. Introduction. *Writing the Female Voice: Essays on Epistolary Literature*. Edited by Elizabeth C. Goldsmith, vii–xiii. Boston: Northeastern University Press, 1989.

González, Pacho, and Fernando Pons. "Outing: Una opción arriesgada." *Entiendes: Actualidad de gays y lesbianas* 48 (1997): 14–19.

"La gripe por correo." *Carteros y Subalternos*, July 1963: 12–13.

Grosz, Elizabeth. "The Labors of Love: Analyzing Perverse Desire: An Interrogation of Teresa de Lauretis's *The Practice of Love*." *Differences* 6, nos. 2–3 (1994): 274–95.

Guasch, Oscar. *La sociedad rosa*. Barcelona: Anagrama, 1991.

Guillén, Claudio. "On the Edge of Literariness: The Writing of Letters." *Comparative Literature Studies* 31, no. 1 (1994): 1–24.

———. "El pacto epistolar: Las cartas como ficciones." *Revista de Occidente* 197 (1997): 76–98.

Guilleragues, Gabriel Joseph de Lavergne, vicomte de, and Mariana Alcoforado. *Lettres portugaises*. Edited by Frédéric Deloffre and Jacques Rougeot. Genève: Droz, 1976.

Gullón, Ricardo. *Autobiografías de Unamuno*. Madrid: Gredos, 1964.

Gutiérrez, Luis. *Cornelia Bororquia o la víctima de la Inquisición.* Edited by Gérard Dufour. Alicante: Instituto Juan Gil-Albert, 1987.

Gutiérrez Llamazares, Miguel Ángel. *Manual básico de legislación de Correos y Telégrafos.* Barcelona: Omnia, 1995.

Halberstam, Judith. "Queering Lesbian Studies." In *The New Lesbian Studies: Into the Twenty-first Century,* edited by Bonnie Zimmerman and Toni A. H. McNaron, 256–61. New York: Feminist Press at CUNY, 1996.

Halperin, David M. *How to Do the History of Homosexuality.* Chicago: University of Chicago Press, 2002.

———. *One Hundred Years of Homosexuality and Other Essays on Greek Love.* New York: Routledge, 1990.

———. *Saint Foucault: Towards a Gay Hagiography.* New York: Oxford University Press, 1995.

Hanson, Ellis. "The Telephone and Its Queerness." In *Cruising the Performative: Interventions into the Representation of Ethnicity, Nationality, and Sexuality,* edited by Sue-Ellen Case, Philip Brett, and Susan Leigh Foster, 34–58. Bloomington: Indiana University Press, 1995.

Herrán Ortiz, Ana Isabel. *El derecho a la intimidad en la nueva ley orgánica de protección de datos personales.* Madrid: Dykinson, 2002.

Hocquenghem, Guy. *Homosexual Desire.* 1978. Durham, N.C.: Duke University Press, 1993.

Hoff, Ruth J. "The Trouble with Truth, Gender, and Desire in *Pepita Jiménez.*" *Revista de Estudios Hispánicos* 35, no. 2 (2001): 215–38.

Iborra, Josep. "La generació del 70: Una nova narrativa al País Valencià." In Salvador and Piquer, *Vint anys,* 47–68.

Ingenschay, Dieter. "Identidad homosexual y procesamiento del franquismo en el discurso literario de España desde la transición." In *Disremembering the Dictatorship: The Politics of Memory in the Spanish Transition to Democracy,* edited by Joan Ramon Resina, 157–89. Amsterdam: Rodopi, 2000.

Jagose, Annamarie. *Inconsequence: Lesbian Representation and the Logic of Sexual Sequence.* Ithaca, N.Y.: Cornell University Press, 2002.

Joan i Tous, Pere. "Sade y Stirner o la tradición imposible del anarquismo español." In *El anarquismo español y sus tradiciones culturales,* edited by Bert Hofmann, Pere Joan i Tous, and Manfred Tietz, 163–75. Frankfurt am Main: Vervuert; Madrid: Iberoamericana, 1995.

Johnson, Barbara. *The Critical Difference: Essays in the Contemporary Rhetoric of Reading.* Baltimore: Johns Hopkins University Press, 1980.

Jones, Constance. Preface. *The Love of Friends: An Anthology of Gay and Lesbian Letters to Friends and Lovers.* Edited by Constance Jones, 7–9. New York: Simon and Schuster, 1997.

Jost, François. "L'Evolution d'un genre: Le roman épistolaire dans les lettres occidentales." *Essais de littérature comparée.* Vol. 2, 89–179. Fribourg: Editions Universitaires, 1968.

Kamuf, Peggy. *Fictions of Feminine Desire: Disclosures of Heloise.* Lincoln: University of Nebraska Press, 1982.

Kant, Immanuel. *The Doctrine of Virtue: Part II of the Metaphysic of Morals.* Translated by Mary J. Gregor. New York: Harper and Row, 1964.

Kany, Charles E. *The Beginnings of the Epistolary Novel in France, Italy, and Spain.* Berkeley: University of California Press, 1937.

Kauffman, Linda S. *Discourses of Desire: Gender, Genre, and Epistolary Fictions.* Ithaca, N.Y.: Cornell University Press, 1986.

———. *Special Delivery: Epistolary Modes in Modern Fiction.* Chicago: University of Chicago Press, 1992.

Keenan, Thomas. *Fables of Responsibility: Aberrations and Predicaments in Ethics and Politics.* Stanford, Calif.: Stanford University Press, 1997.

Kennedy, Hubert. "Johann Baptist von Schweitzer: The Queer Marx Loved to Hate." *Journal of Homosexuality* 29, nos. 2–3 (1995): 69–96.

Kerr, Lucille. *Reclaiming the Author: Figures and Fictions from Spanish America.* Durham, N.C.: Duke University Press, 1992.

Kopelson, Kevin. *Love's Litany: The Writing of Modern Homoerotics.* Stanford, Calif.: Stanford University Press, 1994.

Krauel, Ricardo. *Voces desde el silencio: Heterologías genérico-sexuales en la narrativa española moderna, 1875–1975.* Madrid: Libertarias, 2001.

Kristeva, Julia. *Black Sun: Depression and Melancholia.* Translated by Leon S. Roudiez. New York: Columbia University Press, 1989.

Lacan, Jacques. "Intervention on Transference." In *Feminine Sexuality: Jacques Lacan and the* école freudienne. Edited by Juliet Mitchell and Jacqueline Rose. Translated by Jacqueline Rose, 62–73. New York: Norton, 1982.

———. "Kant with Sade." Translated by James B. Swenson. *October* 51 (1989): 55–75.

———. "The Meaning of the Phallus." In *Feminine Sexuality,* 74–85.

———. *Le Séminaire. Livre VIII. Le transfert, 1960–61.* Edited by Jacques-Alain Miller. Paris: Seuil, 1991.

———. *Le Séminaire. Livre XX. Encore, 1972–73.* Edited by Jacques-Alain Miller. Paris: Seuil, 1975.

———. *The Seminar of Jacques Lacan. Book VII: The Ethics of Psychoanalysis.* Edited by Jacques-Alain Miller. Translated by Dennis Porter. New York: Norton, 1992.

———. *The Seminar of Jacques Lacan. Book XI: Four Fundamental Concepts of Psychoanalysis.* Edited by Jacques-Alain Miller. Translated by Alan Sheridan. New York: Norton, 1998.

———. "Seminar on 'The Purloined Letter.'" Translated by Jeffrey Mehlman. In Muller and Richardson, *The Purloined Poe*, 28–54.

Laclos, Pierre Choderlos de. *Les liaisons dangereuses*. Edited and translated by Douglas Parmée. Oxford: Oxford University Press, 1995.

Lane, Christopher. *The Burdens of Intimacy: Psychoanalysis and Victorian Masculinity*. Chicago: University of Chicago Press, 1999.

———. "Freud on Group Psychology: Shattering the Dream of a Common Culture." In Dean and Lane, *Homosexuality and Psychoanalysis*, 147–67.

———. "The Testament of the Other: Abraham and Torok's Failed Expiation of Ghosts." *Diacritics* 27, no. 4 (1998): 3–29.

Lanser, Susan S. "Queering Narratology." In *Ambiguous Discourse: Feminist Narratology and British Women Writers*, edited by Kathy Mezei, 250–61. Chapel Hill: University of North Carolina Press, 1996.

La Rubia Prado, Francisco. *Unamuno y la vida como ficción*. Madrid: Gredos, 1999.

Leader, Darian. *Why Do Women Write More Letters than They Post?* London: Faber and Faber, 1996.

Lev, Leora. "Redressing Inquisitional Logic: Lluís Fernàndez and Postmodernist Peninsular Camp." *Antípodas* 11–12 (1999–2000): 263–72.

———. "Lluís Fernàndez." In Foster, *Spanish Writers on Gay and Lesbian Themes*, 64–69.

Levine, Linda Gould. "Carmen Martín Gaite's *El cuarto de atrás:* A Portrait of the Artist as Woman." In Servodidio and Welles, *From Fiction to Metafiction*, 161–72.

Lewis, Tom. "Aesthetics and Politics." Afterword. *Critical Practices in Post-Franco Spain*. Edited by Silvia L. López, Jenaro Talens, and Darío Villanueva, 160–82. Minneapolis: University of Minnesota Press, 1994.

Likosky, Stephan, ed. *Coming Out: An Anthology of International Gay and Lesbian Writings*. New York: Pantheon, 1992.

Llamas, Ricardo. Introduction. *Construyendo sidentidades: Estudios desde el corazón de una pandemia*. Edited by Ricardo Llamas, ix–xx. Madrid: Siglo XXI, 1995.

———, and Fefa Vila. "Spain: Passion for Life: Una historia del movimiento de lesbianas y gays en el estado español." In Buxán, *ConCiencia de un singular deseo*, 188–224.

———, and Francisco Javier Vidarte. *Homografías*. 2d ed. Madrid: Espasa Calpe, 2000.

Llanos y Torriglia, Félix. "De la propiedad material e intelectual de la correspondencia epistolar." *Correos: Revista Profesional Ilustrada*, April 1946: 7–8.

Longhurst, C. A. Introduction to *San Manuel Bueno, mártir and La novela de Don Sandalio, jugador de ajedrez*, by Miguel de Unamuno, vii–lii. Dover, N.H.: Manchester University Press, 1984.

Lorenzo, Ricardo, and Héctor Anabitarte. *SIDA: El asunto está que arde*. Madrid: Revolución, 1987.

Loureiro, Angel G. *The Ethics of Autobiography: Replacing the Subject in Modern Spain.* Nashville, Tenn.: Vanderbilt University Press, 2000.

Lowe, Jennifer. "The Loneliness of the Long-Distance Letter-Writer: Reflections on and in Unamuno's *La novela de Don Sandalio, jugador de ajedrez."* *Forum for Modern Language Studies* 29, no. 1 (1993): 62–74.

Lucey, Michael. *Gide's Bent: Sexuality, Politics, Writing.* New York: Oxford University Press, 1995.

MacArthur, Elizabeth Jane. *Extravagant Narratives: Closure and Dynamics in the Epistolary Form.* Princeton, N.J.: Princeton University Press, 1990.

Marañón, Gregorio. *La evolución de la sexualidad y los estados interesexuales.* 1930. 2d ed. *Obras completas.* Vol. 8, 498–710. Madrid: Espasa-Calpe, 1972.

———. "Diálogo antisocrático sobre Corydon." Prologue to *Corydon,* by André Gide. Translated by Julio Gómez de la Serna. 3rd ed. Madrid: Oriente, 1931. n. pag.

Marichal, Juan. *El designio de Unamuno.* Madrid: Taurus, 2002.

Martín Gaite, Carmen. *The Back Room.* Translated by Helen Lane. San Francisco: City Lights, 2000.

———. *La búsqueda de interlocutor y otras búsquedas.* Madrid: Nostromo, 1973.

———. *El cuarto de atrás.* Barcelona: Destino, 1978.

———. *Desde la ventana: Enfoque femenino de la literatura española.* 1987. Madrid: Espasa Calpe, 1993.

———. Letter to the author. April 9, 2000.

———. *Nubosidad variable.* Barcelona: Anagrama, 1992.

———. *Usos amorosos de la postguerra española.* Madrid: Anagrama, 1987.

Martínez Expósito, Alfredo. *Los escribas furiosos: Configuraciones homoeróticas en la narrativa española.* New Orleans: University Press of the South, 1998.

Marx, Karl. "From *The Conspectus of Bakunin's Book* State and Anarchy." *Anarchism and Anarcho-Syndicalism,* 147–52. New York: International, 1972.

Matamoro, Blas. "Carmen Martín Gaite: El viaje al cuarto de atrás." *Cuadernos Hispanoamericanos* 351 (1979): 581–605.

McBride, Dwight. *Impossible Witnesses: Truth, Abolitionism, and Slave Testimony.* New York: New York University Press, 2001.

Meese, Elizabeth A. *(Sem)Erotics: Theorizing Lesbian: Writing.* New York: New York University Press, 1992.

Mendicutti, Eduardo. *Siete contra Georgia.* Barcelona: Tusquets, 1987.

Meyer, François. *L'ontologie de Miguel de Unamuno.* Paris: Presses Universitaires de France, 1955.

Mira Nouselles, Alberto. "After Wilde: Camp Discourse in Hoyos and Retana, or The Dawn of Spanish Gay Culture." *Journal of Spanish Cultural Studies* 5, no. 1 (2004): 29–47.

―――. "De lo patológico a lo político: La articulación de la identidad gay en el teatro homosexual." In Buxán, *ConCiencia de un singular deseo*, 225–56.

―――. "Esta noche SIDA: Comentarios a algunos tratamientos del sida en prensa y televisión." In Aliaga and Cortés, *De amor y rabia*, 145–63.

―――. "Modernistas, dandis y pederastas: Articulaciones de la homosexualidad en 'la edad de plata.'" *Journal of Iberian and Latin American Studies* 7, no. 1 (2001): 63–75.

Mirabet i Mullol, Antoni. *Homosexualitat avui: Acceptada o encara condemnada?* Barcelona: Edhasa/Institut Lambda, 1984.

―――, ed. *Homosexualitat à l'inici del segle XXI.* Barcelona: Claret, 2000.

Montaigne, Michel de. "Of Friendship." *The Complete Works of Montaigne: Essays, Travel Journal, Letters.* Translated by Donald M. Frame, 135–44. Stanford, Calif.: Stanford University Press, 1967.

Montesinos, José Fernández. *Introducción a una historia de la novela en España en el siglo XIX.* Valencia: Castalia, 1955.

Muller, John P., and William J. Richardson. *The Purloined Poe: Lacan, Derrida and Psychoanalytic Reading.* Baltimore: Johns Hopkins University Press, 1988.

Muñoz y Pabón, Juan Francisco. *Amor postal: Novela comprimida.* Sevilla: Imp. de Izquierdo y Cª, 1903.

Nash, Mary. "La reforma sexual en el anarquismo español." In *El anarquismo español y sus tradiciones culturales,* edited by Bert Hofmann, Pere Joan i Tous, and Manfred Tietz, 281–96. Frankfurt am Main: Vervuert; Madrid: Iberoamericana, 1995.

Nicholas, Robert L. *Unamuno, narrador.* Madrid: Castalia, 1987.

Nichols, Geraldine C. *Escribir, espacio propio: Laforet, Matute, Moix, Tusquets, Riera y Roig por sí mismas.* Minneapolis: Institute for the Study of Ideologies and Literature, 1989.

Norton, Rictor. *My Dear Boy: Gay Love Letters through the Centuries.* San Francisco: Leyland, 1998.

"El número de nuevos casos de sida cae un 20% en un año." *El Mundo,* February 15, 1999. December 1, 2003. http://www.elmundo.es/elmundo/1998/febrero/15/ciencia/sida.html.

Ochoa, Eugenio de. Introduction. *Epistolario español: Colección de cartas de españoles ilustres antiguos y modernos.* Edited by Eugenio de Ochoa. Biblioteca de Autores Españoles. Vol. 13, v–xi. Madrid: Rivadeneyra, 1850.

Ocón Alonso-Barroeta, Serafín. *El Correo y la República.* Madrid: M. Aguilar, 1934.

Odets, Walt. *In the Shadow of the Epidemic: Being HIV-Negative in the Age of AIDS.* Durham, N.C.: Duke University Press, 1995.

Oleza, Joan. "La situació actual de la narrativa: Entre l'autofagià i la passió de contar." In Salvador and Piquer, *Vint anys,* 69–93.

Orr, Mary. *Flaubert: Writing the Masculine.* Oxford: Oxford University Press, 2000.

Ortega, Soledad, ed. *Cartas a Galdós.* Madrid: Revista de Occidente, 1964.

Ortega y Gasset, José. "Psicoanálisis, ciencia problemática." 1911. *Obras completas I (1902–1916).* 2d ed, 216–38. Madrid: Revista de Occidente, 1950.

Ortiz, Christopher. "The Politics of Genre in Carmen Martín Gaites's *Back Room.*" In *Autobiography and Postmodernism,* edited by Kathleen Ashley, Leigh Gilmore, and Gerald Peters, 33–53. Amherst: University of Massachusetts Press, 1994.

Ortiz del Barco, Juan. *Propiedad de la correspondencia privada.* Madrid: n.p., 1909.

Pagés-Rangel, Roxana. *Del dominio público: Itinerarios de la carta privada.* Amsterdam: Rodopi, 1997.

Parcerisas, Francesc. "Poder, traducció, política." *Catalan Review* 14, nos. 1–2 (2000): 35–52.

Pardo de Figueroa, Mariano. *Legislación de Correos (servicio interior e internacional).* Madrid: Sucesores de Cuesta, 1893.

Pascual de Sanjuán, Pilar. *Manual epistolar, para las señoritas.* 1877. 11th ed. Barcelona, 1927.

Patton, Cindy. *Globalizing AIDS.* Minneapolis: University of Minnesota Press, 2002.

Pérez, Carlos D. "Notas sobre autobiografía, psicoanálisis y género epistolar." *Inti* 49–50 (1999): 173–76.

Pérez Canovás, Nicolás. *Homosexualidad, homosexuales y uniones homosexuales en el derecho español.* Granada: Comares, 1996.

Pérez Galdós, Benito. *La estafeta romántica.* 1899. Madrid: Hernando, 1918.

———. *La incógnita.* Madrid: Rueda, 2001.

———. *Realidad: Novela en cinco jornadas.* Edited by Ricardo Gullón. Madrid: Taurus, 1977.

———. *The Unknown/La incógnita.* Translated by Karen Austin. Lewiston: Edwin Mellen, 1991.

Perriam, Chris. *Desire and Dissent: An Introduction to Luis Antonio de Villena.* Oxford: Berg, 1995.

Perry, Ruth. *Women, Letters, and the Novel.* New York: AMS, 1980.

"La peste bubónica." *Boletín de Correos,* August 30, 1899: 2243–44.

Petty, Celia, Deborah Roberts, and Sharon Smith. *Women's Liberation and Socialism.* London: Bookmarks, 1987.

Phillips, Adam. *On Flirtation.* Cambridge, Mass.: Harvard University Press, 1994.

Piquer, I. "Apoyo español." *El País,* June 26, 2001, natl. ed.: 25.

"Podemos confesarnos por carta." *Carteros y Subalternos,* February 1963: 13–14.

Poe, Edgar Allan. "The Purloined Letter." In Muller and Richardson, *The Purloined Poe,* 3–27.

"El problema de los Idiomas en Correos." *La Valija,* April 1976: 5.

Quiroga, José. *Tropics of Desire: Interventions from Queer Latino America*. New York: New York University Press, 2000.

Radway, Janice. *Reading the Romance: Women, Patriarchy, and Popular Literature*. Chapel Hill: University of North Carolina Press, 1984.

Rajchman, John. *Truth and Eros: Foucault, Lacan, and the Question of Ethics*. New York: Routledge, 1991.

Rambuss, Richard. *Closet Devotions*. Durham, N.C.: Duke University Press, 1998.

Ramella, Agostino. *Tratado de la correspondencia en materia civil y mercantil seguido de un estudio referente á la legislación española por Lorenzo Benito*. Madrid: Hijos de Reus, 1897.

Real Academia Española. *Diccionario de la lengua española*. 21st ed. 2 vols. Madrid: Espasa Calpe, 1992.

Resina, Joan Ramon. "Hi ha futur per als estudis catalans a l'Amèrica del Nord?" *Catalan Review* 14, nos. 1–2 (2000): 17–33.

Restuccia, Frances. "The Subject of Homosexuality: Butler's Elision." In *Lacan in America*, edited by Jean-Michel Rabaté, 349–60. New York: Other Press, 2000.

Reyes, Alfonso. Introduction. *Literatura epistolar*. Edited by Alfonso Reyes, xi–xxiii. Barcelona: Océano, 1999.

Rheingold, Howard. *Virtual Reality*. New York: Simon and Schuster, 1991.

Richardson, Samuel. *Clarissa, or The History of a Young Lady*. 1747–48. Edited by Angus Ross. Harmondsworth: Penguin, 1985.

Riera, Carme. "Confesión general." In *Contra el amor en compañía y otros relatos*, 215–17. Barcelona: Destino, 1991.

———. "Grandeza y miseria de la epístola." In *El oficio de narrar*, edited by Marina Mayoral, 147–58. Madrid: Cátedra, 1990.

———. "I Leave You, My Love, the Sea as a Token." Translated by Alberto Moreiras. In *On Our Own Behalf: Women's Tales from Catalonia*, edited by Kathleen McNerney, 31–45. Lincoln: University of Nebraska Press, 1988.

———. *Jo pos per testimoni les gavines*. 1977. Barcelona: Columna, 1998.

———. *Palabra de mujer (Bajo el signo de una memoria impenitente)*. Barcelona: Laia, 1980.

———. *Qüestió d'amor propi*. Barcelona: Laia, 1987.

———. *Te dejo el mar*. Translated by Luisa Cotoner. Madrid: Espasa Calpe, 1991.

———. *Te deix, amor, la mar com a penyora*. Barcelona: Laia, 1975.

Robinson, Paul. "Freud and Homosexuality." In Dean and Lane, *Homosexuality and Psychoanalysis*, 91–97.

Rodríguez, María Pilar. *Vidas im/propias: Transformaciones del sujeto femenino en la narrativa española contemporánea*. West Lafayette, Ind.: Purdue University Press, 2000.

Román, David. "'It's My Party and I'll Die If I Want To!'" In *Camp Grounds: Style and Homosexuality,* edited by David Bergman, 206–33. Amherst: University of Massachusetts Press, 1993.

Romero, Leonardo. Introduction to *Pepita Jiménez,* by Juan Valera, 9–91. Madrid: Cátedra, 2000.

Rose, Jacqueline. *Sexuality in the Field of Vision.* London: Verso, 1986.

Rousseau, Jean-Jacques. *The Confessions.* 1781. Translated by J. M. Cohen. London: Penguin, 1953.

Rueda, Ana. *Cartas sin lacrar: La novela epistolar y la España ilustrada, 1789–1840.* Madrid: Iberoamericana; Frankfurt am Main: Vervuert, 2001.

———. "*La novela de Don Sandalio:* Un tablero epistolar para jugar con Unamuno." *Revista de Estudios Hispánicos* 33, no. 3 (1999): 539–61.

———. "El poder de la carta privada: *La incógnita* y *La estafeta romántica.*" *Bulletin of Hispanic Studies* 77 (2000): 375–91.

Ruiz, Francesc, Rosa Sanz, and Jordi Solé i Camardons. *Història social i política de la llengua catalana.* 3rd ed. Valencia: Edicions 3 i 4, 1999.

Salinas, Pedro. "Defensa de la carta misiva y de la correspondencia epistolar." In *El defensor,* 17–114. Madrid: Alianza, 1967.

Salvador, Vicent, and Adolf Piquer. Introduction. *Vint anys de novella catalana al País Valencià.* Edited by Vicent Salvador and Adolf Piquer, 7–40. Valencia: Eliseu Climent, 1992.

Sánchez-Mellado, Luz. "Las últimas del armario." *El País Semanal,* June 29, 2003: 36–46.

Sanchis Guarner, Manuel. *La llengua dels valencians.* 8th ed. Valencia: Eliseu Climent, 1983.

Santana, Mario. "National Literatures and Interliterary Communities in Spain and Catalonia." *Catalan Review* 14, nos. 1–2 (2000): 159–71.

Sanz Cid, Marta, Javier Vega Gutiérrez, and Pelegrín Martínez Baza. *SIDA: Aspectos médico-legales y deontológicos.* Valladolid: Universidad de Valladolid, Secretariado de Publicaciones e Intercambio Editorial, 1999.

Scanlon, Geraldine. *La polémica feminista en la España contemporánea (1868–1974).* Madrid: Akal, 1986.

Schiesari, Juliana. *The Gendering of Melancholia: Feminism, Psychoanalysis, and the Symbolics of Loss in Renaissance Literature.* Ithaca, N.Y.: Cornell University Press, 1992.

Sedgwick, Eve Kosofsky. *Epistemology of the Closet.* Berkeley: University of California Press, 1990.

———. "Paranoid Reading and Reparative Reading; or, You're So Paranoid, You Probably Think This Introduction Is about You." Introduction. *Novel Gazing: Queer Readings in Fiction.* Edited by Eve Sedgwick, 1–37. Durham, N.C.: Duke University Press, 1997.

Senabre, Ricardo. *Literatura y público.* Madrid: Paraninfo, 1987.

Servodidio, Mirella. "Doing Good and Feeling Bad: The Interplay of Desire and Discourse in Two Stories by Carme Riera." In Glenn et al., *Moveable Margins*, 65–82.

———. Introduction. In Glenn et al., *Moveable Margins*, 7–16.

———, and Marcia Welles, eds. *From Fiction to Metafiction: Essays in Honor of Carmen Martín Gaite*. Lincoln, Neb.: Society of Spanish and Spanish-American Studies, 1983.

Shaw, D. L. "Concerning Unamuno's *La novela de Don Sandalio, jugador de ajedrez*." *Bulletin of Hispanic Studies* 54, no. 2 (1977): 115–23.

Shepherdson, Charles. *Vital Signs: Nature, Culture, Psychoanalysis*. New York: Routledge, 2000.

Showalter, English. *The Evolution of the French Novel, 1641–1782*. Princeton, N.J.: Princeton University Press, 1972.

"El sida disminuye ligeramente en España, pero aumenta la transmisión heterosexual." *El Mundo*, August 8, 2003; December 1, 2003. http://www.elmundo.es/elmundosalud/2003/08/08/medicina/1060342413.html.

Sieburth, Stephanie. *Inventing High and Low: Literature, Mass Culture, and Uneven Modernity in Spain*. Durham, N.C.: Duke University Press, 1994.

Siegert, Bernhard. *Relays: Literature as an Epoch of the Postal System*. Translated by Kevin Repp. Stanford, Calif.: Stanford University Press, 1999.

Silverman, Kaja. *The Acoustic Mirror: The Female Voice in Psychoanalysis and Cinema*. Bloomington: Indiana University Press, 1988.

Sinclair, Alison. *Uncovering the Mind: Unamuno, the Unknown, and the Vicissitudes of the Self*. Manchester: Manchester University Press, 2001.

Sinfield, Alan. *The Wilde Century: Effeminacy, Oscar Wilde, and the Queer Moment*. New York: Columbia University Press, 1994.

Singer, Godfrey Frank. *The Epistolary Novel: Its Origin, Development, Decline, and Residuary Influence*. Philadelphia: University of Pennsylvania Press, 1933.

Sinnigen, John H. *Sexo y política: Lecturas galdosianas*. Madrid: Ediciones de la Torre, 1996.

Smith, Paul Julian. *Laws of Desire: Questions of Homosexuality in Spanish Writing and Film, 1960–1990*. Oxford: Oxford University Press, 1992.

———. *Vision Machines: Cinema, Literature, and Sexuality in Spain and Cuba, 1983–93*. London: Verso, 1996.

Sommer, Doris. "Taking a Life: Hot Pursuit and Cold Rewards in a Mexican Testimonial Novel." *Signs* 20, no. 4 (1995): 913–40.

Spires, Robert. "Intertextuality in *El cuarto de atrás*." In Servodidio and Welles, *From Fiction to Metafiction*, 139–48.

Stoler, Ann Laura. *Race and the Education of Desire: Foucault's History of Sexuality and the Colonial Order of Things*. Durham, N.C.: Duke University Press, 1995.

Tambling, Jeremy. *Confession: Sexuality, Sin, the Subject.* Manchester: Manchester University Press, 1990.

Thebussem, El Doctor. "Las cartas tarjetas." *Revista de Correos,* September 1871: 764–67.

———. "Más datos: Acerca de las tarjetas postales de España." *Revista de Correos,* June 1874: 68–71.

Thomas, Paul. *Karl Marx and the Anarchists.* London: Routledge and Kegan Paul, 1980.

Treichler, Paula A. "AIDS, Homophobia, and Biomedical Discourse: An Epidemic of Signification." In *AIDS: Cultural Analysis, Cultural Activism,* edited by Douglas Crimp, 31–70. Cambridge, Mass.: MIT Press, 1988.

Tsuchiya, Akiko. "*La incógnita* and the Enigma of Writing: Manolo Infante's Interpretive Struggle." *Hispanic Review* 57, no. 3 (1989): 335–56.

———. "The Paradox of Narrative Seduction in Carmen Riera's *Cuestión de amor propio.*" *Hispania* 75, no. 2 (1992): 281–86.

Turner, Kay. "Sealed with a Kiss: Introducing Lesbian Love Letters." Introduction. *Dear Sappho: A Legacy of Lesbian Love Letters.* Edited by Kay Turner, 9–32. London: Thames and Hudson, 1996.

Unamuno, Miguel de. "La balada de la prisión de Reading." 1897. *Obras completas (OC)* 8: 729–31.

———. "Carta abierta a Casimiro Muñoz." 1899. *OC* 8: 69–75.

———. "Cartas." 1922. *OC* 10: 521–24.

———. "Cartas a mujeres." 1912. *OC* 8: 903–11.

———. "La comunión de los solitarios." *OC* 11: 941–44.

———. "El contra-mismo." 1918. *OC* 9: 76–80.

———. *Ficciones: Four Stories and a Play.* Edited by Martin Nozick. Translated by Anthony Kerrigan. Princeton, N.J.: Princeton University Press, 1976. Vol. 7 of *Selected Works of Miguel de Unamuno.* 7 vols. 1967–1984.

———. "La intimidad de los escritos." *OC* 11: 937–40.

———. "La moralidad artística." 1923. *OC* 8: 1165–69.

———. "El morillo al rojo (Confesiones cínicas al lector amigo)." 1916. *OC* 10: 373–78.

———. *Obras completas.* Edited by Manuel García Blanco. 16 vols. Madrid: A. Aquado, 1958–64.

———. *El Otro: Misterio en tres jornadas y un epílogo. OC* 12: 800–63.

———. *San Manuel Bueno, mártir, y tres historias más.* Madrid: Espasa-Calpe, 1989.

———. *Del sentimiento trágico de la vida; La agonía del cristianismo.* Madrid: Akal, 1983.

———. "Sobre mí mismo (Pequeño ensayo cínico)." 1913. *OC* 10: 243–48.

———. "Soledad." 1905. *OC* 3: 881–901.

"Un joven profesor zaragozano ha elaborado un interesante estudio sobre el Servicio Público de Correos." *La Valija,* October 1981: 15–16.

Valera, Juan. *Pepita Jiménez.* Edited by Leonardo Romero. Madrid: Cátedra, 2000.

———. *Pepita Jiménez.* Translated by Harriet de Onís. Woodbury, N.Y.: Barron's Educational Series, 1964.

Valis, Noël. "True Confessions: Carme Riera's *Cuestión de amor propio.*" *Revista Canadiense de Estudios Hispánicos* 23, no. 2 (1999): 311–27.

Valverde. "Adios a las cartas de amor." *La Valija,* February 1975: 9.

Vásquez, Mary. "Textual Desire, Seduction, and Epistolarity in Carme Riera's 'Letra de ángel' and 'La seducción del genio.'" In Glenn et al., *Moveable Margins,* 177–99.

Velázquez, José Luis, and Javier Memba. *La generación de la democracia: Historia de un desencanto.* Madrid: Temas de Hoy, 1995.

Verdegay y Fiscowich, Eduardo. *Historia del correo desde sus orígenes hasta nuestros días.* Madrid: Ricardo Rojas, 1894.

Vilarós, Teresa. *El mono del desencanto: Una crítica cultural de la transición española (1973–1993).* Madrid: Siglo XXI, 1998.

Villena, Luis Antonio de. "El amor celeste." 1986. *La fascinante moda de la vida: Relatos sobre rareza y bizarría.* Barcelona: Planeta, 1999. 43–60.

———. *Amor pasión.* Barcelona: Laertes, 1986.

———. *Amor pasión.* Madrid: Espasa Calpe, 2000.

———. *Fuera del mundo (Una novela romántica).* Barcelona: Planeta, 1992.

———. "Insólitos y exquisitos (Lo hermoso de ser banal y singular)." *Lecciones de estética disidente,* 75–77. Valencia: Pre-Textos, 1996.

———. *El libro de las perversiones.* Barcelona: Planeta, 1992.

———. *El mal mundo (Dos relatos sobre el amor masculino).* Barcelona: Tusquets, 1999.

———. *La tentación de Ícaro.* Barcelona: Lumen, 1986.

Violi, Patrizia. "La intimidad de la ausencia: Formas de la estructura epistolar." *Revista de Occidente* 68 (1987): 87–99.

Vivas Marzal, Luis. *Contemplación juridico-penal de la homosexualidad: Discurso de ingreso en la Academia Valenciana de Jurisprudencia y Legislación.* Valencia: Academia Valenciana de Jurisprudencia y Legislación, 1963.

Warner, Michael. "Homo-Narcissism; or, Heterosexuality." In *Engendering Men: The Question of Male Feminist Criticism,* edited by Joseph A. Boone and Michael Cadden, 190–206. New York: Routledge, 1990.

———. *The Trouble with Normal: Sex, Politics, and the Ethics of Queer Life.* New York: Free Press, 1999.

Welles, Marcia. "Carmen Martín Gaite: Fiction as Desire." In Servodidio and Welles, *From Fiction to Metafiction,* 197–207.

Whiston, James. *Valera: Pepita Jiménez.* London: Grant and Cutler, 1977.

Wilde, Oscar. *De Profundis*. New York: Modern Library, 2000.

Wittig, Monique. *The Straight Mind and Other Essays*. Boston: Beacon, 1992.

Wyers, Frances. "Unamuno and 'the Death of the Author.'" *Hispanic Review* 58, no. 3 (1990): 325–46.

Zaczek, Barbara. *Censored Sentiments: Letters and Censorship in Epistolary Novels and Conduct Material*. Newark: University of Delaware Press, 1997.

Žižek, Slavoj. *For They Know Not What They Do: Enjoyment as a Political Factor*. London: Verso, 1991.

———. *The Plague of Fantasies*. London: Verso, 1997.

———. *The Sublime Object of Ideology*. London: Verso, 1989.

———. *Tarrying with the Negative: Kant, Hegel, and the Critique of Ideology*. Durham, N.C.: Duke University Press, 1993.

———. *The Ticklish Subject: The Absent Centre of Political Ontology*. London: Verso, 1999.

INDEX

Abellán, José Luis, 6, 9, 15

Abraham, Nicolas, 97, 190n11

AIDS: and autobiography, 154; blame for, in gay community, 169; and camp, 161–62, 168; coming out as HIV-positive, 155, 156; and computer viruses, 149, 164, 173–74; and gay activism in Spain, 152–53, 161, 166–67, 170; as gay disease, 152, 154, 172–73, 175–76; geographic prevalence of, 157, 211nn2–3; and homophobia, 174; invisibility of, 151–52, 153–54, 156–57, 158; and language, 163, 212n16; media representation of, 153; and prevention campaigns in Spain, 149, 151–52, 175–76; and safe sex, 150, 165; and shame, 155–56, 167–69; testimony and witnessing, 155, 158

Alas, Leopoldo, 202n38

Alas, Leopoldo (Clarín), xxix, xxxv, 9

Alcoforado, Mariana, 34, 42

Aliaga, Juan Vicente, 120, 121, 122, 163

Almodóvar, Pedro, 118, 119, 161

Altman, Janet, x, xxv

Anabitarte, Héctor, 152

anarchism: history in Spain, 122–24; and homosexuality, 208n19, 209n31; individuality and community in, 140; limitations of, 140, 142, 144; and Marxism, 124–25; 126; and sexuality, 128, 130–31; and violence, 131, 132, 134–35

Aristotle, 18

Augustine, Saint, 61

Babuscio, Jack, 168

Bacarisse, Pamela, 194n21

Bakunin, Mikhail, 134, 208n17, 208n19, 209n21

Balzac, Honoré de, 34

Barthes, Roland, xvii–xviii; *A Lover's Discourse*, xl–xli; "The Death of the Author," 192n3

Bayly, Jaime, 177

Beebee, Thomas, xviii, xix, xxviii

Benstock, Shari, 34

Bentham, Jeremy, xxiii

Bergeron, David, 189n1

Bergmann, Emilie L., 121, 146

Bersani, Leo, 212n22

Beverley, John, 205n34

Bieder, Maryellen, 204n12
Blanco Aguinaga, Carlos, 22
Bordowitz, Gregg, 155
Bower, Anne, 32
Brooks, Peter, 107
Brooksbank Jones, Anny, 199n38
Bush, Andrew, 196n8
Butler, Judith: on attachments to
    power, 139–40; on instability of
    identity, 71–72; on lesbianism, 49;
    theory of melancholia and gender,
    100–101, 205n32; treatment of
    psychoanalysis, 182; on the
    unconscious, 189n4; on U.S. military
    policy, 173
Buxán, Xosé, 122

Cadalso, José, 127
Camí-Vela, María Antonia, 204n18
camp, 138, 161–62, 168
Cardín, Alberto, 150, 156, 175, 207n11
Carrillo, Santiago, 135
Castán Vásquez, José María, 191n18
Castillo, Debra, 38
Castle, Terry, xix, 195n33, 199n47
Castro, Fidel, 208n19
Catalan language: compared with
    Castilian, 91–92, 105–6, 203n9,
    204nn11–12; and Valencian, 116–17,
    206n3
Chabran, Rafael, 20
Chambers, Ross, 158, 163
Chartier, Roger, xix
Clarín. See Alas, Leopoldo, (Clarín)
Climent, Eliseu, 116
closet, ix–x, 60–61, 76, 155; applic-
    ability to Spain, 68–69, 109–11; out-
    ing and, 80–81, 89. See also letter
    writing; queer desire
confession: and Catholic Church, xxiv,

199n4; Christian and Greek models
    of, 67; confidentiality in, 63; as
    disciplinary tool, xxiv; as literary
    genre, 89; and moral authority, 63;
    pleasure of, 79; in psychoanalysis,
    53, 69, 199n50; sincerity and truth
    of, 102–3
Copjec, Joan, 189n4
Cortés, José Miguel G., 82, 151, 167,
    200
Cotoner, Luisa, 110
Cousineau, Diane, 32
Crimp, Douglas, 169
Crowder, Thomas, 140
Cvetkovich, Ann, 102

Davidson, Arnold, xi, 189n4
Day, Robert Adams, 189n2
Dean, Tim, 212n22
Decker, William, 212n18
de Lauretis, Teresa, 99–100
Delgado, Elena, 192n27
de Man, Paul, 102–3
Derrida, Jacques, xl–xli, xlii; The
    Post Card, xl–xli, 28, 34; on
    psychoanalysis, 190n11, 196n1; truth
    of testimony, 104
Domingo Lorén, Victoriano, 83–84
Donato, Emilio, 17
Dupláa, Cristina, 92
Düttmann, Alexander García, 155
Duyfhuizen, Bernard, 5, 202n37

Eagleton, Terry, 127–28, 195n33
Edelman, Lee, 163, 171, 173
Ellis, Robert Richmond, 120, 190n7,
    199n2
e-mail. See letter writing
Engels, Friedrich, 208n19, 209n21
Enguix Grau, Begoña, 210n31

epistolary fiction, ix; and authentic letters, xvii–xviii; characteristics of, xliii; definition of, x, 54, 75; didactic function of, xix–xxi, 84, 191n16; historical development of, xvi, xix, xxv–xxvii; history of, in Spain, xxvi–xxviii, xxx–xxxi; readers and, x–xi; relationship to postmodernism, 126; role of editor in, 26–27, 141; subgenres of, xiii; and technological advancement, 150; treatment of community, 126, 140; treatment of desire, xii, xxx–xxxi; and women's desire, xxxi. *See also* letters; letter writing

Epps, Brad, 91, 175, 212n16; on Catalan language, 105, 112; on lesbianism in Carmen Martín Gaite, 36; on lesbianism in Carme Riera, 94–96

Eslava Galán, Juan, 50

Espaliú, Pepe, 154

Espinosa, Miguel, 177

ethics, 62, 77–78, 79, 80–81, 84–85

Fabregat, Amadeu, 116

Favret, Mary, xviii, 32, 33, 127

Felman, Shoshana, 108

Fernàndez, Josep-Anton, 116, 118, 122, 131, 139

Fernàndez, Lluís, xiii, xiv, 115, 178, 179; *L'anarquista nu*, xiv, 115, 118–19, 122–23, 125–126, 128–32, 134–47, 150; *Desiderata*, 118; *Espejo de amor y lujo*, 118; lack of critical attention, 118, 206n4; *Una prudente distancia*, xiv, 150–51, 154–72, 175–76

Findlay, Heather, 47, 198n34

Flaubert, Gustave, 15

Foucault, Michel: on ethics and morality, 62, 67, 200n15; on gay courtship, 202n35; *The History of Sexuality*, xi, xxiv, 62, 70, 132; and psychoanalysis, xi, 189n4, 208n16; theorization of sexuality, xi–xii, xv, 28, 189n5

Franco, Francisco, xv, 18, 39, 59, 78, 124–25

Franco regime, xiv, 37, 38, 39, 115, 146, 147; and anarchism, 123–25; criminalization of homosexuality, 82–84, 119, 121–22, 135–36, 145–46, 202n39, 203n41, 203n2; prohibition of Catalan, 105; surveillance of mail, 124–25, 201n30, 202n34; transition to democracy, 124–25; treatment of lesbianism, 49, 88–89, 95–96; Women's Section of the Falange, 39

Franz, Thomas, xxxiv

Freud, Sigmund, xi, xxii; case history of "Dora," 47, 198n34; death drive, 171; on fantasy in desire, 24; and Wilhelm Fliess, 195n34; on group identification and homosexuality, 16; *Group Psychology* 16; "Mourning and Melancholia," 97–98, 169; and the Oedipal complex, 25; presence in Unamuno's library, 13; "Psychogenesis of a Case of Homosexuality in a Woman" 99; "The Question of Lay Analysis," 53; *Three Essays on the Theory of Sexuality*, 194n24, 195n32; *Totem and Taboo*, 133. *See also* psychoanalysis

Fuss, Diana, 198n36

Fuster, Joan, 116–17, 206n3

Galdós, Benito Pérez. *See* Pérez Galdós, Benito

Ganivet, Ángel, 10

García Lorca, Federico, 10–11, 20

García-Posada, Miguel, 11
gender, 38–40; and letter writing, xx,
    xxi, xl, 32–34, 44; and melancholy,
    98–99; narrative expectations and,
    40, 54–55
Gener, Pompeyo, 195n30
Gide, André, 17, 18, 194n20
Gil-Albert, Juan, 24
Gil de Biedma, Jaime, 153
Gilroy, Amanda, xix
Glenn, Kathleen, 93, 103
Goethe, Johann Wolfgang von, 4;
    The Sorrows of Young Werther, xxvi,
    xxvii, 127
Gold, Hazel, xxvii, xxviii, xxx, 191n16
Goldsmith, Elizabeth, ix, 32
Goya, Francisco de, xxv
Goytisolo, Juan, 154, 175
Guasch, Oscar, 82, 207n9
Guibert, Hervé, 154, 161
Guilleragues, Gabriel, 4, 33
guilt: and AIDS, 152, 155–56, and
    heternormativity, 109, 110; and
    morality, 73–74; and queer desire,
    89, 95, 101–3, 199n2
Guirao, Olga, 177
Gullón, Ricardo, xxxvii–xxxviii, 20

Halberstam, Judith, 48
Halperin, David: critique of Sedgwick,
    182–83; on Foucault, 189n5; on
    Greek sexuality, 66–67; on sexual
    terminology, 198n35
Hanson, Ellis, 165
Hill, Rowland, xxi, xxiii
Hocquenghem, Guy, 131
homosexuality. *See* queer desire
homosociality, 15–18, 45–46, 79–80
Hoyos y Vinent, Antonio de, 20,
    194n22

Iborra, Josep, 118
identity, xl–xli, 6, 23–24, 27–29,
    110–11; resistance to, 51, 71–72; self-
    perception of, 52; Spanish models
    of, 68–69, 120, 146
Ingenschay, Dieter, 206n6, 207n10
Irigaray, Luce, 98

Jagose, Annamarie, 199n39
Joan i Tous, Pere, 134
Johnson, Barbara, 196n1
Jost, François, 75

Kamuf, Peggy, 33
Kant, Immanuel, 18, 73–74, 133
Kany, Charles, 190n12
Kauffman, Linda, ix, xli, 33
Keenan, Thomas, 85
Kerr, Lucille, 204n15
Kopelson, Kevin, 200n17
Kramer, Larry, 168
Krauel, Ricardo, 195n30
Kristeva, Julia, 97, 99

Lacan, Jacques: death drive and
    jouissance, 171; definition of desire,
    14; definition of love, 70, 85; ethics
    of psychoanalysis, 73–74, 200n15;
    "Intervention on Transference," 47,
    99; "Kant avec Sade," 133–34,
    201n22; "The Meaning of the
    Phallus," 70; on "The Purloined
    Letter," 32, 196n1; symbolic and
    political laws, 133, 208n16; theories
    of lesbianism, 47, 99. *See also*
    psychoanalysis
Laclos, Choderlos de: *Les liaisons dan-
    gereuses*, xxvi, xxvii, 34, 127; trans-
    lation into Spanish, xxvii
Lane, Christopher, 16, 190n6, 193n17;

on psychoanalysis and queer theory,
179–81, 183–85
Lanser, Susan, 198n31
La Rubia Prado, Francisco, 6
Leader, Darian, 45
Lebowitz, Fran, 168
lesbianism: absence in fiction, xxxi;
compared with "queer," 47–48; in
Franco regime, 49–50, 88–89;
invisibility of, 49–50, 52, 89; and
loss, 50, 99–101, 108; and memory,
49–50, 89, 96–98, 104
letters: and authorial identity, 4–5, 9;
and autobiography, xvi–xvii; and
contagion, 149, 151, 166, 173–74;
and confidentiality, ix, xvi–xvii,
xxvi, 77; dead letters, 141–42; and
epistles, xxviii; as expressions of
sexual desire, ix, 11, 19, 28, 36; and
moral instruction, xx, 207n12; in
postal system, xviii; and poststructuralism, xxii; privacy and
inviolability of correspondence,
xvii–xviii, xxviii, 9–11, 78, 201n31,
202n34; as psychological explorations, xiii, xxi, xxxiii–xxxvii, 4–5,
27–29, 32; reading of, xvii–xviii;
rights to publication of, xxix,
201n31; and romantic love, 32, 35,
198n29; as substitutes for the body,
54, 96, 163, 164–65; as weapons,
159–61, 163, 166–67. See also
epistolary fiction; letter writing;
postal system
letter writing: addressees in, 43, 75, 93;
and the closet, ix, x, 27–28, 36, 54;
and electronic mail, xvi, 149–50,
164, 212n17, 212n18; between men,
xxi, 7; pleasure of, 54; as substitute
for conversation, 109; between

women, 45–46, 55, 96–97; and
women writers, xx, xxviii, 32–34,
42, 44, 203n3. See also epistolary
fiction; letters; postal system
letter-writing manuals, xix–xx, 190n14
Lev, Leora, 118, 126, 138, 206n5
Levine, Linda Gould, 46, 175
Llamas, Ricardo: on AIDS, 151; on the
closet, 82, 109; on gay liberation in
Spain, 207nn7–8, 209n24
Longhurst, C. A., 20
Lorca, Federico García. See García
Lorca, Federico
Lorenzo, Ricardo, 152
Lowe, Jennifer, 192n4
Lucey, Michael, 193n18

MacArthur, Elizabeth, xxx
Marañón, Gregorio, 18, 194n20, 194n24
Martí Ibáñez, Félix, 128
Martínez Expósito, Alfredo, 190n8,
199n3
Martín Gaite, Carmen, xii, 151, 178;
"La búsqueda del interlocutor," 37;
El cuarto de atrás, xiii, xiv, 35–55;
Desde la ventana, 42; Entre visillos, 38;
epistolary response to author, 52; on
Franco regime, 37, 39; and historical
memory, 37–38; and interlocutors,
37, 42–43; Nubosidad variable,
198n30; resistance to psychoanalysis,
53; Retahílas, 53; Ritmo lento, 38;
treatment of gender, 38, 39–40, 44,
46, 49–50; Usos amorosos de la
postguerra, 42
Marx, Karl, 208n17, 208n19, 209n21
Marxism: history in Spain, 135; homosexuality and, 135–36; representation
in L'anarquista nu, 135–37. See also
anarchism

McBride, Dwight, 206n36
Meese, Elizabeth, 48
Memba, Javier, 124–25
memory, 38–40, 49–50, 89, 96–98, 104
Mendicutti, Eduardo, 212n23
Meyer, Francois, 5
Michaels, Eric, 154
Mira, Alberto, 18, 23, 145–46, 194n23
Moix, Ana Maria, 111
Monette, Paul, 154
Montaigne, Michel de, 18
Montesquieu, Baron de (Charles-Louis de Secondat), 127
Montseny, Federica, 128
movida, 119, 121, 145, 161, 167
Muñoz y Pabón, Francisco: Amor postal, xxxi, xxxviii–xliii, 84; treatment of homosexuality, xl–xlii; use of postcards, xxxix

Nash, Mary, 128
Nicholas, Robert, 6
Nichols, Geraldine, 111, 204n19
Nordau, Max, 195n30
Norton, Rictor, 189n1

Ochoa, Eugenio de, xxvi, 9, 33
Odets, Walt, 210n1
Olavide, Pablo de, xxxviii
Ortega y Gasset, José, 13
Orr, Mary, 193n16
Ortiz, Christopher, 40
Ortiz, Tomás, 177
Ortiz del Barco, Juan 9–10
Ovid, 33

Pagés-Rangel, Roxana, xxv, 27, 190n14
Parcerisas, Francesc, 204n11
Pascual de Sanjuán, Pilar, xx

Patton, Cindy, 163
Pérez-Cánovas, Nicolás, 146
Pérez Galdós, Benito, xxvii, xxix; Doña Perfecta, xxxv; La estafeta romántica, xxvi, xxxi; La incógnita, xxvii, xxx, xxxi, xxxiv–xxxviii, xliii; Realidad, xxxv, xxxvi, xxxvii–xxxviii; representation of enigmatic desire, xxxvii; Tristana, xxxi, xxxv; use of epistolary form, xxxv–xxxvii
Perriam, Chris, 60, 79–80
Perry, Ruth ix, xviii
Petit, Jordi, 210n32
Phillips, Adam, 39, 77
Piquer, Conchita, 40
Poe, Edgar Allan: "The Purloined Letter," 31–32, 55
postal system: development in Spain, xxviii–xxix; inviolability of correspondence in, xvii–xviii, xxviii, 9–11, 78, 202n34; and postcards, xxxix; relation to subjectivity, xxi–xxiii; surveillance under Franco, 124–25, 201n30, 202n34; suspicion of, in Spain, xxix, xxxix, 201n30. See also letters; letter writing
privacy, xxvi, xxviii–xxix; 9–11, 76–78, 81–84, 93, 105, 111, 191n15, 191n19; media violations of, 153, 167; in Spanish law, 202n32
Proust, Marcel, 21
psychoanalysis, xi; analytic sessions in, 13, 47; and confession, 53, 69; conscious and unconscious desires in, 54; death drive and homosexuality, 171, 200n18; desire and identification in, 48, 52, 198n36; and postal system, xxii; relation to autobiography, 77; resistance to, 53; as theory of sexuality, 26, 99, 183–85;

transference and countertransference in, 47–48; and the unconscious, 183–85. *See also* Freud, Sigmund; Lacan, Jacques

Puig Antich, Salvador, 124, 144

queer desire: and the closet, ix–x, 60–61, 68–69, 76, 89, 109–11, 189n1; as contagion, 172–74, 213n24; criminalization of, in Spain, 82–84, 119, 121–22, 145–46, 202n39, 203n41, 203n2, 207n10; and friendship, 18–19, 64–65, 81; and gay and lesbian liberation, xiv; in Gide's work, 17; history of gay liberation in Spain, 119–21, 129–30, 145–47, 159, 202n38, 206n7–9, 210n32, 210n34; homosexuality in ancient Greece, 65–67; as homoeroticism, x, xxi, xxv, xxxi, xl, 7, 20, 64, 65, 79–80; homophobia and, xli, 16, 17, 72, 74, 143, 146–47; and love, 69–70, 142–43; minoritizing and universalizing approaches to, 81; before nineteenth century, xxv; stigma of, xiv, xli, 145–46, 155, 178–79; terminological debates, xv, 198n35

queer theory, xi–xii, 137; hermeneutics of suspicion in, 180–83; in literary studies, 179–85. *See also* Foucault, Michel

Quiroga, José, 193n6

Radway, Janice, 197n18

Rajchman, John, 200n15

Rambuss, Richard, ix

reading, x; fiction and reality, 175; letters, xvii–xviii, 43, 45, 112; and reader-response criticism, 108; and

responsibility, 75–76, 85, 112, 158, 174–75; as sexual activity, 149–51, 163, 172, 173–75. *See also* epistolary fiction; letters

Resina, Joan Ramon, 203n8

Restuccia, Frances, 205n32

Reyes, Alfonso, 9

Rheingold, Howard, 165

Rich, Adrienne, 49

Richardson, Samuel, xix, xxvi; *Clarissa*, xix, xx, xxvi, xxvii, 84, 126, 127; *Pamela*, xx, xxvi, xxvii; translation into Spanish, xxvii

Riera, Carme, xiii, xiv, 87, 151, 178; characteristics of fiction, 89–90; "Confesión general," 203n7; *Contra el amor en compañía y otros relatos*, 90; *Dans el darrer blau*, 91; *Jo pos per testimoni les gavines*, 92; "Jo pos per testimoni les gavines," xiv, 87–89, 91, 92, 93–98, 101–12, 126, 158; and linguistic diversity, 91–92, 204nn12–14; *Palabra de mujer*, 92; *Qüestió d'amor propi*, 90–91, 93, 106; relationship to lesbianism, 93, 110; "Te dejo, amor, en prenda el mar," 92; *Te deix, amor, la mar com a penyora*, 87, 92, 94; "Te deix, amor, la mar com a penyora," 87, 88, 90, 93–97; use of epistolary form, 90, 112, 203n6; use of translation, 92–93; "Y pongo por testigo a las gaviotas," 92, 96

Riera, Miguel Àngel, 177

Robinson, Paul, 195n32

Rodríguez, María Pilar, 103, 204n18

Román, David, 168

Romero, Leonardo, xxxiii

Rose, Jacqueline, 139, 189n4

Rotello, Gabriel, 169

Rousseau, Jean-Jacques, xxvi, 84,
    102–3; *Julie*, xxvi, xxvii, 84, 127
Rueda, Ana, xxvii, 191n15, 191n16,
    191n17, 193n13

Sackville-West, Vita, 34
Sade, Marquis de, 74, 133–34
Sahuquillo, Ángel, 207n11
Salinas, Pedro, 32, 77, 165, 190n10
Sánchez-Mellado, Luz, 111
Santana, Mario, 204n9
Scanlon, Geraldine, 197n12
Schiesari, Juliana, 98
Sedgwick, Eve Kosofsky, 189n3;
    criticism of queer literary studies,
    179–83; on historical development
    of sexuality, 61–62, 81
Senabre, Ricardo, xxvii
Servodidio, Mirella, 93, 101, 102, 204n18
sexuality, 53, 60–62; and closet, 61;
    normative models of, 7, 22, 26, 40,
    44, 80, 143; *See also* Foucault,
    Michel; psychoanalysis; queer desire
Shaw, D. L., 6
Shepherdson, Charles, 208n16
Shilts, Randy, 168
Showalter, English, xix
Sieburth, Stephanie, 197n17
Siegert, Bernhard, xxi–xxiv, xxxii
Silverman, Kaja, 98
Sinclair, Alison, 7, 9, 20, 22
Sinfield, Alan, 194n23
Singer, Godfrey, 190n12
Sinnigen, John, xxxviii
Smith, Paul Julian, 68, 121, 146, 154
Sommer, Doris, 104, 204n15
Sontag, Susan, 163
Spires, Robert, 46
Stoler, Laura Ann, xi
Sullivan, Andrew, 169

testimony, 154–55, 169; authenticity
    and sincerity of, 106–7; and bearing
    witness, 104, 107–9, 206n36;
    characteristics of, 88, 103; and
    fiction, 94, 103–4, 204n15, 205n34
Thomas, Paul, 142
Todorov, Tzvetan, 37, 43
Torok, Maria, 97, 190n11
transgenderism, 137–39
Treichler, Paula, 163
Tsuchiya, Akiko, xxxvi, xxxvii, 90, 106
Turner, Kay, 196n3

Unamuno, Miguel de, xii, 151, 178;
    Abel Sánchez, 194n25; *La agonía del
    cristianismo*, 5; "La balada de la
    prisión de Reading," 19; "Carta
    abierta," 9; "Cartas," 9; "Cartas a
    mujeres," 24; "El contra-mismo," 13;
    La esfinge, 23; and Freudian psycho-
    analysis, 13; "La intimidad de los
    escritos," 8; on letter writing, 8–9;
    "La moralidad artística," 20, 21; and
    motherhood, 21; *Nada menos que
    todo un hombre*, 194n25; narrative
    enigmas in, 3–4; *La novela de Don
    Sandalio*, xiii, xiv, 3–5, 6–8, 11–16,
    19–27; *El otro*, 27; philosophical
    concerns of, 5, 6, 24; on reader's
    interpretation, 27; relationship to
    homosexuality, 20–21; *San Manuel
    Bueno, mártir*, 4, 5–6; *Del sentimiento
    trágico de la vida*, 194n25; on sexual-
    ity and procreation, 21, 194n25;
    "Sobre mí mismo," 8; "Soledad," 8;
    La tía Tula, 26, 194n25; treatment of
    confession, 8–9

Valera, Juan, xxvii; and aesthetics,
    xxxii; *Pepita Jiménez*, xxvi,

xxx–xxxiv, xliii; treatment of
Catholicism, xxxii–xxxiii
Valis, Noël, 91
Vásquez, Mary, 90
Velázquez, José Luis, 124–25
Verhoeven, W. M., xix
Vidarte, Francisco Javier, 109
Vila, Fefa, 206n7, 207n8, 209n24
Vilarós, Teresa, 119, 121
Villalobos, Celia, 175
Villena, Luis Antonio de, xiii, 151, 178;
"El amor celeste," 60; *Amor pasión*,
xiii, 59–60, 62–85, 112, 126; "La
bendita pureza," 60; characteristics
of fictional works, 60–61, 201n24;
Fuera del mundo, 61; and homo-
sexuality, 61; *El libro de las perver-
siones*, 65–66; *El mal mundo*, 60; on
revision of *Amor pasión*, 201n25;
virtues of banality, 200n16

virtual reality, 165, 174–75
Vivas Marzal, Luis, 82–83

Warner, Michael, 168, 200n18
Watney, Simon, 163
Welles, Marcia, 53, 199n49
Whiston, James, xxxiv
Wilde, Oscar: *De Profundis*, 18–19; and
homosexuality, 21, 23; and Lord
Alfred Douglas, 19
witnessing. *See* testimony
Wittig, Monique, 49
Woolf, Virginia, 34
Wyers, Frances, 192n3

Zaczek, Barbara, 33
Žižek, Slavoj, 133, 190n11, 196, 201n22,
205n32

Patrick Paul Garlinger is assistant professor of Spanish at Northwestern University.